12.50

The IMF and the Debt Crisis

The IMF and the Debt Crisis

A Guide to the Third World's Dilemma

Peter Körner
Gero Maass
Thomas Siebold
Rainer Tetzlaff

translated from the German by
Paul Knight

Zed Books Ltd.

The IMF and the Debt Crisis was first published in German under the title *Im Teufelskreis der Verschuldung* by Junius Verlag GmbH Hamburg, Von-Hutten-Strasse 18, 2000 Hamburg 50, Federal Republic of Germany, in 1984. The English translation was first published by Zed Books Ltd., 57 Caledonian Road, London N1 9BU, and 171 First Avenue, Atlantic Highlands, New Jersey 07716, USA, in 1986.

Copyright © Junius Verlag Hamburg, 1984.
Translation copyright © Paul Knight, 1986.

Cover designed by Andrew Corbett.
Diagrams by Editpride.
Printed by The Bath Press, Avon.

Second impression, 1987.

British Library Cataloguing in Publication Data

The IMF and the debt crisis : a guide to the Third World's dilemma.
1. International Monetary Fund. 2. Balance of payments—Developing countries
I. Körner, Peter. II. Im Teufelskreis der Verschuldung. *English*
382.1′7′091724   HG3890

ISBN 0-86232-487-4
ISBN 0-86232-488-2 Pbk

Library of Congress Cataloging-in-Publication Data

Im Teufelskreis der Verschuldung. English.
The IMF and the debt crisis.

Translation of : Im Teufelskreis der Verschuldung.
Bibliography : p.
Includes index.
1. International Monetary Fund. 2. Debts, External
—Developing countries. I. Körner, Peter. II. Title.
HG3881.5.I58I3713 1986   336.3′435   86-18889
ISBN 0-86232-487-4
ISBN 0-86232-488-2 (pbk.)

Contents

Tables

Diagrams

This study was supported financially by the German Society for Peace and Conflict Research, Bonn.

List of Abbreviations

AC	Africa Confidential
ARB	African Research Bulletin
bfai-Mitteilungen	Mitteilungen der Bundesstelle für Aussenhandelsinformationen
BW	Business Week
DU	Der Überblick
FAZ	Frankfurter Allgemeine Zeitung
FAZ, BdW	Frankfurter Allgemeine Zeitung, Blick durch die Wirtschaft
F&D	Finance & Development
FEER	Far Eastern Economic Review
FR	Frankfurter Rundschau
FT	Financial Times
HB	Handelsblatt
ICR	International Currency Review
IHT	International Herald Tribune
LARR	Latin America Regional Report
LAWR	Latin America Weekly Report
MTM	Marchés Tropicaux et Méditerranéens
NfA	Nachrichten für den Aussenhandel
NYT	New York Times
NZZ	Neue Zürcher Zeitung
SZ	Süddeutsche Zeitung
WA	West Africa
WSJ	Wall Street Journal
Ww	Wirtschaftswoche

Introduction: The Developing Countries in the Debt-Trap or the Limits of IMF Crisis Management

August 1982: the supposedly rich oil-producing state of Mexico, pumped full of loans by major international banks seeking short-term profits, faced bankruptcy. It suddenly became clear that not only borrowers — developing countries and socialist states — but also creditors were caught in a debt trap. As long as 'only' countries such as Ghana, Zaire, Bolivia, Peru, Bangladesh or Sri Lanka had been threatened with insolvency, public opinion in industrial countries had scarcely noticed debt crises in the Third World. But now debt crises no longer affected merely the people of the developing countries; the financial collapse of a number of major borrowers posed a serious threat to the world monetary and financial system. Calm indifference suddenly gave way to alarmed solicitude as the possibility of an international bank crash reared its head. Many major international banks had loaned amounts totalling several times their original capital to major creditors who had now suddenly become insolvent.

A coordinated rescue operation by private banks, governments, the International Monetary Fund (IMF) and the Bank for International Settlements (BIS) managed to restore the major debtors' ability to pay in the short term and for the time being a collapse was averted. This did not, however, constitute a solution to the debt crisis. It was merely 'a cobbling operation on a world scale' (Schubert, 1983a) which seems unlikely to prevent debtor countries collapsing under the weight of their debts in the future. (These debts totalled at least US $900 thousand millionat the end of 1984.) Even though only major debtors and banks make the headlines, the dynamics of debt have affected almost all the developing countries. The world economic recession has meant that most Third World countries face difficulties in servicing their debts on time.

It is hardly surprising, therefore, that the Second Report of the Brandt Commission published at the beginning of 1983 considered Third World indebtedness to be a focal point in the North-South conflict. The report stressed that it affected the living conditions of most of humanity. Rising debt-servicing commitments are in many countries reducing what is available to satisfy basic needs. The debt crises of most developing countries do not endanger the world monetary and financial system, but they do have wide-ranging consequences which indirectly affect industrial

1

countries: insolvent countries cannot be considered as possible trade partners and the political consequences of indebtedness can destabilise entire regions. In extreme cases they may even lead governments to risk foreign policy and military adventures to distract the population from the internal consequences of debt — as in the case of Argentina and the Falklands-Malvinas War of 1982.

Indebtedness and debt crises are certainly not a new historical phenomenon. While countries such as England, the USA, Canada and Australia were able to initiate self-sustaining development with foreign loans, the new Latin American states and the countries of the Near East were already caught in the debt trap in the 19th Century. In those days, the repayment discipline of debtor countries was maintained if necessary by gunboat diplomacy. Today, it is the IMF, with its stabilisation programmes, which acts in the interests of the creditors. In the acute debt crises of major debtors, the IMF has become the major international organisation, centrally important as a crisis manager for the Third World — important both to creditors and debtors. Since the mid-1970s, an increasing number of developing countries has had to turn to the IMF and negotiate economic stabilisation programmes in order to receive the Fund's standby credits. These credits in turn are an indispensable precondition for regaining creditworthiness with international creditors. The IMF's seal of approval indicates to the financial world that a government is prepared to carry out austerity policies to ensure its solvency. Only then do financial markets open and rescheduling and refinancing arrangements become possible.

The crises of major debtors have, however, revealed the limits of IMF crisis management. Loans worth thousands of millions of dollars to India, Brazil, Mexico, Yugoslavia, Argentina and Rumania almost depleted the IMF's funds. The industrial countries were then forced to increase IMF quotas and expand its credit framework; but they did not provide the Fund with the necessary finance to live up to its role as a crisis manager. The industrial countries, themselves struggling with severe economic difficulties, decided at the IMF annual meeting in 1983 to limit the Fund to being a financer of short-term bridging loans in cases of payments difficulties. Somewhat hesitant attempts at a redefinition of the Fund's role had been going on since the mid-1970s. Stabilisation programmes over longer periods had been introduced to take account of the growing difficulties of the developing countries. In the crisis, however, the terms of lending were made harsher, so that now more than ever the burdens of adjustment were placed on the shoulders of the debtor countries.

The experiences of the 1960s and 1970s had already shown that it was above all the poorer sections of the population which suffered from the effects of IMF stabilisation programmes. Austerity programmes *à la* IMF in many cases brought unemployment, rising prices for basic items and a deterioration in health, education and social services. Radical austerity measures often fuelled social conflicts and led to violent confrontations. The IMF drove developing countries into recession, usually without achieving its targets of reducing inflation and restoring a sound balance of payments. IMF stabilisation programmes proved at best to be effective only in the short term. The number of the IMF's permanent customers itself shows that the Fund is not helping to solve the structural problems revealed by the debt crises. Instead of seeing debt crises as evidence of development problems requiring long-term solutions, the IMF regards them as short- to medium-term economic imbalances, the causes of which are primarily home-made. It argues that erroneous economic and financial policies lead to balance-of-payments deficits and that the developing countries have failed to 'adjust' to changing world economic conditions.

The diagnosis of the crisis, and the therapy derived from it, are based on a monetarist economic philosophy whose implementation has had dubious results even in industrial countries. This therapy is even less successful in developing countries without the economic cycles, entrepreneurial initiative, efficient banks, productive capacity and social security systems which are necessary if a system of market-economy stimuli such as the IMF prescribes is to function. Although the IMF, in introducing three-year stabilisation programmes in 1974 and in cooperating with the World Bank in the framework of Structural Adjustment Programmes (since 1980), has implicitly recognised that debt crises can only be solved in the long term, it continues to insist on its own inadequate diagnosis and therapy model.

In fact, debt crises are virtually pre-programmed in the economic, financial and development policies of governments which use foreign capital unproductively. Yet the IMF fails to realise that legacies from colonial history such as monocultural exports and rigid social structures severely limit developing countries' room for manoeuvre. (But to put all the blame on global economic factors such as the oil-price and interest-rates shocks, protectionism or recession in industrial countries and to absolve Third World governments from all responsibility is no more realistic.)

An analysis of specific cases shows that although there are various routes into debt the social and economic structures inherited from colonialism impede the productive use of capital and make it more difficult to earn the foreign exchange needed to service debts. The ruling classes and governments of developing countries must also take part of the blame because they do not use the available room for manoeuvre but thoughtlessly pursue economic and financial policies which are viable only in favourable economic conditions. If external factors (drops in raw materials prices, oil-prices and interest-rate rises) supervene, debt crisis is inevitable.

In contrast with the IMF, but equally incorrectly, developing countries argue that debt crises result primarily from such external shocks and they regard IMF terms as injustified interference in their national sovereignty. For years developing countries at international conferences, particularly at the UN Conference on Trade and Development (UNCTAD), have called for a softening of IMF terms and a substantial rise in the money available for loans. An automatic transfer of resources — which is in effect what the developing countries are demanding — would not necessarily bring about development but might instead lead many governments to squander even more money on measures which are futile in developmental terms. The unsuccessful IMF interventions in Zaire and Haiti, where loans were pocketed by 'cleptocratic' state-classes and stabilisation programmes were thwarted at every possible turn, demonstrate graphically where the automatic transfer of resources can lead. These examples also show that the IMF will treat a government more leniently if the USA, for political, economic or strategic motives, is interested in its survival. But the IMF is also capable of drastically changing the economic and political balance of power in a country. This has been particularly true for reform-oriented governments which looked likely to swerve from a pro-US line — as in the cases of Jamaica under Manley and Portugal after the revolution in 1974/5.

In positive terms, intervention would be required to bring about a reformed, development-oriented conditionality — if necessary over the heads of the ruling classes. Unlike the so far ineffectual IMF resolution of 1979 to take into account the political and social compatibility of stabilisation programmes, it would be essential to combine 'adjustment' with socio-political reforms designed to bring about a more just distribution of income. The burdens of the crisis would not be loaded onto the shoulders of social groups (urban wage- and salary-earners, smallholders, tenant farmers and agricultural workers) who were not responsible for the crisis. Above all, adjustment measures should not affect the satisfaction of basic needs. The success or failure of IMF programmes should not, as has hitherto been the case, be measured solely by monetary criteria. Qualitative criteria such as progress in domestic food production, socio-political improvements and social reforms should also be introduced. Creditors — as co-authors of crises — should be held jointly responsible and obliged to provide rescheduling and refinancing terms which would allow Third World countries more room to manoeuvre in their development policies. If we regard not only balance-of-payments deficits but also balance-of-payments surpluses as crisis-provoking, then we can argue that Third World countries in deficit should be given an opportunity to draw on at least part of these surpluses — through expansion of the IMF's Compensatory Financing Facility, for example. In the long term, a conditionality oriented towards development should promote low-debt development strategies which help to mobilise internal resources and reduce developing countries' traditional dependence on world markets.

1. The Debt Crisis of the Third World — A Crisis of Development

The Vicious Circle of Indebtedness

The World Bank estimated the Third World's total debt at the end of 1984 at US $ 895 thousand million. The figure includes IMF loans totalling US $ 33 thousand million (see Table 1.5). In fact, the developing countries' liabilities are probably far greater than this, since international statistics do not take 'military aid' loans into consideration and do not adequately register loans which run for less than a year. If 'military aid', estimated at $80–100 thousand million (Madeley, 1982, p. 184) is also taken into account, then the Third World's overall debt at the end of 1984 was probably close to one billion (1,000,000,000,000) dollars.[1]

The extent of the debt problem is indicated by the fact that the four major Latin American debtor states — Brazil, Mexico, Argentina and Venezuela — earned far less foreign exchange from exports in 1982 and 1983 than they needed to meet interest and principal repayments on their debts. New loans constantly have to be raised to pay off liabilities. The debt crisis is not confined to 'a number of countries with temporary liquidity difficulties' as World Bank President Clausen has diplomatically claimed (HB, 18 March 1983) but affects large and small countries, the poor and the not so poor. In 1984 over $100 thousand million were rescheduled in twenty-four Third World countries. Reschedulings, however, provide only short-term relief for debtor countries. Another debt catastrophe seems possible in the second half of the 80s. Projections by the Morgan Guaranty Trust Company indicated a further sharp increase in developing countries' foreign debt. (*World Financial Markets*, June 1983). 'The specter of an international financial collapse has receded', wrote *Fortune* in early 1985 (18 February, p. 29) but 'the economic agony goes on.'

It all began harmlessly. In the mid-1950s foreign debts which had been held in abeyance during the Second World War began to accumulate again. The development aid granted by the industrial countries to colonies which were gradually becoming independent played an important part in this process (Abbott, 1979, pp.35 ff.). In 1960 Third World debt stood at $18 thousand million; within ten years it had rocketed to $75 thousand million and at the beginning of the 'oil crisis' it had reached $112 thousand million (See Table 1.5). But acute debt crises requiring rescheduling arrangements remained comparatively rare until the mid-1970s.

Up to 1973, the developing countries had managed to reduce their balance-of-payments deficits either with their own income (export earnings and remittances by emigrant workers) or with other forms of capital inflow. In the 1960s, favourably-termed development aid credits, the granting of special drawing rights and direct investments by transnational corporations financed two-thirds of the balance-of-payments deficits in the Third World. In 1973, the proportion had dropped to a half and by 1981 it was down to just over a quarter (Betz, 1983, p. 33). The gaps increasingly had to be plugged with expensive private loans.

In 1970, almost half of the foreign loans raised by developing countries came from public sources (excluding IMF loans). By 1984 this proportion had dropped to 32% (IMF, 1984). Public funds are allocated either bilaterally or through a multilateral institution, mainly the World Bank. For some years the 31 so-called 'Least Developed Countries' (LDCs) have received development aid in the form of non-repayable subsidies. The necessities of development rarely play an important part in determining the amount of aid. Allies or geo-strategically important countries receive more than others. Industrial countries use development aid as a means of securing their interests in the Third World. The USA, for example, concentrated its aid payments on Israel and Egypt — which in 1981 received 19 and 14% respectively of all aid — and on a number of other strategically important countries (Garcia-Thoumi, 1983, p. 30).

Since the oil crisis of 1973/4, private banks have considerably increased their loan allocations to developing countries. In 1971, bank loans constituted 24% of total debt. By 1984, this had doubled to 49% (OECD, 1984; IMF, 1984). If we add to this the short-term loans given by private banks, their share comes to well over 60%. Apart from public and private loans, there is another category, private state-guaranteed export credits. They are used by developing countries to pay their import bills; from the viewpoint of the exporter or of the exporting country they are a well-tried means of improving competitiveness against other industrial countries and of opening up new markets. These suppliers' credits are granted either by the suppliers themselves or by a state export bank.[2]

Developing countries' growing indebtedness consists mainly of loans raised on the Eurocredit market. This market — sometimes also called the Eurodollar market because this is by far its largest sector — is a free international capital market largely independent of government and central bank controls (Schubert, 1982; June, 1976). Here dollar credits from dealings outside the USA deposited with transnational banks are passed on as loans to transnational corporations and to industrial, developing and East European countries. Private banks lend one another most of this money.

When the OPEC countries quadrupled crude oil prices in 1973, commercial moneylenders suddenly found themselves rolling in capital as many oil-producing countries transferred their surplus petrodollars to international bank accounts. Because of the recession, however, the banks could not profitably direct this money to the industrial countries, their traditional customers. The pressure to invest these vast sums led the banks to grant requests for loans from developing countries, although in previous years only a few Third World countries had been creditworthy on the Euromarket. Two years before the oil crisis, the number of developing countries which had taken up Euromarket loans was only 16. Two years after the crisis, this number had risen to 43 (Wagner, 1980, p. 144).

The banks, however, managed to shift some of their increased risk on to the developing countries by granting loans with variable interest rates, and they tried to reduce it by consortium loans. For an increasing number of Euro-loans the banks, instead of demanding a rate of interest fixed at the beginning of the loan term, periodically adjusted the rate of interest to the general interest trend, normally the LIBOR (London Inter-Bank Offered Rate), the rate at which international banks in London lend money to one another. On top of this basic interest rate the banks added a risk premium ('spread') and a one-off completion fee. The less creditworthy a country was, the higher the risk premiums and hence the loan costs which it had to pay. Consortium loans enabled the banks to raise huge sums and so to spread the credit risk. This practice also tempted medium-sized banks to take part in the lucrative Euro-loan business.

Private banks rapidly became the main financiers of the developing countries. It is impossible to ascertain exactly how high the medium- and long-term and above all short-term indebtedness of the Third World to private banks is because no international institution keeps a complete record of such data. Indeed none *can* keep a record, as the banks are not obliged to provide details of their credit operations on the Euromarket. The only information available is the estimates of the OECD, the World Bank, the Bank for International Settlements (BIS) and the IMF.[3] For 1984, the IMF estimated outstanding debts from private sources — finance and export loans — at US $559 thousand million, over two-thirds of overall debts (IMF, 1984, p. 68).

The governments of developing countries cannot provide complete information either. State institutions in these countries often do not know the precise level of indebtedness as they have no adequate records. This is especially true of loans raised by private borrowers from private banks. In many cases the right to take up foreign loans is not centrally regulated. State enterprises can take up loans without consulting the government or separate ministries may sign loan agreements without coordination with one another (F & D, 3/83, pp. 23 ff.). The real extent of the debacle generally becomes apparent only when a detailed report has to be presented to creditors. When in 1982 the debt crisis came to a head in Mexico and in Brazil, the governments of these countries started counting their cash and the data on foreign indebtedness had to be revised upwards several times in a short period. At this other debtor countries plucked up courage and corrected their debt statistics.

The foreign debts of developing countries are registered in the World Bank's debtor reporting system (for 105 states) on which IMF data also rely, and in the OECD's creditor reporting system (for 157 states). As the data of the debtors and of the creditors are generally incomplete, the OECD and World Bank data have considerable margins of error; the actual indebtedness of developing countries is far higher than the published figures suggest. Neither the OECD nor the World Bank in their individual country statistics take short-term loans into account (except for major debtors), yet both provide estimates of the overall total of the Third World's short-term liabilities. Taking into account all available data, the IMF and the World Bank estimated that developing countries' short-term debts at the end of 1977 totalled US $57 thousand million and had risen to $155 thousand million by 1982. More and more governments had financed balance of payments and budget deficits with expensive short-term loans (see Table 1.1).

Table 1.1 Short-term liabilities expressed as a percentage of developing countries' overall debt (excluding OPEC)

1971–2	*1973–6*	*1977–8*	*1979*	*1980–2*	*1983*	*1984*
10	15	18	17	20	16	14

Source: 1971–2 and 1973–6: OECD, 1984, p. 35; 1977–82: calculations on the basis of IMF, 1984, p. 68; 1983–4: World Bank, *World Debt Tables 1985–85*, p. ix.

In 1983 and 84, because of the dramatic increase in credit risk, the banks drastically reduced their loans to the Third World. The short-term indebtedness of developing countries dropped again to $122 thousand million (IMF 1984, p. 68; World Bank, *World Debt Tables 1984–85*, p. ix). If short-term credits are left out of account the spread of debt is highly uneven, especially among major debtors. In Israel, according to estimates made by the Morgan Guaranty Trust Company for 1982, short-term indebtedness accounted for 48% of total borrowing. The corresponding figures for other countries were: Venezuela 45%, the Philippines 38%, Colombia 32%, Mexico 30%, Peru 29%, South Korea 28%, Nigeria 27% and Brazil, Argentina, Chile and Turkey all 19% (*World Financial Markets*, June 1983, p. 8). The increasing tendency among Third World governments to take up expensive short-term loans has changed the debt structure and intensified their payment problems.

The Third World's debt servicing requirements grew much faster than its foreign liabilities. Between 1977 and 1984, interest and principal payments (of 123 developing countries) rose from 40 to $121 thousand million (IMF, 1984, p. 72). This would not be problematic if developing countries' export earnings had also increased. But in fact their capacity to service their debt has dropped

Table 1.2 Debt servicing ratios for all developing countries (1977–84)

Countries	1977	1980	1982	1984
All developing countries	15.1	17.4	24.4	21.5
Asia	7.6	8.2	11.2	9.9
Africa	11.9	16.5	22.2	24.9
Middle East	14.1	16.9	22.9	23.1
Latin America	32.0	35.7	55.1	44.6
Europe	14.9	18.8	22.1	21.4

Source: IMF, 1984, pp. 172f.

off considerably. The average debt service ratio — the ratio of interest and principal payments to export income — rose in two years from 17.4% in 1980 to 24.4% in 1982 (see Table 1.2).

The debt-service ratio is not in itself a reliable indicator of the point at which foreign debt becomes critical. All attempts to fix threshold values (or other indicators of indebtedness) which, when exceeded, lead to a debt crisis, have proved empirically untenable; the usefulness of a single indicator taken out of context is limited.[4] Mexico and Brazil, for example, continued to be granted new loans despite their high debt-service ratios until the middle of 1982, whereas other debtor countries with far lower debt-service ratios were forced to negotiate rescheduling agreements. What determines whether debt becomes critical is the point at which banks decide that a debtor is no longer creditworthy. This means that current refinancing of liabilities is no longer guaranteed — a decision that is not purely economic but is frequently also politically motivated.

The 'interest shock' (Schubert, 1983, pp. 233 ff.) hit the Third World countries even harder than their declining capacity to service their debts. From 1974–78 interest on bank loans was sometimes below the rate of inflation in industrial countries and the debtor countries benefited from a negative real interest-rate. But from 1977–81 the USA's high-interest policies forced interest on Euroloans up from 7.8 to 17.5%.[5] The newly industrialising countries, as well as a number of heavily indebted OPEC and raw-materials exporting countries, were severely hit by this development because their oil debts largely consisted of private loans with a variable rate of interest. According to the World Bank, medium-and long-term private debts with variable rates of interest totalled $190.3 thousand million at the end of 1982 (World Bank, 1984, p. xxiii). If LIBOR rises or falls by 1%, the debt burden for the developing countries changes by $1.9 thousand million. Including the cost of interest on short-term loans, the interest service ratio — the ratio of interest payments to export income — amounted in 1982 to 45% in Brazil, 44% in Argentina, 40% in Chile and 37% in Mexico (*World Financial Markets*, October 1982, p. 5).

Higher debt-service burdens and shorter loan terms meant that more and more developing countries had to use more and more loans to settle old debts, with the result that the net inflow decreased. According to World

Bank estimates, the net capital transfer to developing countries on medium-term and long-term debts in 1984 was an outflow of $7 thousand million, the first-ever negative balance. According to the same estimates, the 12 major debtor countries as early as 1982 were repaying some $300 million more than they were receiving. In 1984, this difference rose to $15 thousand million (World Bank, *World Debt Tables* 1984–85, p. xi).

The scope for financing future-oriented investments with foreign loans was consequently reduced; foreign money no longer supplemented national investment capital and foreign debt lost its developmental legitimation. The greater the proportion of the debt which would only be repaid by raising new loans, the more dependent the debtor countries became on their creditors' assessment of their creditworthiness. Economic and political 'misbehaviour' was immediately punished: new loans were not granted and even in the most favourable cases the creditworthiness of the countries concerned suffered considerably. This in turn had repercussions on the fixing of the risk supplement when interest was being calculated. The banks imposed further burdens on countries in severe financial difficulties and plunged them into further debt.

Although almost all developing countries are caught in the vicious circle of indebtedness, its dynamics affect different countries in very different ways. A mere 20 major debtors, mainly newly industrialising countries and creditworthy oil states, owed almost three-quarters of all the Third World's foreign debts in 1984 (see Table 1.3).

Table 1.3 Foreign debt of the 20 major Third World debtors (1984) (In thousands of millions of dollars)*

Brazil	103	Yugoslavia	24
Mexico	98	Chile	21
Argentina	48	Nigeria	21
South Korea	43	Algeria	18
Venezuela	35	India	18
Indonesia	32	Malaysia	17
Israel	29	Portugal	15
Philippines	27	Peru	14
Turkey	25	Thailand	14
Egypt	22	Pakistan	13

* Very little information is available on the debts of Iraq, which were estimated at $32–40 thousand million in 1985. (*NZZ*, 18 April 1985 and *FT*, 7 May 1985).

Sources:World Financial Markets, October/November 1984, p. 5; daily newspaper reports.

In contrast, low income developing countries (most black African countries, Haiti and some Asian countries) have foreign debts which are low in absolute terms or when measured against GNP. This cannot however, be described as development at a low level of debt. The economic growth of these countries is dependent on the inflow of favourable development aid loans. Many countries could not survive without such payments from abroad.[6] They have not been spared by the intensification of the debt crisis — from 1981 to 1984 15 of the 50 or so black African countries had to reschedule their debts (see Appendix).

The following example illustrates that even the payment of small sums in debt-service often means that the poorest developing countries have to make greater sacrifices than countries with high income. The ratio of debt to GNP is often used as an indicator to measure a country's capacity to produce real resources which in turn can be used to finance debt-servicing. In 1980, per capita debt in South Korea was US $461 and in Bangladesh US $41. The ratio of debt to GNP in South Korea (a newly industrialising country) was 30% and in Bangladesh, the fourth poorest country in the world, it was 33%. The burden of debt thus seems at first sight to be roughly equal for both countries.

Calculations of this kind disregard the fact that only a certain proportion of the gross national product — a proportion which differs from country to country depending on the level of development — is actually available for new investment. The proportion of the GNP which is needed for the satisfaction of basic requirements has to be subtracted from the whole. If this necessary consumption — marked by the poverty limit — is subtracted, then the remainder is disposable income or hypothetical economic surplus.[7] If the debt is now in each case measured against the surplus, it becomes apparent that the burden is greater for the poorest developing countries. In South Korea, where income and therefore disposable income is high, the ratio rises to only 34% whereas in Bangladesh — despite a comparatively low overall level of debt — it rockets to 111%. This calculation is merely illustrative, as disposable income is a purely statistical quantity, but it does draw attention to the limitations and the often misleading nature of the commonly used statistical indicators.

Table 1.4 The burden of indebtedness in countries with different levels of development

	South Korea	Bangla desh	
Per capita gross national product	1528	126	$
Per capita debt	461	41	$
Debt as percentage of GNP	30	33	%
Poverty limit	155	89	$
Disposable income (statistical)	1373	37	$
Debt expresed as a percentage of disposable income	34	111	%

The above amounts are all in US dollars (1980 prices)

Sources: Authors' calculations based on FAO, *The State of Food and Agriculture 1981*, Rome, 1982; World Bank, *World Development Report*, 1982; OECD, *External Debt of Developing Countries*, 1982 Survey, Paris, 1982.

Table 1.5: Public and private debts of developing countries, 1970–84 (in thousands of millions of US dollars)

	1960	1970	1973	1975	1977	1979	1980	1981	1982	1983	1984
Overall debt according to World Bank estimates (133 developing countries)[1]							610	702	775	843	895
Short-term debts							119	145	155	134	122
Public and private, medium- and long-term debts according to World Bank Debtor Reporting System (105 developing countries)		63.5	109.2	161.9	240.1	353.0	412	470	525	598	655
Debt-service payments		9.4	16.0	23.0	33.1	63.4	71.1	83.0	81.1	85.4	92
Net transfer[2]		5.9	10.8	23.6	24.9	31.2	26.4	31.2	14.5	− 1.0	− 7
Public and private, medium- long-term debt according to OECD Creditor Reporting System (157 developing countries)	17.9	74.7	112.4	173	262	391	445	501	552	606	n.a.
Debt service payments		10.2	17.2	25.1	40.1	71.2	82.3	99.7	107.6	96.1	n.a.
Debts to IMF	0.4	0.8	1.2	4.8	7.9	8.3	9.5	14.0	22.0	30.0	33

[1] Including short-term loans and IMF loans

[2] Payments minus debt servicing payments

Sources: OECD/DAC, Statistical Appendix to 1977 *Annual Report;* OECD, *External Debt of Developing Countries, 1982 Survey,* Paris, 1982; OECD, *External Debt of Developing Countries, 1983 Survey,* Paris, 1984; World Bank, *Developments and Prospects for the External Debt of the Developing Countries, 1970–80 and Beyond,* Washington, 1981; World Bank, *World Debt Tables* for various years; IMF, *International Financial Statistics,* various years.

Only a few developing countries opted for a development path with a low level of debt and avoided dependence on commercial or concessionary loans. The outstanding example is Albania, which is almost self-sufficient. Its constitution forbids the government to raise foreign loans (except for short-term suppliers' credits) because foreign debt is regarded as a potential threat to national independence.[8] All other socialist developing countries are dependent on loans from western creditors or else on injections of finance from the Soviet Union and Eastern Bloc countries. Examples of development with low levels of debt have been and still are rare because only states consistently pursuing a de-linking development strategy (one aimed at uncoupling from world markets) can dispense with foreign loans. But almost all developing countries pursue policies of integration into world markets — and such policies have always been connected with indebtedness.[9]

Indebtedness and Development — The Lessons of the Past

The flow of finance across national borders is not an exclusively twentieth-century phenomenon.[10] Even in the late Middle Ages and in the early modern era — when credit operations and modern banking were gradually beginning to develop — state spending was often financed with foreign money. Dutch manufacturing was built up with the aid of Italian capital. Dutch capital helped to finance English factories and to launch the industrial revolution. Soon the increased allocation of credit necessitated the establishment of central banks. These alone could ensure the stability of currencies and provide protection for private banks. After the founding of the Bank of England in 1694, London developed, especially from the beginning of the 19th Century, into the world centre of finance (to be joined in the 20th Century by New York). The year 1817 marks the beginning of the granting of foreign loans as we know it today. The English family bank Baring, the most powerful banking house of the time, lent 100 million francs to France, which had been hard hit by the Napoleonic Wars (Greayer, 1978, p. 298).

Foreign loans have always been two-edged instruments for debtor countries. At the beginning of this century, Rosa Luxemburg (1975, p. 376) aptly summed up the contradictory nature of the international loan system: foreign debt, she wrote, was

> indispensable for the emancipation of rising capitalist states and at the same time the surest means for the old capitalist states to patronise the young ones, to control their finances and to exert pressure on their foreign customs and trade policies.

In countries such as England, the USA, Canada and Australia, foreign loans helped to promote industrialisation to a level at which independent, self-sustaining development was possible. But in most cases attempts by developing countries to free themselves from colonial and post-colonial dependence by foreign loans have merely increased this dependence.

Loans raised abroad, far from helping developing countries to escape the clutches of the colonial metropoles and to modernise their industries, often plunged them into debt crises. Insolvency meant that the debtor countries were subjected to international financial control by creditors and their room for manoeuvre in foreign policy seriously reduced; revolutionary upheavals and sometimes even military occupation resulted. At times, the imperial powers deliberately used the allocation of loans as a means of bringing about colonial dependence and legitimating military occupation. The histories of Egypt, Morocco, Tunisia and the Ottoman Empire provide graphic illustrations of this. A glance at developments in Latin America, which suffered several debt crises in the 19th and 20th Centuries, reveals astonishing parallels between the 1920s and 30s and the present situation: world economic crisis, American high interest policies, unproductive use of credit by debtors and ill-considered loan allocation policies designed only to make short-term profits for creditors.

Egypt

'My country is no longer part of Africa, we are part of Europe'[11] — this was the motto with which the Egyptian *khedive* (viceroy) Ismail, from 1863 onwards, attempted to accelerate the modernisation and 'Europeanisation' of Egypt and to bring it to the level of the leading industrialised countries of Europe. He financed this programme by raising loans first on the Paris and later on the London money markets (Landes, 1958; Ducruet, 1964). The modernisation of industry and the army was intended in the first place to finally liberate Egypt from Ottoman rule and later to protect it from the clutches of the imperial powers of England and France. But this programme only led to bankruptcy in 1876 and to the setting up of joint Anglo-French financial control. It ended with military occupation by the British in 1882.

The construction of modern irrigation plants and of new roads, the purchase of steamships, and — the most ambitious project of all — the building of the Suez Canal, pushed Egypt's foreign debt from £3.2 million (1862) to £68.5 million (1876). The large-scale projects were carried out by foreign, mainly English firms who were often able to charge excessive prices by bribing the Egyptian bureaucracy. Egypt was to repay the debts by increasing the cultivation and export of cotton.

When the Civil War cut back cotton production in the USA and the price of cotton shot up, Egypt was gripped by cotton fever. To expand production, traditional methods of farming were modernised, irrigation plants, steam-ploughs and modern devices for processing raw cotton were imported from England on credit. When the Civil War in the USA ended, cotton speculation collapsed and prices fell drastically within a few days. As cotton-growing was no longer attractive, but sugar prices were now high, cane-sugar production and sugar export seemed to be a lucrative alternative. Egyptian agriculture was again turned upside down and new machines were introduced, again on credit. By the mid-1870s the brief boom had ended and in 1876 the *khedive* had to declare Egypt's insolvency.

To reduce its budget deficit the Egyptian state transferred much of its landed property to joint-stock companies, most of them English. It had already sold its share in the Suez Canal Company to the English majority shareholders in 1875. Further tax increases (which had to be borne mainly by small farmers or *fellaheen* who had already been bled dry) were introduced in the hope of mastering the crisis. In 1879, the imperial powers successfully insisted on the setting up of a control organ, the *Commission de la Dette Egyptienne*, whose job was to ensure the repayment of loans. In 1880, Egypt's debt-servicing payments ate into 50% of its export earnings and two-thirds of the state budget (Corm, 1982, p. 40). The political situation was disastrous: the *khedive* was overthrown and the farmers revolted. An uprising of national forces in Alexandria in 1882 provided England with a pretext for marching into Egypt and incorporating it in the British Empire.

Egypt was not unique. The colonisation of Tunisia (1881) and of Morocco (1912) by France followed a similar pattern. The national elites' attempts to modernise the economy led to imports of technology financed from abroad and to increasing foreign liabilities which the countries soon found themselves unable to repay. Financial control was followed by military occupation. Unlike the case of Egpyt, where it had to give precedence to England, France forestalled the claims of Italy to Tunisia and of Germany to Morocco (Fieldhouse, 1977, pp. 142 ff.; Feiss, 1930, pp. 397 ff,; Corm, 1982, pp. 45 ff.).[12]

The Ottoman Empire (Turkey)

The feudal ruling class in the Ottoman Empire was forced to modernise its infrastructure and military power to prevent the disintegration of the empire and to arm itself against Russian attempts to gain control of the Bosphorus and the Dardanelles. The costs of the Crimean War (1853–6), ambitious railway projects, the construction of ports and excessive military expenditure put severe strains on the budget. Modernisation could not be funded with domestic finance because no more money could be squeezed out of the farmers and the taxation system was extremely generous to great landowners. The Ottoman Empire therefore had to fall back on foreign loans. The imperial powers — England, France, and increasingly from the 1880s onwards, Germany — were seeking spheres of influence and therefore provided the necessary finance. New loans could be obtained so easily that the ruling class had no need and no incentive to draw more on domestic funds.

Indebtedness — in 1858, 5.5 million Turkish pounds; in 1874, 218 million (Corm, 1982, p. 41) — developed a dynamism of its own which could not be stopped. A snowball effect ensued:

The more money Europe lent, the more ways Turkey spent. The Imperial Government sought the loans. It was simpler to pledge next year's tithes as guarantee for a new loan than to effect economies in the local administration and to retain control of the tithes in order to meet current expenses. Or it was easier to fund a constantly reappearing floating debt by a foreign loan than to abolish wasteful methods in the central administration. (Blaisdell, 1966, p. 38.)

In 1875 the Ottoman Empire had to suspend repayments of its foreign debts. England and France thereupon forced through international control of Turkish finance. The control organ, the *Conseil d'Administration de la Dette Publique Ottomane*, received taxes on salt, tobacco and spirits, the tithe on silk, fishery taxes and 10% of the railway companies' income. Although the Ottoman Empire never lost its sovereignty in international law, without control of its own finances its national independence existed on paper only. As the British Foreign Secretary Lord Derby put it in 1879: 'The daily surveillance of which Turkey is the object in her domestic affairs has reduced her sovereign authority to practically zero.' (Quoted from Blaisdell, 1966, p. 26.)

Latin America
Latin America, whose nation states — with only a few exceptions — have enjoyed national sovereignty for 160–70 years, has always been the major debtor region of the Third World. Here foreign loans were used to establish infrastructures — often railways — to develop exports from the mining and agriculture industries or to finance military equipment and military operations (Corm, 1982, p. 47). From 1822–6, English banks granted several loans worth a total of about £21 million to a number of former Spanish colonies which had just gained their independence — including Chile, Peru, Argentina, Mexico and Guatemala. The wars of independence of Colombia and Venezuela were financed partly with British loans (Galeano, 1980, p. 225; Greayer, 1978, p. 299). By exporting capital and goods, England, the first industrial nation, replaced Spain and Portugal as the metropole of Latin America (Rippy, 1959). The majority of Latin American countries, of course, over-reached themselves with their debts. All the debtor countries of the region — apart from the former Portuguese colony of Brazil, which had also raised capital on the London financial market — found themselves in serious repayment crises from 1825–7.

Falling prices for export goods, coupled with constant price levels for imported goods, forced the Latin American countries even after this to fall back on foreign loans to finance their balance-of-payments deficits. In Brazil, which had to adjust to constantly sinking terms of trade, debt-service payments in the middle of the 19th Century ate into almost 40% of the budget (Galeano, 1980, p. 226). In the 1870s, Latin America experienced its second debt crisis. Argentina, Brazil and Chile were the only countries to escape insolvency.

In 1914, Argentina (US $784 million) and Brazil (US $717 million) had the highest debts in Latin America. The foreign debt of the entire region totalled about US $2.2 thousand million. After the First World War, the USA replaced Great Britain as the major supplier of finance. The 1920s saw a huge increase in Latin America's overall debt. In 1929 the region's foreign liabilities reached US $4.1 thousand million. Argentina accounted for US $1.2 thousand million and Brazil for US $1.1 thousand million of this, while Mexico and Chile accounted for US $826 million and 499 million respectively (Kneitschel/Burdach, 1974, p. 65 f.).

A substantial part of the investments financed with foreign loans went into the agricultural and mining industries to increase foreign exchange earnings and service debts. In many cases, however, foreign money was not used to expand productive capacity and earn foreign exchange. Many projects financed with foreign capital proved to be misplanned — for example, the building of an expensive railway in the Colombian mountains (Aldcroft, 1978, p. 287). Frequently loans were raised to pay off debts, to avoid delays in payment or simply to finance budget deficits — regardless of whether it would in future be possible to service these increasing foreign liabilities.

The creditors were partly to blame for this development. Their checks on the creditworthiness of debtor countries were superficial. Indeed, they virtually forced money on the finance-hungry Latin American countries with no regard for whether debtors were using the money for development or for whether they could earn the necessary foreign exchange to pay off interest and principal. As today, the creditors tacitly assumed that in the event of repayment difficulties the debtor countries could be forced to adopt the necessary stabilisation measures. According to Aldcroft (1978, p. 298)

> the creditor countries' crucial error was that they turned their backs on the debtor countries at the worst possible moment, like pulling a man up a cliff with a rope and then, before he reaches the top, letting the rope go and plunging him to the ground.

In the second half of the 1920s, Latin America's debt-service commitments became alarmingly high. The costs of interest and principal repayments reached almost three times the level of capital inflow, yet they could at first be covered by balance-of-trade surpluses. But from 1928/9 onwards the catastrophe could no longer be averted. The last American boom before the world economic crisis, and the US government's high interest policies from 1928 onwards, attracted capital to the US market and brought about a drastic reduction in the supply of credit for Latin American countries. From 1929 on, the US economy gradually slumped into recession. Latin America now found it increasingly difficult to sell its exports in the US market. At the same time the prices of its major exports sank lower and lower. Foreign exchange earnings dropped substantially. Since creditors now left the region in the lurch by refusing to grant further loans, current account and budget deficits could no longer be financed by foreign loans. The Latin American governments tried to master the situation with import restrictions, foreign exchange controls and devaluation. Finally they were forced to sell part of their gold reserves. But in the course of the 1930s Latin American countries found it impossible to service their debts and almost all of them became insolvent. Bolivia in 1930 was the first country to stop servicing its debts. By the end of 1933 all the countries of the region except Argentina and Haiti had followed Bolivia's example (Aldcroft, 1978, p. 288; Abbott, 1979, p. 24).[13]

USA, Canada, Australia, New Zealand, Japan

Unlike the North African, Near Eastern and Latin American countries discussed above, which are all today — indeed today more than ever — still struggling with the debt problem, the USA, Canada, Australia, New Zealand and Japan, like the industrialised countries of Europe before them, have succeeded with the aid of foreign loans in establishing and maintaining self-sustaining development.

Until the First World War, the USA was the major debtor country. Its foreign trade structures, characterised by imports of manufactured goods and exports of raw materials, were very similar to those of a developing country. In the 1840s and in some cases even later, some federal states defaulted on payments when raw materials prices dropped. The ratio of foreign debt to GNP in the USA in the 1830s has been estimated at 40%. The figures for 1869 and 1899 are 24% and 20% respectively, and even in 1914 it was still as high as 18% (McMullen, 1979, p. 3).

Development in Canada, Australia and New Zealand was even more heavily dependent on foreign finance. In Canada the ratio of foreign debt to GNP in 1900 was 114%, in 1910 111% and in 1920 88%; by 1960 it had dropped to 42.7% (McMullen, 1979, p. 4). In 1930, the ratio of foreign loans to the national debt was 63% in Canada, 52% in Australia and 37% in New Zealand (Aldcroft, 1978, p. 294). Whereas Canada, Australia and New Zealand remained net debtors and were hard pressed to service their debts during the world economic crisis (Aldcroft, 1978, p. 295), the USA, thanks to its rapid emergence as a powerful industrial state, soon progressed from debtor-country to creditor-country status. The defeat of the southern states in the American Civil War put an end to slavery and contributed to the breakthrough of agrarian-capitalist relations throughout the USA. Democratic institutions enabled the labour movement to force through relatively high wages, which in turn triggered off a mass demand for consumer goods and the opening of the domestic market. Thanks to its highly qualified labour force, the USA soon succeeded in independently developing new technology and by the beginning of the 20th Century it was an exporter of manufactured goods. The First World War marks the USA's definitive breakthrough as the world's leading industrial nation. While the European countries were weakened by military conflict, the USA, which did not enter the war until 1917, enjoyed an export boom. It supplied the *entente* powers with arms, ammunition, raw materials and food and also penetrated other markets which the European countries were forced to neglect because of the war. Thus the USA achieved high trade and balance-of-payments surpluses and became a creditor of European and non-European countries (Hardach, 1973, pp. 271 ff.)

Like the USA, Japan also progressed from debtor to creditor status as a result of the First World War. Loans from England had helped to finance the wars against China in 1897 and Tsarist Russia in 1905 (Corm, 1982, p. 55; Sampson, 1981, p. 41). During the First World War, Japan benefited above all from the American export boom and the falling-off of European exports to Asian countries. High balance-of-payments surpluses enabled Japan to become a creditor. In the 1920s, however, Japan financed its industrial development with capital imports which again made the country a net debtor (Hardach, 1973, pp. 278 ff.).

Wars, as two world wars and the example of the USA have shown, can qualitatively change the balance of power between imperial powers. In some cases, they enabled countries to make the qualitative leap from debtor to creditor status. But this does not identify the economic and social structures which allowed countries such as the USA, Canada, Japan and Australia to achieve a self-sustaining development with a relatively high standard of living for large sections of the population whereas the majority of countries which try to achieve such a development with the aid of foreign loans are constantly falling into debt crises.

Extravagance and over-ambitious modernisation projects have in many cases been a major factor in debt crises; but the failure to expand productive capacity to earn enough money to service debts is rooted in the *economic and social structures of the debtor countries*. Following Senghaas' analysis (1982) of the economic development of Europe a number of development-inhibiting factors can be discerned:

Monoculture

The money for debt servicing was, and generally still is earned from a few export goods and often from only one product. As with cotton production in Egypt, the export sector in many developing countries is still a kind of enclave and has not dovetailed with the domestic market. Many of today's industrial countries also had one-sided export economies in their early stages. Yet they constantly expanded their range of exports until it included manufactured goods and they also succeeded in linking export production to production for the domestic market. While the industrial countries became increasingly resistant to price slumps or drops in demand caused by world market factors, countries with less flexible development were plunged again and again into crisis.

The Narrowness of the Domestic Market

A national domestic market of mass demand for consumer goods and less

19

sophisticated means of production has not emerged in developing countries because of extremely unequal distribution of land and of wealth, which disproportionately benefits great landowners and mining companies. In all the examples quoted above, the consumption requirements of the great landowners and of the urban upper-classes could not be adequately met by domestic production; their demands could only be satisfied by sophisticated luxury goods to be imported from industrial countries. Equipment for agriculture and the mining industry also had to be imported. The foreign exchange earned by exports was not sufficient to pay for all these imports, which consequently had to be financed with loans. In contrast, the distribution of land and of property in the industrial countries allowed a wider spread of income from the export industry, often through the taxation system or through political reforms. Domestic demand for mass-consumer goods was sufficient to stimulate the production of investment goods necessary for their creation.

Failure to Introduce Social Reforms
The economic and social development of the industrial countries was possible only because the decline of feudalism allowed capitalist structures to form in industry. Political power gradually shifted from great landowners to an industrial bourgeoisie, from whom the emergent labour movement wrested higher wages and social reforms. In contrast, no agrarian reforms or revolutions which would have modernised agriculture took place in the developing countries. Political power remained largely in the hands of parasitic oligarchies and unproductive state-classes. The demands of workers and peasant farmers for a greater share in social wealth were crushed with repressive methods, as the history of the authoritarian military regimes in Latin America or in Turkey in the 19th and 20th Centuries bears witness.

Deficits in Education and Technology
High levels of literacy and the establishment of education and research institutes from the early stages of industrialisation onwards enabled the industrial countries to develop their technology independently and to train skilled workers. Third World countries had few educational and research institutions of their own and thus remained dependent on foreign aid. Where sufficient local experts were lacking, they were forced to import technologically sophisticated goods and to pay for them partly with foreign loans. The modernisation of Egyptian agriculture by imported (and loan-financed) English steam-ploughs in the middle of the 19th Century to be repaid from the heavily fluctuating proceeds of cotton sales is still the classic example of technology imports.

Limited National Sovereignty
All industrial countries were at any early stage able to control their own resources and attained complete sovereignty in their foreign trade and

foreign policy. National independence was the precondition for the productive use of export earnings according to national priorities. But in the developing countries even today a significant proportion of resources is controlled by foreign companies. Export income benefits the economy and society of the country concerned only to a limited extent because the state cannot tax foreign companies at more than nominal levels. The international financial controls imposed on Egypt and the Ottoman Empire illustrate how in times of severe debt crisis domestic tax income had to be pledged directly to foreign creditors and sovereignty in foreign trade matters (such as the imposition of duties) was lost. Such interference in the foreign trade and foreign policies of other countries is not confined to the 19th Century. Even today, some IMF terms resemble such intervention. In its stabilisation programmes the Fund insists on the abolition of import controls and quotas. In the case of Zaire, the IMF even appointed its officials to leading posts in the Central Bank and the Customs Authority (see Chapter 3).

Indebtedness and Creditworthiness: Who Gets Money and Who Does Not

As the historical examples show, the question of whether a debtor country could or would repay interest or principal was always the central consideration for creditors when granting loans. In the age of imperialism (1880–1914), countries unable or unwilling to pay were simply occupied militarily. Since then, creditors have above all relied on the fact that in the event of balance-of-payments and debt crises the debtor countries would have to take the necessary stabilisation measures. Admittedly, creditors have on several occasions had to write off debts; but on the whole, the granting of loans has proved a lucrative business in which most of the risks are borne by the debtor. Whereas in the past repayment 'morale' was, if necessary, restored by gunboat diplomacy, the methods of disciplining a debtor country today are more subtle. The IMF's stabilisation programmes achieve the same goal without sabre-rattling. Few countries are prepared to risk the stigma of debt-repudiation because this could permanently ruin their creditworthiness.[14]

Modern communications systems have greatly improved methods of assessing debtor countries' creditworthiness as compared with the 19th Century, when news took weeks and months to arrive from distant continents. Yet even today creditors often find themselves facing the ruins of their credit policies. When the banks were overflowing with liquidity and the demand for credit in industrial countries was relatively weak, they frequently granted generous loans even to unreliable customers. As a banker has put it: 'a lack of first-class debtors led to the granting of loans to less solvent debtors, and the element of security was neglected in favour of the profit component.' (Rhein, 1980, p. 180.) Fierce competition among the banks themselves intensified this trend. So far, all attempts to develop early warning systems to provide advance information on debtors' impending inability (or unwillingness) to pay have failed. In the mid-1970s, raw-materials exporters such as Zaire and Peru were unwittingly financed into crisis by the banks. And in 1982/3, the near-collapse of the major debtors Brazil and Mexico took the banks completely by surprise.

The shock of the Mexico and Brazil crises made the banks realise that the international debt crisis is no longer solely a crisis of debtors but also one of creditors. The criteria to assess creditworthiness have radically changed. A large number of studies have been published since the beginning of the 1980s analysing credit risk in terms of the banks' own interests (Guth, 1980; Abs, 1981; Group of Thirty, 1982; Eaton/Gersovitz, 1982). But despite the impending collapse of the international monetary and financial system, no generally recognised assessment criteria have yet been developed. The Group of Thirty — founded in 1978 to study the basic problems of the world monetary and financial system on behalf of the banks — analysed the assessment systems of 11 major banks and concluded that there were as many criteria catalogues as there were banks (Group of Thirty, 1982, pp. 45 f.). What all assessment systems have in common is an attempt to ascertain and to quantify the economic performance, debt-servicing capacity, administrative capacity and political stability of debtor countries. The Group of Thirty report contains the following list of indicators, some quantifiable, others not:

Debt-service ratio (used as criterion by 10 out of 11 banks)
Growth of GDP (9)
Export structure (9)
Per capita income (8)
Export growth (8)
IMF loans and foreign exchange reserves (8)
Foreign debt (8)
Monetary and budgetary policies (8)
Import structure (7)
Labour potential, numbers and level of training/education (7)
Ratio of imports to foreign exchange reserves (6)
Structure of foreign debt (6)
Capacity for peaceful change (6)
Probability of internal conflict (6)
Minority problems (6)

plus a number of other factors which only a minority of the banks took into account.[15]

With the aid of these criteria the banks produce national risk tables which read like hit-lists of creditworthiness. It is virtually impossible for the layman to work out how these figures are arrived at. All the major banks in the world apparently have such lists, according to which loans are granted to industrial and to developing countries, to capitalist and to socialist states alike.[16]

Specialist publications which are widely read and highly influential in the world of banking have also tried to establish uniform assessments and standardised criteria. The best-known aids to risk-assessment are the country risk tables in *Euromoney* (London) and in the *Institutional Investor* (New York). The following league table for Third World countries was published in the *Institutional Investor* of March 1984 (this list awarded the USA 96.0 out of a possible 100 points):

Table 1.6 Creditworthiness of Third World Countries, March 1984 (Expressed in points, maximum 100)

North Africa and Near East		One year change			One year change
Saudi Arabia	72.2	−0.5	Nigeria	32.4	−10.1
Kuwait	65.5	−1.1	Kenya	26.7	−3.1
United Arab Emirates	60.9	+0.7	Zimbabwe	19.2	−4.5
Bahrain	56.8	0	Mauritius	17.1	−2.1
Qatar	55.9	+1.0	Congo	16.1	−0.8
Algeria	54.5	0	Senegal	16.0	−1.1
Oman	49.1	+2.4	Malawi	14.7	−2.8
Tunisia	45.2	−1.7	Angola	12.6	−2.7
Jordan	35.9	−1.5	Seychelles	11.3	−1.4
Libya	33.4	−3.7	Liberia	10.3	−1.0
Cyprus	32.8	−2.0	Ethiopia	9.1	−0.4
Egypt	32.3	−2.1	Zambia	8.9	−1.4
Israel	28.3	−4.1	Tanzania	8.4	−1.4
Turkey	27.3	+5.4	Sierra Leone	7.9	2»1.7
Morocco	25.4	−4.8	Sudan	7.7	−0.5
Iraq	20.0	−11.0	Zaire	5.5	+0.1
Iran	18.4	+4.6	Uganda	4.4	+0.4
Syria	17.4	−3.7			
Lebanon	14.1	−1.7	*Latin America*		
			Trinidad and Tobago	50.3	−3.8
			Colombia	49.1	−6.4
			Venezuela	37.7	−19.7
Asia and Oceania			Mexico	36.2	−0.7
Singapore	78.0	+0.5	Paraguay	35.4	−5.2
Taiwan	68.4	+2.2	Panama	34.2	−4.3
Malaysia	67.2	−3.6	Barbados	30.5	—
Hong Kong	65.6	−7.1	Brazil	30.0	−18.1
PR China	63.6	+2.6	Uruguay	28.6	− 8.3
South Korea	54.5	−2.0	Chile	27.3	−16.7
Thailand	52.3	+1.1	Ecuador	25.4	−8.2
Indonesia	49.7	−4.3	Argentina	25.0	−5.3
India	47.6	+1.3	Peru	24.6	−9.7
Papua New Guinea	39.0	−3.5	Dominican Republic	15.1	−2.0
Sri Lanka	27.6	−2.6	Jamaica	15.0	−2.0
Philippines	24.3	−11.4	Costa Rica	13.3	+0.4
Pakistan	21.1	−0.4	Guatemala	12.4	−1.5
Bangladesh	12.3	−1.0	Cuba	10.4	−1.6
North Korea	3.6	−0.8	Honduras	10.3	−2.3
			Haiti	10.2	—
Africa south of the Sahara			Bolivia	9.6	−2.5
Cameroon	35.5	−0.6	Grenada	6.4	−1.3
Gabon	34.4	−2.1	El Salvador	6.4	−0.5
Ivory Coast	32.6	−4.0	Nicaragua	5.3	−0.8

Source: Institutional Investor. International edition, March 1984, p. 68

Figure 1. The Creditworthiness of Selected Third World Countries, 1981-1983.

(For comparison: Federal Republic of Germany.)

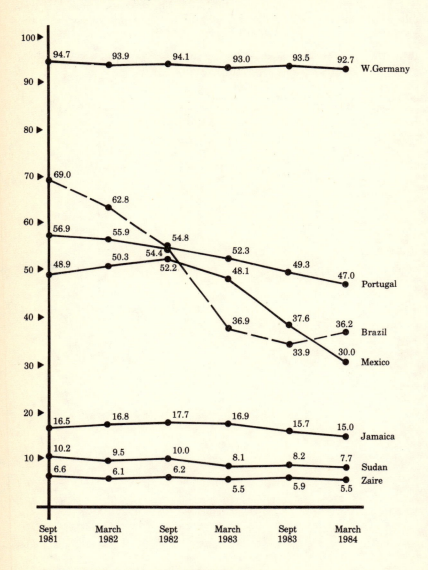

Based on *International Investor*, International edition,
September 1982, September 1983 and March 1984.

International creditors have been regularly surprised by debt crises in the Third World. The creditworthiness of Mexico and Brazil was drastically reduced only *after* crisis point had been reached — despite the data-gathering and analyses of the World Bank, the OECD and the Bank for International Settlements. Creditors still have insufficient information to gain a reliable early warning technique, primarily because the short-term debt records of developing countries are incomplete.

To achieve a better overview of credit risks, several dozen banks founded the Institute of International Finance (IIF) in 1983 in Washington — the headquarters of the IMF, the World Bank and the US government. Its purpose is to gather, analyse and disseminate data and information on the economic and financial situation and the development policies of debtor countries (IIF Foundation Statute, January 1983). Detailed information on the short-, medium- and long-term development of debtor countries is vitally important for banks. Oriented exclusively towards profit, it is essential for them to know if they can do business with countries in the short, the medium or the long term. From the perspective of their own interests 'banks need a clear picture in order to be able to make a decision for the entire period of the credit commitment.' It is therefore indispensable for banks to know 'if a country is creditworthy for two, five or ten years' because 'the prediction of greater uncertainty in five years may certainly justify the decision to do business with this country for a further three years. To ignore this temporal aspect is to deprive the bank's management of an important component for optimal planning' (Jahn, 1980, p. 502.) The business motto: suck to the last drop of blood and then move on to another victim, could hardly be more clearly expressed. And it shows not only that the debt crisis of the Third World is also a creditors' crisis but that the creditors must bear a large responsibility for the catastrophe.

The major international banks, in assessing the creditworthiness of debtor countries, are primarily interested in whether these countries have received the stamp of approval of the World Bank or the IMF for their economic and financial policies. Countries which get into debt crises and then refuse to apply IMF-style stabilisation measures risk incurring the banks' displeasure and having their flow of credit severely reduced or cut off altogether. A further factor influencing the assessment of a country's creditworthiness is its relation to the USA and its strategic importance for the West in the East-West confrontation. Countries which receive the USA's seal of political approval and obtain continuing financial support (including substantial IMF funds) also receive a bonus from the banks, whereas states with reform-oriented or populist governments which attempt to break away from US influence have great difficulties on international capital markets and with the IMF. Jamaica under the Manley government is an example (see Chapter 3). Countries which keep their distance from the USA – such as Algeria — are assessed primarily in terms of their economic potential and of how profitable such a loan would probably be for the banks.

To sum up: the creditworthiness of developing countries is judged not only in terms of their economic potential and ability to service their debts but also in terms of their overall social structure and their domestic and foreign policy orientation. Economists have tried in vain to predict debt crises or to establish 'scientifically' based critical threshold values for indebtedness; yet the fact remains that acute debt crises have arisen only when banks declare a country uncreditworthy and withhold their funds.

Routes to Debt Crisis: Are the Causes National or International?

To avoid debt crises, countries taking up loans — whether they are industrial states such as France, market-economy oriented developing countries such as Brazil, state-capitalist countries like Algeria or socialist countries such as Poland — must above all use foreign money in a way which ensures their continuing solvency. The ability to repay interest and principal depends on whether foreign loans are invested productively so that the profit from the projects so financed and the growth rate of the GDP enable the country to earn the funds needed to service its debts. It is not, however, enough to boost the domestic economy with foreign loans. Foreign capital ought to be invested so as to earn enough foreign exchange to meet interest and principal repayments. Debt servicing — and *a fortiori* interest payments — must at no point exceed the amount of foreign exchange earned from growth in production. If the state takes up foreign loans, it must also ensure that it increases its tax revenue so that it can meet its debt-service requirements. In principle, the continued use of foreign loans for consumption only is disastrous, because it means that neither the economic growth necessary within an overall development strategy nor the necessary foreign exchange targets can be achieved (OECD, 1974, pp. 32ff.; Holthus, 1981, pp. 249 ff.).

The reasons why these basic conditions for the productive use of foreign capital are not met are generally manifold and complex; but they can be broken down into three groups:

— the colonial legacy, which bequeathed to the developing countries certain economic, social and political structures which already contained the germs of 'indebted' development within them;

— the debt-ridden economic, financial and development policies of governments and ruling classes in the developing countries;

— external 'shocks', world market tendencies which affect the developing countries.

A number of articles have identified external factors as the main cause of indebtedness, blaming the two oil-price shocks of 1973 and 1979/80 and the drop in raw materials prices as the main factors behind the disaster. Whereas one group (UNCTAD, 1979; Dell/Lawrence, 1980) argues that the developing countries are helpless in the face of such developments and require additional aid, the IMF and the World Bank stress that the developing countries ought to have adjusted to these new world market conditions and that the failure to do so caused the crisis (IMF, 1981; *World Development Report*, 1981). They allege that the debt crisis in the Third World is primarily home-made. A closer analysis of the causes of the crisis shows, however, that there are huge methodological difficulties in making precise distinctions between home-made, world-market-related and colonial-historical factors. The three groups are often almost inextricably inter-connected.

Many authors regard the oil-price policies of OPEC as the starting point for the Third World's debt problems. According to this view, increases in the current account deficits of oil-importing developing countries precisely mirror their higher oil bills. These countries responded by taking up more foreign loans to balance the deficits caused by OPEC and this set the debt-avalanche moving. Oil-price increases undoubtedly imposed severe strains on the balance of payments of developing countries; but OPEC alone cannot take all the blame. The industrial countries and the transnational corporations, themselves affected by oil price rises, passed the higher import and production costs on to the developing countries, which had to pay far higher prices for necessary imports of investment and consumer goods as well as food. All of these were indispensable within the framework of import-dependent industrialisation strategies. The debt of major oil-exporting countries such as Mexico, Indonesia, Venezuela, Algeria and Nigeria proves conclusively that higher oil prices cannot have been the decisive factor in the creation of colossal debts. The oil-exporting countries were after all not the victims but the beneficiaries of the oil-price shock. It is paradoxical that it was in 1982, the year in which oil prices showed a clear downward tendency for the first time in ten years, that the debt crisis crashed over debtors and creditors. And it was the oil-exporting countries such as Mexico, Venezuela and Nigeria who were hardest hit.

Along with the rise in the price of imports went a drop in export earnings, a problem which almost every Third World country — apart from the oil-exporting countries — had to face. Falling prices for raw materials and shrinking sales markets in the recession-torn industrial countries brought serious difficulties for developing countries. The raw materials price index, always subject to considerable fluctuations, slumped dramatically from 1974 onwards. In the period 1980–82 alone, raw materials prices dropped by an average of 25% (World Bank, *Annual Report 1983*, p. 28). In a favourable world economic climate, developing countries can make up for price-related reductions in export earnings by increasing sales. But they were doubly affected by the recessions in the industrial countries in 1974/75 and 1980/82 (*World Development Report 1983*, pp. 12 ff.). The substantial balance-of-payments deficits which now emerged were willingly financed by the transnational banks, which were unable to lend enough of their liquid funds to the crisis-ridden industrial countries. They even granted generous loan facilities to several unreliable customers among the developing countries.

The bill for this 'generosity' was soon presented to the Third World countries in the form of higher interest-rates which brought the banks substantial profits. The USA's high-interest policies — necessitated by huge budget deficits caused by excessive military expenditure — had sent interest-rates rocketing to giddy heights on the Euromarkets. Newly industrialising countries, oil exporters and some major raw-materials exporters which financed their balance-of-payments deficits largely with private loans, were severely affected by this 'interest shock' (Schubert, 1983). Developing countries found their debt-servicing repayments an even worse drain on their resources than the higher oil prices (LAWR, 6 March 1981).

The high interest-rates had lasting effects — via exchange-rates — on those import and debt bills of the Third World that were expressed in dollars. Lured by high interest-rates in the USA, investors and speculators throughout the world switched their funds from the Japanese *yen* and European currencies to the US dollar and invested in the USA. As a result, the dollar rate of exchange on all the exchange markets of the world shot far higher than the level which its true purchasing power justified. This placed a considerable extra burden on the developing countries. As most of their debts were expressed in dollars, their foreign liabilities, measured against their own currencies, increased. Exports to Europe and Japan, which are not paid in dollars, merely brought the comparatively cheap currencies of Europe and Japan into the developing countries, whereas the vast majority of their debt-service repayments had to be made in expensive US dollars.

One of the reasons why countries such as Brazil, which have made considerable efforts to boost their exports, face balance-of-payments problems is the protectionism of industrial countries. Duties and other protective measures are designed to keep Third World products off their markets. Manufactured products from newly industrialising countries are most affected by this — they are often equal in quality and more competitive in price than comparable goods from industrial countries (textiles, watches, radios, cameras, even ships). Protectionist pressure has intensified particularly since the beginning of the 1980/82 recession. Industrial countries, hit by a severe economic crisis have had to struggle with the problem of unemployment and have therefore increasingly resorted to measures designed to defend their economies from world market competition.

. Direct investments by transnational corporations can be another major cause of the debt problems of developing countries. Advocates of direct investments such as W. Guth, Chairman of the Deutsche Bank, argue that 'a liberal policy towards foreign private capital' must be an integral component in policies designed to overcome the debt problem (1965, p. 163). According to this view, direct investments provide developing countries with long-term capital, which brings profits for the corporations and relief for the balance of payments of the countries concerned (in the form of additional foreign exchange earnings through exports or the saving of foreign exchange through import substitution). In contrast to loans, direct investments do not produce debt — on the contrary, the transfer of profits is dependent on the profitability of the projects.

But in fact these capital inflows also bring in their wake some negative effects on the balance of payments (Glaubitt/Lütkenhorst 1980; UNCTC, 1983, pp. 17 ff.). Direct investments are frequently conditional upon advance concessions — the building of infrastructure such as roads, ports, airports — which the governments of developing countries generally have to finance by taking up loans. Subsequently, the capital inflow is often offset by a considerable foreign exchange outflow in corporation profits, royalty and patent fees and salaries paid to foreign experts — all of which are difficult to quantify because transnational corporations, in internal dealings between subsidiary and parent companies, have numerous possibilities of transferring profits in disguised form. Over and above this, the corporations import considerable amounts of capital goods, working funds, spare parts, semi-manufactured goods and raw materials, the value of which exceeds foreign exchange earnings from exports or savings of foreign exchange from import substitution. As the corporations use the most modern technology, these imports are far greater than those of domestic companies. Foreign companies also have the possibility of artificially hiking prices of imports from the parent company via the transfer-pricing system.

All these external factors have contributed, especially since 1980, to the eruption of the debt crisis in the developing countries. Yet they do not in themselves provide a sufficient explanation. The debt crises are in most cases built into the economic, financial and development policies of the governments of the developing countries. They often fail to make productive use of foreign loans, and corruption and mismanagement often prevent the effective deployment of funds. Instead of giving equal priority to agriculture and industry and using relatively low amounts of capital together with appropriate technology, governments often squander loans on capital-intensive, technologically complex prestige projects or arms programmes. A good part of the money is wasted in the luxury consumption of the middle- and upper-classes which imitate the consumption patterns of the industrial countries. These consumption requirements can only be satisfied — in the absence of domestic production — by imports which use up large sums in foreign exchange. Even policies of social reform may violate the basic principles of the productive use of foreign capital unless they are coupled with radical economic and social structural reforms and a more intensive use of domestic resources.

The governments of developing countries are dependent on foreign loans precisely because domestic funds are inadequately mobilised. National savings ratios are, as a rule, relatively low, and as the distribution of income is frequently very unequal only the middle- and upper-classes would be able to save appreciably. In general these classes prefer to indulge in luxury consumption rather than invest their money productively. The income surpluses of these classes are very lightly taxed. As the middle- and upper-classes are closely connected with the state bureaucracy, they can block all attempts at tax reform or other reforms designed to bring about a fairer distribution of income. Existing laws are side-stepped in the jungle of corruption and nepotism, and tax evasion — often connived at by the state — is common practice. Rigid traditional social and political structures prevent economic development in general and the productive use of foreign capital in particular. Administrative incompetence intensifies the debt crisis. The poor education and training of financial personnel and inadequate coordination make effective debt management impossible.

These factors are especially evident in the case of state enterprises (*World Development Report 1983*, pp. 88 ff.; Elsenhans, 1982a). Created in order to open up the resources of the developing countries and to contribute decisively to modernisation, these enterprises control the economies of many Third World countries. State enterprises have overall economic, labour market, social and industrial functions. In Latin America they contribute above all to the development of domestic raw materials industries whereas in Africa — given the absence of a traditional bourgeoisie — their function is generally productive. They are also usually overstaffed — a means of mopping up unemployment. In order to restrain the dynamism of inflation, they sell their products at prices which do not cover costs. They keep the cost of living artificially low and increase the profitability of domestic private companies which they supply with subsidized inputs for production. Many state enterprises cannot operate economically — they do not need to do so because they are not exposed to market competition.

To cover their deficits, state enterprises have become increasingly dependent on subsidies from the state budget or have fallen back on foreign finance. Another reason for their high levels of foreign debt is that they act on behalf of the state in bringing loans and therefore foreign exchange into the country — a device which relieves the state budget and 'doctors' the level of state debt downwards. In Mexico in 1981, the state oil company **PEMEX** alone had foreign liabilities of US $20 thousand million — 40% of the country's total public liabilities (Schubert, 1982, p. 81). According to the Central Bank, state enterprises accounted for 57% of all foreign loans in Portugal in 1982 (Banco de Portugal, boletim trimestral 2/1983, p. 39).

Debt crises in the Third World are therefore to a large extent the responsibility of the governments and ruling classes of independent states who, given the nature of their interests, are virtually bound to violate the basic principles of the productive use of capital. But as we have said, their room for manoeuvre is narrowly delimited by the colonial legacy. The colonial centres forced the developing countries to adopt one-sided monocultural export structures. The colonies provided agricultural and mineral raw materials which were essential for the industrialisation process of the metropoles. At the same time, the colonies served as sales markets for the manufactured products of the metropolitan powers and as spheres of investment for their surplus capital. This basic pattern still characterises the export structures of developing countries and economic relations between industrial and developing countries. These structures do not allow the majority of developing countries to earn the foreign exchange necessary for development. The one-sided orientation towards the needs of the colonial metropoles has prevented the development of domestic markets. Traditional agriculture has been destroyed, and the growing of cotton, sisal, coffee, cocoa, bananas and sugar for export has taken the place of food production for domestic requirements. Even today these countries have to import substantial amounts of food. Prospering domestic industries — such as textile manufacturing in India — were destroyed. Industrialisation could not, therefore, build on traditional modes of manufacture — an advantage available to the major industrialised nations.

After independence, developing countries found it difficult to press ahead with independent industrialisation because the colonial system of education, oriented towards the socio-cultural norms and values of the former colonial powers, had completely disregarded the needs of the developing countries. Even today, skilled workers, technicians and managers are in short supply. Developing countries remain technologically dependent on transnational corporations — a dependence prefigured in colonialism. The political and administrative structures, the central governments, local administration, army and police in these countries were all oriented towards the needs of the colonial centres; after independence they were unable to set in motion a self-sustaining process of development.

The rigid, development-inhibiting social structures in most Third World countries are rooted in the economic and political structures created by colonialism. On independence, political power was transferred from the colonial governments to agricultural oligarchies and urban upper classes. Under colonialism, these classes earned a living exclusively from the monocultural export sector. Landed proprietors controlled the land where the export goods were produced and urban classes profited from trade with agricultural and mineral raw materials. Given their economic base, these classes were, and are, far more oriented towards trade and consumption than productive activity. There was, therefore, little scope for an interest in the productive use of foreign capital to develop. Apart from the analytical distinction between internal, external and colonial factors, seven typical causes of debt crisis can be distinguished:

1) indebted industrialisation;
2) neglect of agricultural development;
3) failure to diversify exports;
4) debt-inducing social reforms;
5) cleptocracy;
6) developmental gigantomania;
7) indebted militarisation.

Indebted Industrialisation
Almost all developing countries have in principle followed the path of

'indebted industrialisation' (Frieden, 1981). In periods when the industrial countries were weakened by economic crises or wars and the developing countries' sales opportunities for their raw materials were drastically reduced, import substitution — the substitution of imported consumer goods, and later of investment goods by domestic production — was regarded almost everywhere in the Third World as the only viable development alternative. It 'was not the product of a sovereign decision derived from an industrial philosophy' but rather 'the only socially viable alternative, as a consequence of the international economic crisis of the 1930s, and later of the Second World War' (Canitrot, 1980, p. 918). Because foreign exchange inflows from raw-materials exports dropped or dried up altogether, foreign exchange was to be saved for imports. This strategy was first applied in Latin America in the 1930s and was later adopted by Asian and African countries.

In the strict sense, as a term which describes a typical path to indebtedness, 'indebted industrialisation' refers primarily to newly industrialising countries such as Brazil, Mexico, South Africa, South Korea, Taiwan and Portugal. Compared with most developing countries, they have developed rapidly and extensively and have already begun to compete with the industrial countries in some sectors of world markets for industrial goods.

In most of these countries the state and state enterprises played an important part in directing economic development and in building up raw materials industries (such as steel). But the consumer goods and later the capital goods industries which emerged from this process soon came under the control of transnational corporations; the national bourgeoisies were mostly reduced to the role of junior partners. The state and the transnational corporations became the driving forces behind 'indebted industrialisation'. Industrial development necessitated substantial state investments, which could only be financed by inflationary budget deficits and even by the supplementing of domestic savings with foreign loans. The transnational corporations and state enterprises were only able to start and maintain the capital-intensive domestic production of raw materials, consumer goods and capital goods because the newly industrialising countries constantly imported capital goods — semi-manufactured products and machines — from industrial countries capable of technologically-complex production techniques. But as a rule, every phase of import substitution led to the importing of more and more sophisticated goods. This resulted not in the saving of foreign exchange and an improvement in the balance of payments but in additional deficits which had to be financed with foreign loans. In many cases, industrialisation, by diverting domestic resources away from agriculture and into industry, caused food production to stagnate and even to drop. The food imports which then became necessary were often a severe drain on the balance of payments. The activity of transnational corporations also ate dramatically into foreign exchange. Profit transfers and artificially high-priced imports (via the transfer-pricing system) put the balance of payments of newly industrialising countries under considerable pressure.

Usually, import substitution industrialisation can only be implemented if it is financed with foreign loans. In most cases, countries find it impossible to earn enough foreign exchange to meet their debt-service requirements, especially when US high-interest policies drastically increase the interest burden. Debt and liquidity crises are therefore normally built into this development path.

After a phase of import substitution some countries consequently switched to export industrialisation, in an attempt to stop the debt spiral and meet debt-service requirements by exporting manufactured goods. The example of Brazil, which has pulled out all the stops to export its industrial goods —including weapons — in order to overcome the problem of its foreign debt, emphasises that this strategy does not avoid the debt trap. The world economic crisis and protectionism in the industrial countries severely limit sales opportunities.

Neglect of Agricultural Development

Strictly speaking, neglected agricultural development as a route towards indebtedness is merely a variant of 'indebted industrialisation'. It does, however, indicate a shift of emphasis. It takes as its starting point the realisation that in most Third World countries, and above all in the least developed (LDCs), most people live and work on the land. Agricultural development, the building of regional and sub-regional production and supply structures should have absolute priority in development planning.

Most countries with low-income levels — African countries south of the Sahara, poorer Asian countries such as Bangladesh, Nepal and Laos — now practise import substitution industrialisation, though generally on a far more modest level than in the newly industrialising countries. This strategy can only be financed and implemented by foreign loans, massive state intervention, inflationary budget deficits and diverting agricultural resources into small-scale industrial development by means of taxation and state price policies. As the political backing for governments comes primarily from the urban middle- and upper-classes and not from small-holders, urban and industrial interests largely determine the planning and financing of development.

If governments do anything at all for the agricultural sector, their efforts are one-sidedly directed towards export-oriented agriculture. In this they are simply imitating the policies of their former colonial masters, who often confined the agricultural sector to the export of one product only — as a cheap raw material for use in the colonial centres.

Agribusiness — transnational corporations involved in the production, processing and marketing of agricultural goods — is also interested in Third World export production and, in alliance with the ruling classes in the countries concerned, intensifies the one-sided orientation of agriculture (Dinham/Hines, 1983).

Discrimination against the agricultural sector frequently led to stagnation or even a drop in food production, which in turn meant that substantial imports of food — as well as of energy and capital goods — were necessary. In many cases, this caused a severe strain on import capacity and a scarcity of foreign exchange. This was further aggravated in the 1970s and the early 1980s by price increases for imported food coinciding with the oil-price shock and the rise in the cost of capital goods — and, at the beginning of the 1980s, with the 'interest-shock'.

Neglect of agricultural policy ultimately leads to a vicious circle. More and more people migrate to the towns in the hope of a better standard of living and a better income; consequently more funds must be taken out of the agricultural sector to feed the urban population. The demand for food imports — which have to be financed with foreign loans — keeps growing. To pay off these debts, agricultural export production is increased, often at the expense of food production for domestic requirements. There comes a point at which this 'development' path cannot be financed — the state goes bankrupt, foreign exchange reserves run out.

Table 1.7 Average index of food production per capita 1979/81 (1969/71 = 100) (1)
Proportion of food exports to overall exports in % (2)

	(1)	(2)		(1)	(2)
Sudan	98	63	Mali	88	31
Madagascar	94	13	Ethiopia	85	21
Tanzania	91	28	Sierra Leone	81	37
Togo	90	14	Senegal	76	51
Haiti	89	39	Somalia	65	79

Sources: World Development Report 1983, p. 184; FAO, Trade Yearbook 1981

Failure to Diversify Exports
Many countries have to calculate their state and foreign exchange budgets on the basis of income from one, two or at most three raw materials. As a rule, their exports are scarcely diversified and economic development, development planning and financing are based on the uncertain foundation of prices which are sometimes subject to abrupt changes. In 1974/5, the price of copper soared to an all-time high only to plunge subsequently by a half. Countries such as Zambia, Chile and Zaire, which depended heavily on copper for their revenue, suddenly faced serious problems. Over-ambitious development projects — and unproductive state apparatuses — could now no longer be financed. In Zaire the main cause of indebtedness — universal and systematic corruption — became evident (see Chapter 3).

In the 1970s, governments which had based their development planning on a favourable (but by no means at that time unrealistic) price level for their main export goods frequently found their planning in ruins because the international raw-materials markets, affected by the world economic situation, did not provide the expected foreign exchange. When such price slumps occurred — and their effect was frequently intensified by price rises for imports of oil, capital goods and food — governments such as that of Zambia opted to stop their financial gaps with foreign loans. They feared that austerity would plunge their countries into recession and bring a loss of popular support in its wake. Yet compensatory financing with foreign money can only be sustained if the price slump is temporary and is soon followed by a rise. In many cases the raw materials price 'stabilises' at a low level. State revenue and foreign exchange reserves then drop and a debt crisis is inevitable.

Dependence on the export of a few raw materials means that reliable medium- and long-term planning is impossible. Price slumps always come as a shock and there is no way of calculating whether income is likely to drop in the short, medium or long term, whether compensatory financing through foreign loans would be advisable or whether it would be better to pass an austerity budget immediately. Whereas a far-sighted development policy would include a spread of products for export, the state classes frequently pursue their personal short-term interest in maintaining their main source of income, based on the export of a few traditional products.

Table 1.8 Main export product revenues expressed as a percentage of overall export earnings (average for 1980/2)

Uganda (coffee)	96	Madagascar (coffee)	47
Burundi (coffee)	90	Mali (cotton)	46
Zambia (copper)	89	Guyana (aluminium)	45
Jamaica (aluminium)	73	Chile (copper)	45
Ruanda (coffee)	68	Zaire (copper)	43
Ethiopia (coffee)	65	Grenada (cocoa)	43
El Salvador (coffee)	60	Bolivia (tin)	43
Ghana (cocoa)	59	Burkina Faso (cotton)	40
Colombia (coffee)	58	Dominican Republic (sugar)	40
Papua–New Guinea (copper)	50	Sudan (cotton)	39

Source: American Express Bank, quoted from *NZZ*, 18 February 1983

Debt-Inducing Social Reforms
Social reforms are likely to lead to debt crises if basic economic and social structures remain unchanged, if integration in the world market is not subordinated to domestic economic development and if political-military orientation towards the USA is not abandoned. Loans taken up to finance the budget and the balance of payments are not adequately invested in the earning of foreign exchange but instead are used to finance ambitious social and consumption-oriented goals (Griffith-Jones, 1981). Chile under Allende (1970–73), Jamaica under Manley (1972–6) and Portugal after the military coup of April 1974 are classic examples of this basic pattern.

Social injustice resulting from the process of industrialisation provoked such strong political resistance by the underprivileged that social-reformist forces were able to take power. To satisfy the demands of their social base, such governments immediately set about raising real wages, improving educational and health services and extending state social programmes to improve the living standards of the underprivileged and — as economists put it — to increase consumption. Maximum prices were fixed and products were subsidised to ensure that the population would be better supplied with basic articles (above all food). Because demand rose as a result of the distribution of income, imports generally also increased. The resultant gaps in the balance of payments had to be plugged with foreign loans and foreign exchange reserves.

As state expenditure increased faster than revenue, deficits were financed by taking up more loans from domestic banks and by printing money. An inflationary development set in, which ought to have been counteracted by devaluation; but the government refrained for fear of increasing the price of imports. The result was that imported goods kept getting cheaper compared with domestic goods, and this further accelerated the inflow. Exports, on the other hand, lost their competitiveness and deficits increased. Once the foreign exchange reserves had run out, debts became more and more difficult to service and new loans harder to obtain. An acute liquidity crisis followed. A politically-motivated loan boycott by creditors — who saw the spectre of socialism in social reforms — a drastic drop in direct investments and the flight of capital of domestic and foreign entrepreneurs intensified the crisis. Recourse to the IMF now became inevitable. IMF-imposed austerity policies end the process of reform and inaugurate a process of restoration. It is usually only a matter of time before the reformist government loses power.

Cleptocracy

Zaire under Mobutu, Haiti under Duvalier, the Philippines under Marcos, Nicaragua under Somoza, Uganda under Amin, the Central African Republic under 'emperor' Bokassa — these are all examples of 'cleptocracies', where state-classes under the repressive leadership of one clan pile up wealth so uninhibitedly in foreign exchange accounts or squander such huge sums on luxury consumption that corruption and self-enrichment become the central cause of the debt crisis. The direct access of these classes to the finance ministries, the central banks and the customs authorities enables them to operate illegally — in the smuggling of raw materials (a major source of foreign exchange), the diversion of scarce foreign exchange reserves for private use and the forging of import licences. This involves setting the price in foreign exchange of a given import higher than it actually costs — and the difference between the actual and the 'official' price finds its way into private pockets.[17] A further variant of this method of obtaining foreign exchange was discovered by the IMF at the beginning of 1984 in the Philippines: according to reports, members of the government had large numbers of Philippine *pesos* printed, of which no records or statistics were kept. This money was then exchanged for US dollars on the black market.[18]

Cleptocratic practices are not restricted to these few spectacular cases but occur in most Third World countries (*Jeune Afrique Economie*, 3 March 1982; *World Development Report 1983*, p. 139). The outstanding symptom is capital flight, which intensifies as the economy and domestic policies of a debtor country edge nearer to crisis. The major incentive for capital flight is an over-valued currency, which buys foreign exchange at a favourable rate. This foreign exchange then finds its way into foreign bank accounts or is used to purchase property — above all in hard currency countries such as the USA and Switzerland. *Business Week* (3 October 1983, p. 132) estimated that from 1975 to the end of 1982 more than US $120 thousand million were transferred from developing countries to the financial centres, from where the money flowed back to the debtor countries in the form of loans. From 1980–82 alone, capital flight from the developing countries is estimated at US $102 thousand million, of which 71 thousand million came from a mere seven countries. In some cases, these funds formed a high proportion of the new indebtedness (see Table 1.9).

Table 1.9 Capital flight and new indebtedness of certain debtor countries, 1980–82, in thousands of millions US dollars.

	Capital flight	New indebtedness	Capital flight new debt in %
Mexico	26[1]	45	58
Venezuela	18	8	225
Argentina	11[2]	18	61
Nigeria	6	8	75
Indonesia	4	9	44
Philippines	3	9	33
Egypt	3	9	33

Source: Business Week, 3 October 1983, p. 132, authors' calculations.

[1] According to the *Financial Times* (1 December 1983), capital flight from Mexico in 1981 and 1982 totalled $12.3 and $13.15 thousand million as against $4.4 thousand million in 1979. Due to devaluation it slumped to $3.7 and 2.5 thousand million in 1983 and 1984 respectively (LAWR, 31 May 1985, p. 7).

[2] It is estimated that under the military dictatorship in Argentina about $35 thousand million of capital flight money were transferred between 1976 and September 1983. (Information from Argentinian Central Bank quoted in *HB*, 3 November 1983). This sum almost exactly equalled the new liabilities.

Developmental Gigantomania

Developmental gigantomania is the major cause of debt in countries such as Nigeria, Gabon and Sudan. Into this category come attempts — forced through by the state and often financially backed, indeed initiated by Western industrial countries and the World Bank — to realise ambitious infrastructural projects in the shortest possible time. The governments of the developing countries hope that this will bring about a rapid modernisation which will increase state revenue and foreign exchange earnings in the future; the industrial countries, major banks and industrial companies hope that such projects will open up sales markets and investment possibilities for them,[19] as Third World countries buy equipment from the donor countries with the help of development aid loans, which are often contractually tied to specific suppliers.

The costs of realising these projects, and even more the subsequent costs of maintenance and renewal, are generally underestimated by both governments and credit grantors. In many cases, scarce foreign exchange is used up, further loans have to be taken up abroad and the debt increases. Such large-scale investments frequently turn out to be disastrous or at least fail to earn the hoped-for sums of foreign exchange. The example of Sudan shows that a handful of large-scale projects can be responsible for the bulk of foreign debt (see also Chapter 3). Development aid frequently does not 'aid' but contributes significantly to debt misery drama.

Indebted Militarisation
Militarisation is to be found in almost every debtor country. In many Third World countries substantial amounts of the small foreign exchange budget go on military expenditure. The explosive social potential of the industrialisation process, wars and conflicts which result from arbitrary colonial frontiers, undeclared territorial claims and the striving to demonstrate national independence or even greatness — some or all of these induce many governments to increase the strength of the army, to recruit foreign 'advisers' and to purchase ultra-modern arms and military equipment which in most cases is manufactured in the industrial countries.

In many cases, military expenditure is so excessive that budgets are swollen by inflation; the currency and balance of payments are ruined by high inflation rates. As most developing countries have only an embryonic domestic arms production capacity and therefore have to import arms, military equipment, ammunition and production plants, arms imports often compete with civilian imports for scarce foreign exchange (Wulf, 1983). If developing countries are unable to finance arms imports with their depleting foreign exchange reserves, suppliers often grant them substantial military aid loans. Countries such as India, Israel and South Africa hoped that the establishment of independent arms production would significantly accelerate industrialisation as a whole, but such efforts have proven extremely capital- and import-intensive and have merely turned out to be a variant of 'indebted industrialisation'. It has been estimated that arms imports and 'armaments industrialisation' account for a fifth of total foreign debt (Brzoska, 1983, p. 271).

The arms trade has flourished, although sometimes economic recession has reduced world trade. Governments of developing countries did not stop buying arms even when foreign exchange earnings and foreign exchange reserves declined, the debt crisis became acute and recourse to the IMF inevitable. Argentina, for example, quickly replenished its arms arsenals after its defeat in the Falklands-Malvinas war, despite the fact that it suffered an acute debt crisis that year, not least because of the war.

Table 1.10 Developing countries whose military expenditure exceeded 20% of their budget in 1980 (excluding oil exporters).

South Yemen	45.7	Mauretania	25.9
Ethiopia	42.6	Peru	24.4
Syria	35.4	Jordan	23.4
Israel	34.2	Pakistan	23.2
North Yemen	30.0	Burundi	22.2
Chad	29.0	Burma	22.1
Mozambique	28.9	Uganda	20.6
South Korea	28.4	Singapore	20.6
Zimbabwe	25.9	Mali	20.5

Source: US ACDA. 1983.

Notes

1. Developing countries are not the only ones with a high level of foreign debt. Others include the East European countries, which owed $79 thousand million to western creditors at the end of 1984 and France, which at the end of 1984 had foreign liabilities totalling $54 thousand million (NZZ, 5 May 1985).

2. German exporters, for example, can insure themselves by paying a premium to the Hermes Credit Insurance Company, which operates on behalf of the Bonn government. As early as 1952 a consortium of West German banks formed the Export Credit Company (Ausfuhrkredit-Gesellschaft), which grants medium- to long-term export loans.

3. Since January 1984, the IMF in its *International Financial Statistics* has reported on loan allocations by international banks; but these statistics still provide only an inadequate picture of developing countries' indebtedness to banks.

4. 20% was a threshold value frequently quoted (Betz, 1983, p. 35).

5. In 1983 interest rates dropped to 12.7% (OECD/DAC, 1983, p. 215).

6. Bilateral development aid loans in Black African countries in 1982 amounted on average to over a fifth of gross domestic investments. In Burkina Faso, Burundi, Central African Republic, Chad, Gambia, Guinea-Bissau, Liberia, Madagascar, Mali, Mauretania, Niger and Senegal at least they amounted to more than 50% (World Bank, 1984a, p. 74).

7. The concept of hypothetical surplus was introduced by Baran (1971, pp. 85 ff.).

8. Even Albania could not get by completely without loans. After the

Albanian government broke off relations with the Soviet Union in 1960, it received considerable sums to finance its development plans from the People's Republic of China. An interest-free loan of US $180 million from China helped to finance ambitious industrialisation projects in the fifth five-year plan. But because of ideological differences, Albania broke off financial relations with China in 1978 (Statistisches Bundesamt, Länderkurzbericht Albanien, 1983, Stuttgart/Mainz 1983, pp. 21 f.).

  9. Malaysia, a newly industrialising country whose foreign debts were comparatively low in relation to its economic potential, pursued a cautious policy with regard to foreign debts until 1980. Since the beginning of the 1980s, however, Malaysia has increasingly financed its balance-of-payments deficits by raising loans abroad. Its foreign liabilities rose from US $6.3 thousand million in 1981 to about US$17 thousand million in 1984 (*World Financial Markets*, October/November, 1984, p. 5).

  10. See: Kulischer, 1976 passim; Krippendorff, 1975, p. 85; Sampson, 1981, pp. 27 ff.; Kindleberger, 1981; Abbott, 1979, pp. 11 ff.

  11. Quoted from Corm, 1982, p. 38.

  12. The imperial powers' disputes over colonies brought them close to war on several occasions: for example between England and France over Egypt in 1898 and between France and Germany over Morocco (in 1905 and 1911). The *Entente Cordiale* (1904) between England and France was to a large extent the result of mutual acceptance of their respective spheres of influence in Egypt and Morocco. See: P. Gifford/W.R. Louis (eds.), *France and Britain in Africa. Imperial Rivalry and Colonial Rule*, New Haven/London, 1971.

  13. Most Latin American countries resumed their debt-service payments in the 1940s and 50s, but creditors had to accept substantial write-offs. Mexico in 1943 was the first country to start repaying debts again — but it paid only $50 million of $500 million due to be repaid (*FT*, 28 December 1983).

  14. Since the Second World War, only a handful of governments have refused to honour the foreign liabilities of previous governments. These include Fidel Castro's government in Cuba and the Acheampong regime in Ghana. After the debt repudiation of 1972, Ghana's creditworthiness was for many years as good as nil (see Chapter 3). Jamaica's ex-Premier Manley, who during his term of office clashed violently with the IMF and the creditor countries, still rejects debt repudiation as a way out of his country's debt crises. He points to the negative experiences of Cuba, which, after the repudiation of its old debts, did not receive any Western loans for many years. (Authors' interview with Manley, Kingston, August 1982.) Before the Second World War, debt repudiations were also rare, one of the most spectacular examples being that of Mexico in 1867. At the beginning of the 1860s France occupied Mexico, which was weakened by war and unable to honour its debts. The USA then pressed the French troops to withdraw, at which point the Mexican president, Benito Juárez, repudiated his foreign debt (Greayer, 1978, p. 300).

  15. These include economic, social and political factors. The purpose is to ascertain the likelihood of internal and external conflicts.

  16. For the criteria of the Commerzbank compare Jahn 1980.

  17. Some especially blatant examples of these practices are described in Chapter 3 (Zaire).

  18. In subsequent negotiations with the Marcos regime on a stabilisation programme, the IMF forced the resignation of Central Bank president Laya, who was not only responsible for the printing of the banknotes but had also

doctored the country's foreign exchange reserves upwards by US $600 million (NZZ, 14 January 1984 and FEER, 26 January 1984, p. 42).

19. The companies concerned often advance their cause by means of bribes. In many cases 'large-scale projects were awarded to companies (often multinational companies) on the basis of the amount of their bribes rather than the quality of their services.' (*World Development Report, 1983*, p. 139.)

2. The IMF: Crisis Manager for the Third World?

The IMF's History, Power Structure and Mode of Operating

Not until the 1970s, two decades after its foundation, did the IMF first come to the forefront of public attention. Balance-of-payments and debt crises were forcing more and more developing countries to turn to the IMF and to negotiate stabilisation programmes. The negotiation of such a programme is a *sine qua non* for an IMF standby loan — and only such a loan can restore a country's creditworthiness on the international financial markets. The IMF soon became the most powerful international organisation of the 20th Century, decisively influencing the well-being of a majority of the world's population. Although the developing countries are most affected by the IMF's policies, they have scarcely any influence on their formulation. At the foundation conference of the organisation at Bretton Woods, USA, in 1944, the USA managed to force through its interests against rival industrial countries weakened by the war and to anchor these interests in the structure of the new world monetary system. Most national states of the Third World did not exist at that time and the interests of the developing countries were scarcely represented at Bretton Woods.

During the Second World War, plans for a new world trade and world monetary order were worked out in the USA — plans designed to create conditions which would prevent a repetition of the world economic crisis of the 1920s and at the same time ensure the worldwide expansion of US capital in the postwar era. A system of fixed exchange rates to prevent a new spiral of competitive devaluations to make exports cheaper and the abolition of trade and capital transfer restrictions seemed to be suitable instruments for achieving these ends. The USA soon persuaded leading trading nations to agree on the cornerstones of this new order — free world trade, fixed rates of exchange and equal treatment for trading partners; but there was disagreement for a long time about the mechanisms for reducing balance-of-payments deficits and surpluses without states having to resort to practices which inhibited trade.

John Maynard Keynes, head of the British delegation, drafted a plan proposing that all imbalances in balances of payments should be converted into a new international unit of account — to be known as 'Bancor' — and balanced out in a central 'clearing union'. The 'Bancor' accounts of the surplus countries would thus finance balance-of-payments deficits. The debt of deficit countries would be restricted by the respective national quotas; but debtors and the clearing union would be expected to take graduated measures beforehand to improve the debt position.[1] Keynes' plan meant, however, that creditors would also have to contribute. Both debtors and creditors were to pay progressively increasing duties, the former when using the 'Bancor' facility, the latter when creating 'Bancor'.

The USA, which rightly believed that it would in future have high balance-of-payments surpluses, rejected the Keynes plan. Its counter-proposals, known as the White plan after the head of the US delegation, shifted the burdens of adjustment onto the deficit countries alone.[2] The White plan acknowledged the need to grant deficit countries loans to improve their balance of payments and to prevent them setting up trade barriers; yet it was also designed to provide the new credit-granting organisation with instruments to force the debtor country into balance-of-payments discipline. This function was to be fulfilled by a fund into which all member countries would pay according to a quota system. Its loans — restricted, as in the Keynes plan, by the respective national quotas — were to be tied to conditions for a balance-of-payments oriented policy (Andersen, 1977; Aschinger, 1973).

The USA got its way on all essential points. The White plan shaped the structure of the IMF. With the foundation by 44 countries of the IMF and the World Bank — complementary organisations, the former responsible for short-term balance of payments aid, the latter for long-term, project-related development aid — the USA succeeded in imposing its interests on a world economic order based on free trade and free enterprise. New states could be effortlessly integrated through the Bretton Woods system into the capitalist economic system and bound to its principles: without IMF membership no admission to the World Bank, without conformity to IMF rules no development aid from the World Bank — a classic example of the carrot and stick principle. The power of the industrial countries, particularly of the USA, could not be endangered by the newcomers: a quota system which breaches the 'one country — one vote' system otherwise common in UN organisations guarantees the USA dominant influence in both organisations.

The formulation of the IMF agreement took no account of the specific interests of the developing countries. India's proposal that the agreement should include the formula that the Fund should 'assist in the fuller utilisation of the resources of economically underdeveloped countries' (quoted from Horsefield, 1969, Vol. I, p. 93) was rejected on the grounds that the IMF was an organisation with purely monetary functions. India did, however, succeed in having the 'development of the productive resources of all members' included on a par with 'the promotion and maintenance of high levels of employment and real income', a goal mainly relevant to the industrial countries (Article I.2). This passage is undoubtedly an acknowledgement by the IMF of responsibility for development, and the developing countries can quote this when arguing that the IMF should take more account of their requirements in its policies.

ARTICLE I

Purposes

The purposes of the International Monetary Fund are:

(1) To promote international monetary cooperation through a permanent institution which provides the machinery for con sultation and collaboration on international monetary problems.

(ii) To facilitate the expansion and balanced growth of international trade, and to contribute thereby to the promotion and maintenance of high levels of employment and real income and to the development of the productive resources of all members as primary objectives of economic policy.

(iii) To promote exchange stability, to maintain orderly exchange arrangements among members, and to avoid competitive exchange depreciation.

(iv) To assist in the establishment of a multilateral system of payments in respect of current transactions between members and in the elimination of foreign exchange restrictions which hamper the growth of world trade.

(v) To give confidence to members by making the general resources of the Fund temporarily available to them under adequate safeguards, thus providing them with opportunity to correct maladjustments in their balance of payments without resorting to measures destructive of national or international prosperity.

(vi) In accordance with the above, to shorten the duration and lessen the degree of disequilibrium in the international balances of payments of members.

The Fund shall be guided in all its policies and decisions by the purposes set forth in this Article.

The USA also got its way in having the headquarters of the Bretton Woods twins in Washington rather than in New York, the headquarters of the UN and the choice of most conference members. This means that the top management of both organisations is in close and constant contact with the political and economic establishment in the US capital.

So far 148 countries have signed the IMF agreement. The Soviet Union — which was represented at the Bretton Woods Conference — refused to join an organisation designed to protect the capitalist monetary system, the 'Achilles heel of capitalism' (Lenin). Other socialist countries (Poland, Czechoslovakia) became members but resigned during the period of the Cold War. In the recent past, Hungary and Rumania, both of which have heavy credit requirements in the West, joined the IMF. Poland submitted an application for membership in November 1981. The West is fully represented in the IMF, except for neutrality-conscious Switzerland, which practises 'constructive non-membership'.[3] Developing countries form the largest group: all Third World nation-states are IMF members apart from a few mini-states in the Pacific, and Albania, Angola, Cuba and Taiwan, which was replaced by the Peoples' Republic of China in 1980. Mozambique became the 148th member — the latest example of the draw of the Bretton Woods system.

Despite their numerical superiority, the developing countries have no significant influence in the IMF. The balance of power in the Fund is determined by quotas, on which payment obligations, credit facilities and voting rights of members are based. The quotas were worked out according to a formula — never officially accepted in Bretton Woods — which included countries' national income, gold and foreign exchange reserves, size and fluctuations of foreign trade as well as export dependence, with different weightings given to these factors (Horsefield, 1969, Vol. I, p. 95). The quota structure today still largely reflects the political balance of power of the 1940s. Bretton Woods merely bestowed the respectability of an ostensibly neutral formula on a pecking order previously agreed among the industrial nations. Even after the eighth and latest quota revision, the USA's share of the total quota is 20.1%[4] and it is followed by Great Britain with 6.9% (although this country has lost much of its world economic power). The quota distribution does however represent a relative success for the Third World because according to the calculation formula most developing countries ought to have far lower quotas than they actually have (Jeker, 1978, p. 219).

When votes are taken in the IMF's management committees, every country has 250 basic votes plus one further vote for every 100,000 Special Drawing Rights (SDRs) of its quota. The egalitarian element in the distribution of votes has been eroded to the disadvantage of the developing countries by the quota revisions which take place regularly every five years and above all by the extraordinary quota increase from 61 to 90 thousand million SDRs in 1983 — an increase designed to meet the rapid growth of the Fund's finance requirements. The proportion of basic votes to overall votes, which in 1965 was still almost 14%, is now only 4%. The lion's share of the votes is taken by the five leading industrial countries, led by the USA (19.3%) and followed by Great Britain (6.7%), the Federal Republic of Germany (5.8%), France (4.8%) and Japan (4.6%). Up to 1982, the developing countries increased their share of the vote, not because of their growth in numbers but solely because of the shift of world economic power towards OPEC. As a result of the quota increase of 1983 their share has now dropped to 40.5%. The USA with its share of the vote can still block any change of quotas because such a change would require an 85% majority.

This unequal distribution of votes makes itself felt particularly in the Board of Governors and in the Executive Board of the Fund. The Board

Figure 2. Distribution of Votes within the IMF.

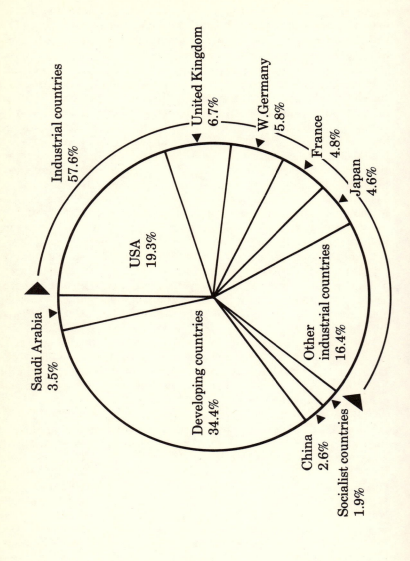

of Governors is the highest body in the Fund, to which every member state delegates a representative, usually the governor of the central bank or the minister of finance. The Board of Governors meets once a year, together with the Board of Governors of the World Bank, at the end of September and decides on matters of fundamental importance such as electing new members or changing quotas.[5] Over the years, the annual meeting of the IMF and the World Bank has developed into an important gathering of the state and the private financial elite. In the background of the meetings, bankers and ministers of finance haggle about loans and financial decisions with wide-ranging international implications are prepared (Sampson, 1981, pp. 14 f.).

The Board of Governors has charged the Executive Board with the management of day-to-day business. This body consists of 22 directors, of which the countries with the largest quotas (the USA, Great Britain, the Federal Republic of Germany, France and Japan) provide 5. Saudi Arabia's huge loans to the IMF since 1978 guarantee it a place on the Executive Board. In 1980, the Peoples' Republic of China was allocated a directorship, to politically smooth its path towards membership. The other 15 Executive Directors are elected by member countries divided into regional voting groups.

The real impulses for the IMF's work come from the Executive Board, which discusses and decides on the controversial standby arrangements. Crucial votes are extremely rare in this body and as a rule decisions are made without votes (Gold, 1972, pp. 195–201; Gold, 1979, p. 11). It would be wrong, however, to deduce from this that there was general agreement among Executive Directors on the scope and stringency of conditionality. The renunciation of formal votes reflects the inferiority of the developing countries, who would suffer political defeats if votes were counted. The two Executive Directors from Niger and Guinea who represent the 40 Sub-Saharan countries do not together even have as many votes as their colleague from the Federal Republic of Germany.

The chairman of the Executive Board is also Managing Director of the IMF. He is elected by the Executive Board for a five-year term of office and has a staff of 1,600. The present Managing Director of the IMF is Jacques de Larosière, former Director of the French Treasury, who has held the post since 1978. He was elected for a second term in May 1983. It has been an unwritten rule since Bretton Woods that the Managing Director of the IMF is always a West European and the President of the World Bank is an American. When the two organisations were founded, it seemed politic to appoint a US citizen President of the World Bank to win the confidence of

US banks as a source of finance for the World Bank capital. It did not, however, seem opportune to insist on the leading position in the IMF as well — so the USA contents itself with the post of Deputy-Executive Director (Gerster, 1980, p. 280).

The main function of the IMF is to provide its members with financial aid to cover short-term gaps in their balance of payments. According to the Bretton Woods philosophy, this was designed to prevent deficit countries resorting to measures which would restrict international trade and money transfers. In economic terms, the financial aid provided for this purpose is a loan; in legal and technical terms it is the purchase ('drawing') of the foreign exchange required in the currency of the deficit country. The sum a country is entitled to draw is determined by its quota. The Fund attaches conditions to the granting of loans; these are meant to persuade the member country to pursue policies which will eliminate the balance-of-payments deficit. The conditionality is dependent on the actual use made of loan facilities and can range from non-binding recommendations to detailed conditions.

No conditions are attached to the first 25% of the quota, which is known as the Gold or Reserve Tranche. Each country deposits foreign exchange (formerly gold) amounting to this sum with the IMF,[6] which is why this Reserve Tranche is generally included with a country's foreign exchange reserves. Four more tranches each equalling 25% of the quota are also available. The first Credit Tranche is not stringently conditioned but the next three Credit Tranches may only be drawn if the country concerned has agreed a stabilisation programme with the IMF and signed a standby arrangement. The government of the country concerned has to sign a letter of intent committing it to wide-ranging economic changes which the Fund believes will restore a healthy balance of payments.

Standby arrangements usually run for a year. In the 1970s it generally came to be accepted, even in the IMF, that the chronic balance-of-payments problems of many developing countries were the result of structural problems which could not be solved in such a short period — a fact to which the IMF responded by creating the Extended Fund Facility in 1974. This permits the drawing of up to 140% of the quota within a period of two to three years if the member country concludes an extended arrangement with the IMF. The conditions for the Extended Fund Facility are at least as stringent as those for the upper Credit Tranches.

In practice, the upper drawing limits are flexible. The so-called 'waiver clause' in the IMF agreement (Article V. 4) permits the Fund to grant member countries sums exceeding their drawing limits in the event of 'periodic or exceptional requirements'. As a rule, however, this is only allowed if the government of the member country commits itself to a particularly wide-ranging stabilisation agreement.

In 1979 the Fund responded to the second oil-price shock and the increasing balance-of-payments problems of the Third World by creating a Supplementary Financing Facility (sometimes also known as the Witteveen Facility after the IMF director in whose term of office it was introduced). This permitted member countries to draw up to 140% of their quotas from the higher credit tranches and from the Extended Fund Facility. Since 1981, another facility, the so-called Policy of Enlarged Access, has fulfilled the same function, though its drawing ceiling was successively reduced to 95% of the quota per annum on the insistence of the Reagan administration. In cases of extreme balance-of-payments problems the upper limit can be raised to 115%. Despite this reduction, the supplementary facilities do enable substantial sums to be mobilised, sums which, unlike the standby arrangements of previous years, make a more than symbolic contribution to the closing of the balance-of-payments deficit. But these facilities are relatively expensive. To finance them, the IMF borrows from surplus countries and has to pay the usual market rates for these loans. For developing countries with very low incomes an interest subsidy account was set up, which is financed from the Trust Fund (see below) and contributions from industrial and developing countries.

At the insistence of the developing countries, the Fund has over the years created further 'finance windows'. These are credit facilities which may be used independently or in connection with other facilities if certain external conditions apply. The Compensatory Financing Facility is designed in particular for raw-materials exporting countries whose balance-of-payments difficulties are (partly) attributable to drops in export earnings for which they are not responsible (for example, a sudden drop in the world market price of their main export product). Although this facility was introduced as long ago as 1963, it only began to be widely used at the end of the 1970s, when the Fund liberalised the drawing conditions. Since 1981 the IMF has also had the right to grant credits from this facility to countries whose balance of payments is especially burdened by the increasing costs of cereal imports (Goreux, 1980; Lelart, 1982). Conditions for drawing up to 50% of the quota in this facility are weak but beyond this sums are only released if the Fund is satisfied with the country's cooperation — as the diplomatic-technocratic language of the IMF phrases it. The upper drawing limit is 83% of the quota (before the 8th quota increase it was 100%). This limit can be raised if both conditions — a drop in exports and high prices for cereal imports — apply.

From 1974 to 1976 the Fund also operated an Oil Facility which was designed to alleviate the balance-of-payments problems of countries especially hard hit by the oil-price rises of those years. The conditions were the same as for the Compensatory Facility; it was financed by special IMF loans from oil-exporting and industrial countries. The drawing limit was 75%

of the quota. The facility for the financing of buffer stocks established in 1969 remains comparatively insignificant. This facility may be used (to up to 45% — formerly 50% — of quotas) by countries which have difficulties making their contributions to international raw materials stocks.[7] By encouraging the setting up of such buffer stocks, the IMF is trying to prevent drops in export earnings.

The Trust Fund, created in 1976 and wound up in 1981, was financed mainly from sales of part of the IMF's gold reserves.[8] Its loans, the terms of which were especially favourable, benefited the 55 poorest developing countries. Usually granted in connection with standby arrangements, the Trust Fund replaced the substantially larger drawing rights of the oil facility.

Member countries may also receive liquidity and thereby finance to improve their balance of payments through the allocation of Special Drawing Rights (SDRs). SDRs were created in 1969 as foreign exchange reserves at an IMF governors' meeting, to ensure that enough liquidity would be available for the expansion of world trade. The traditional forms of reserves — gold and the US dollar — were no longer able to fulfil this function. The value of an SDR is today determined by the value of a 'currency basket' containing the five major Western currencies — the US dollar, the D-Mark, the French franc, the pound sterling and the Japanese yen — variously weighted.[9] The IMF — and increasingly other institutions — uses the SDR, which is especially stable in relation to other currencies, as a unit of account. Since 1969, SDRs have been 'created' by IMF decisions in several stages and allocated to IMF member states according to quotas. These SDRs represent a country's claim over and against all other IMF members to the corresponding sum in foreign exchange. They are real foreign exchange reserves and can therefore be used to finance balance-of-payments deficits. No conditions are attached to the allocation or use of SDRs.[10]

The finance for IMF operations — apart from the Supplementary Financing Facility and the Policy of Enlarged Access — comes from members' contributions. Every country has to pay in a sum related to its quota, usually 25% in foreign exchange and 75% in its own currency. A uniform interest rate, periodically adjusted according to the IMF's financial situation, has to be paid for loans financed from the IMF's own funds. In 1984 this rate was 7%. In 1952, the Executive Board ruled that IMF loans would normally be repayable over a period of three to five years, on the assumption that balance-of-payments difficulties would have been cleared up by the end of this period at the latest. The IMF pays compensation to member countries whose currencies are used to finance withdrawals by other countries, provided the holding of the currency in the Fund falls below a certain norm.

The IMF agreement not only authorises the Fund to grant credits to member countries, it also stipulates that the 'Fund shall exercise firm surveillance over the exchange rate policies of members' (Article IV,3b).

Since the system of fixed rates of exchange has been abolished and member states are free to pursue whatever exchange-rate policies they please, this 'surveillance' has been interpreted to mean that members should periodically 'consult' and 'inform' the Fund. At least once every eighteen months — but as a rule more frequently — IMF experts visit the member state (Hood, 1982; Brau, 1981). They discuss with the authorities not only exchange-rate policies but all important economic questions and insist — if this is at all economically feasible — on the observance of IMF rules (the reduction of existing restrictions on trade and on money transfers). Unless a standby arrangement is being negotiated, the IMF has no power of sanction in such 'consultations'. But the influence of Fund missions on the economic policies of many developing countries should not be underestimated.

The economic philosophy of the Fund finds its way into the economic and financial policy of member countries not least through its 'technical aid', which is used above all by developing countries. The IMF passes on its expertise at seminars, provides advice on the structure and organisation of central banks, backs up administrations in financial, fiscal and statistical matters and sends its advisers to work out and check on the progress of economic programmes (IMF, 1982). The IMF provides a complete programme of technical services which most definitely have political implications. Poorly trained staff from the developing countries not only improve their qualifications but are also taught the economic philosophy of the IMF; conceptually inadequate economic plans are not only made more effective but also brought into line with IMF policies.

It may therefore be concluded that the IMF is an international organisation through which the countries of the capitalist North can impose their financial and monetary interests — and sometimes even other interests — on the countries of the southern hemisphere, beyond national frontiers. The IMF reflects the world economic balance of power and its structure guarantees dominant influence for the industrial nations. The developing countries, once integrated into the capitalist world economy, have virtually no chance of fending off the West's 'financial policeman' — as debtor countries they are dependent on his aid.

The Instruments of the 'Financial Policeman': Meaning and Content of IMF Stabilisation Programmes

Standby arrangements are not mentioned in the Bretton Woods agreement. Not until the 1950s did the IMF develop the policy of conditions and sanctions which had made it the most important but also the most controversial institution in the world economy. The IMF practice of tying loans to conditions — a practice on which the USA, in particular, insists — represents the solution to a conflict which could not be resolved at the Bretton Woods negotiating table. J.M. Keynes, the chief British negotiator, firmly advocated free, and to a large extent unconditional, access for deficit

Table 2.1: Drawing rights within the IMF

Facility	Duration	Drawing Limit (in % of quota)	Repayment Deadline (in years)	Interest rates (in %)[1]	Conditionality
Reserve Tranche	since 1952	25	–	–	none
First Credit Tranche	since 1952	25	3–5	7.0	weak
Upper Credit Tranche	since 1952	75	3–5	7.0	stringent
Extended Fund Facility	since 1974	140	4.5–10	7.0	stringent
Supplementary Financing Facility ('Witteveen-F[2]'),	1979–82	140	3.5–7	prime cost[3] plus 0.2–0.375	stringent
Policy of Enlarged Access[2]	since 1981	95–115 p.a.	3.5–7	prime cost plus 0.2[3]	stringent
Compensatory Financing Facility	since 1963	83	3–5	7.0	weak to stringent
Cereal Import Facility	since 1981	105	3–5	7.0	(dependent on sum borrowed)
Buffer Stock Facility	since 1969	45	3–5	7.0	weak
Oil Facility	1974–76	75	3.5–7	6.875–7.875	weak
Trust Fund	1976–81	–	5–10	0.5	weak

[1] A one-off administrative fee of 0.5% of the loan also has to be paid (except in the case of the reserve tranche).
[2] Could/can only be used in conjunction with standby arrangements (higher loan tranches) or an agreement of the Extended Fund Facility.
[3] An interest subsidy account exists for poorer developing countries.

Source: IMF, *International Financial Statistics*, March, 1984; IMF, *Annual Report*, 1984.

countries to the Fund's finances — a proposal which was strongly rejected by the United States (although neither position was included in the IMF's statutes). Not until the second amendment of the IMF agreement in 1978 was this practice — long since standard — officially written into the IMF statutes. A standby arrangement was defined as a resolution by the Fund entitling a member state to draw sums totalling a certain amount within a certain period of time (Art. XXX. b); another clause states in very vague terms that the IMF may develop economic conditions for the granting of loans (Art. V. para 3). This leaves the Executive Board complete freedom to determine the conditionality of loans.

By the end of 1984, member countries had concluded 550 standby arrangements and 34 Extended Fund Facility arrangements with the IMF. Developing countries were obliged to apply for these strictly conditioned forms of credit with over-proportional frequency. In December 1983 there were 43 standby and extended agreements in force. In more than a quarter of all IMF member-states, economic policies had to be brought into line with IMF stabilisation instructions. With the exception of Hungary and Rumania all the states concerned were developing countries.

Standby arrangements were originally conceived as precautionary measures, allowing countries which had no immediate need but might need to use these funds at some point in the future access to IMF funds (Guitián, 1981, p. 14). In 1952 the Executive Board decided that the drawing of loans over and above the Reserve Tranche could be tied to conditions. At the insistence of the USA this practice was especially applied to Latin American countries, whereas as late as 1956 Great Britain was drawing from the fourth tranche without any conditions attached.

The first standby arrangement concluded by a Latin American country (Peru) with the IMF in 1954 already contained all the major elements of later agreements. The Peruvian government had to agree to a stabilisation programme and commit itself to 'consultations' with the IMF during the period of the loan. If an effective stabilisation of the Peruvian currency was not achieved, the loan could be withheld as a sanction. Private and public moneylenders in the USA insisted — as in the case of Chile in 1956 — on an IMF agreement as an indispensable condition for further loans. Their interest was clear — together with the IMF they could impose their wishes without being accused of 'dollar imperialism' and without harming business. The sums raised through the IMF were not enough to satisfy debtors' demands and so the governments of the developing countries were still obliged to borrow from other US sources (Haumer, 1971, p. 399; Andersen, 1977, pp. 219 ff.).

Even today — in the words of an IMF official — 'the importance of the Fund as a catalyst for other sources of financing cannot be overstressed' (Guitián, 1981a, p. 17). Many governments of developing countries reluctantly decide to sign IMF agreements because this is the only method of restoring the country's creditworthiness on international capital markets. If balance-of-payments and budget deficits have reached such levels that creditors are alarmed about the repayment of their loans, governments have no choice but to negotiate a stabilisation programme with the 'faceless men' of the IMF. Such are the rules of the international finance system. Even today the actual amount of the loan is of secondary importance; the decisive factor is the 'seal of approval' which an IMF agreement gives to the government's economic policy.[11] Such an agreement indicates to creditors that the country concerned is capable of paying and willing to pay and means a green light for further loans. It is only this ascribed competence to judge national economic policies which has given the 'financial policeman' its real power to discipline indebted countries. Both promises of loans from bilateral or multilateral credit grantors and debt reschedulings with private or public creditors are dependent on the IMF.

The 'seal of approval' indicates ability to repay debt — but it should also indicate that a country is on its way back to economic health. The stabilisation programmes which are a compulsory part of IMF agreements aim at achieving monetary and financial stability. But governments are far from enthusiastic about concluding such agreements with the IMF. They are deterred by the tough conditions, which have a powerful impact on the economic, social and, indirectly, the political situation in their countries. This explains why countries frequently delay as long as possible before applying to the IMF if it is still possible to plug their financial gaps from other, often more expensive, sources. Once these sources have run dry and an application to the IMF can no longer be avoided, the Fund insists on even tougher interventions. And at this point minor changes of course are really no longer enough.

From the legal point of view these agreements, which bind governments to wide-ranging changes in their policies and in some cases grant the Fund neo-colonial power, are not international agreements. To seal the agreement, a legalistic trick is used. The government of the country taking up the loan commits itself in a letter of intent, formulated in detail by the IMF, to implement specifically-named stabilisation measures; on the basis of this unilateral declaration the IMF grants the funds requested. This legal construction absolves the government from the need to observe, for example, parliamentary procedures on the ratification of state treaties. It also means that IMF loan agreements do not have to be published because they are not international agreements in the sense of the UN Charter. As the IMF invariably and the governments, with few exceptions, remain silent on the terms it is frequently unclear what measures a government has had to commit itself to[12] (Gerster, 1982, pp. 124 f.). Once the stabilisation programme is implemented, however, typical IMF terms are easy enough to recognise.

Devaluation, reduction of the budget deficit, restrictions on domestic credit and cuts in subsidies for public goods — these are as a rule the major features of IMF stabilisation programmes. It is irrelevant for the IMF whether the causes of the debt crisis are internal or external — the therapy must be applied regardless. The crucial factor is whether the deficit is temporary and can be financed by bridging loans, or permanent (Guitián, 1981, p. 4). If the Fund concludes that the deficit is long-term, then there is only one possibility: the economy of the deficit country must be adjusted to its financial room for manoeuvre — countries with surpluses which are partly responsible for the deficits remain unaffected.

The linchpin of IMF 'adjustment policy' is the fight against inflation. According to the IMF's economic philosophy, inflation is a decisive factor in balance-of-payments deficits. High inflation rates in many developing countries are considered to be a result of 'excessive demand' — a term which in view of the poverty in many developing countries eloquently underlines the ideological nature of economic theory. This means that the available supply of goods and services in the country lags behind demand (demand measured in monetary units and not in terms of need). When large sums of money are chasing a few goods, prices rise. The IMF's objective is to eliminate this imbalance, to bring supply and demand into line with each other.

In the IMF's view, demand is artificially inflated and inflation is due to economic errors and omissions at national level. State expenditure not covered by revenue, subsidies for basic goods, expenditure on transport and social services and the costs of unproductive state enterprises — all these the IMF regards as major causes of inflation.

IMF economists argue that inflation caused by domestic 'excessive demand' puts constant pressure on the balance of payments. The high rate of inflation leads to an over-valuation of the national currency, because its constantly decreasing domestic purchasing power no longer corresponds to the officially fixed rate of exchange. A flood of imports occurs; whereas prices for local products rise with demand, imports remain comparatively cheap because of fixed exchange-rates. At the same time it becomes more difficult for the country to export goods and thus to earn the foreign exchange it needs to improve its balance of payments. On world markets the prices for domestically-produced goods — in terms of the official exchange-rate — are comparatively low. The balance-of-payments gap has to be plugged with foreign loans and the level of debt increases.

This explains why devaluation of the national currency is as a rule one of the central demands of the IMF. Devaluation is intended to improve the balance of payments by making imports more expensive and boosting exports by making them cheaper. Import and foreign exchange controls, as practised by many Third World countries, have no more place in IMF concepts than multiple rates of exchange. As they are both artificial hindrances to trade, the IMF insists on their abolition, or at least gradual reduction. In line with creditors' interests, the elimination of arrears on debt-servicing and on profit transfers are always part of IMF stabilisation programmes. These measures, together with others designed to create favourable conditions for foreign investors, are intended to restore confidence among foreign capital investors and to guarantee a long-term inflow of capital. If debt-service obligations are an extreme strain on the economy, the IMF often insists that new debt be limited for the period of the stabilisation programme and/or that only weakly-conditioned loans should be taken up.

The IMF attempts to tackle 'excessive demand' within the domestic economy by restricting the volume of domestic credit, increasing interest-rates and controlling the money supply. Governments must undertake to finance the budget deficit not by printing money but by taking up loans on the domestic money markets and even here only up to a certain ceiling. Thus the deficit remains limited. The private sector's demand for credit is also restricted, although it is generally given more scope than the state. The purpose of this preferential treatment is to shift economic activities from the state to the private sector because in the view of the IMF private enterprise works more efficiently.

Subsidies for basic foodstuffs and transport (petrol prices) as well as social services which do not cover their costs are hardest hit by the IMF-imposed cutbacks designed to reduce the budget deficit. The IMF economists are not interested in the political and social reasons for these budget items nor in the effects of cutbacks. They are solely concerned with eliminating 'price distortions' which lead to 'excessive demand' and thus prevent 'adjustment'. It is with this argument that prices are decontrolled and the prices of public services (electricity, water) increased.

The Fund insists that state enterprises — even when they fulfil social functions — should at least cover their costs and if this is impossible the Fund frequently insists on their closure. IMF programmes also frequently call for extensive dismissals in the public services — which in developing countries are often over-staffed. Again the purpose of such measures is to improve the balance of payments. Cutbacks in social expenditure and increases in the price of public services often go hand in hand with tax-cuts designed to encourage domestic and foreign investors. These investors also benefit from another measure which the IMF frequently includes in its conditions: the strict limitation of wage increases. This is designed to ensure that trade unions do not conclude wage agreements which make up for the reductions in wage-earners' income caused by price increases and subsidy cutbacks. The free play of market forces is obviously not considered desirable here.

The three cornerstones of IMF economic recovery policies are easy to identify: the application of the principles of the market economy, deflation of the economy through monetary measures and the opening of frontiers for free trade and capital transfers. The IMF's faith in the welfare-promoting effects of market forces and of free enterprise is apparently based more on political convictions than on economic analysis. It is precisely because the free play of market forces did not produce the results which the Fund hoped for that state enterprises were created in many developing countries and governments intervened in market activity with subsidies and price controls. Nonetheless, the Fund continues to insist on cutbacks in public expenditure, the reduction of the state sector (in some cases it even launches regular reprivatisation campaigns) and decontrolling prices — and again and again it is taught the error of its ways by the structures of developing countries' economies. Most developing countries lack coherent economic cycles, market transparency, entrepreneurial initiative, efficient banks, productive capacities and social security systems — all of which are necessary if a system of market-economy incentives is to function satisfactorily and to lead to a distribution of income comparable to industrialised countries.

The Fund argues that inflation and balance-of-payments deficits are the logical results if a national economy consumes more goods and social services than it produces. This perspective leads to two possible remedies. The first is to seek the causes of inadequate production and to take production-stimulating measures (to interpret 'excessive demand' as 'inadequate supply') and the second is to tighten belts and consume less or, in the language of economists, to 'adjust' overall economic demand to the (low) supply. Until the beginning of the 1980s, the IMF concentrated almost exclusively on the second option which, implemented with the classical instruments of monetarism, is still dominant: the economy is deflated, and the IMF attempts to tackle excessive demand — caused in its view by a rampant increase in the money supply — by cutting the volume of domestic credit. The 'pure doctrine' of monetarism insists on equal reductions of all components of overall economic demand. But to encourage private enterprise the IMF puts the main emphasis on the reduction of public expenditure and wages (Daniel, 1981, p. 33).

The IMF's diagnosis is itself dubious. The causes of inflation and balance-of-payments deficits in developing countries are frequently high import bills. Price rises for oil and capital goods imports in particular, as well as high interest levels on money-markets, have imposed severe strains on the balance of payments of Third World countries. If this cost inflation is treated with demand-reducing therapies, the result is inevitably worse than the disease. Economic activity is throttled, the incentives for private investors frequently have no effect and the economy drifts into recession. Inadequate use of production capacities and high unemployment are, however, precisely the reasons for the subsidies and transfer payments in national budgets which the IMF condemns as inflationary. The 'policy of sackcloth and ashes' (Dell, 1982, p. 608) plays around with symptoms but makes the causes of the disaster worse.

An active role for the state in economic activity and subsidy policies for the benefit of the poor — in the face of the IMF's uniform therapy, obsessed as it is with the market economy and deflation, these priorities go by the board, despite the fact that the IMF agreement (Article IV. 3b) and the guidelines for the granting of standby arrangements passed by the IMF Executive Board in 1979 expressly bind the Fund when working out 'adjustment programmes' to 'pay due regard to the domestic social and political objectives, the economic priorities, and the circumstances of members.' (*IMF Survey*, 19 March 1979, p. 82.) In the case of subsidies for basic foods, this obligation is swept aside on the grounds that they are an intolerable strain on the balance of payments. In the case of military expenditure, however, which in many developing countries puts a severe strain on the balance of payments, the Fund insists on every member country's right to defend itself. Exceptions prove the rule: in Peru in 1977 the IMF decided that the country's massive arms imports from the Soviet Union were one of the main causes of the crisis and insisted on their reduction (Rey, 1979); six years later, at the end of 1983, the Fund criticised the high expenditure of foreign exchange on military imports (this time from the West) and finally cancelled the three-year stabilisation programme agreed in June 1983 (LAWR, 23 December 1983). The purchase of aircraft for US $20 million by Bolivia in November 1980 was one reason for the IMF's decision not to pay the last instalment of a standby arrangement of US $17 million and not to complete a projected Extended Fund Facility (LAWR, 28 November 1980).

The stabilising function of the third cornerstone of IMF adjustment programmes is also problematic. With its insistence on reducing trade and capital transfer controls and on liberalising foreign trade relations, the Fund is attempting to implement the goal formulated in Article 1.2 of the IMF agreement: 'to facilitate expansion and balanced growth of international trade.' Behind this goal is a belief in the theory of comparative cost advantage, which states that free and unrestricted trade relations ensure that every country specialises in the production of those goods which, given its natural strengths and advantages, it can sell especially favourably. A worldwide division of labour based on cost advantages would, as it were, automatically guarantee the well-being of all concerned.

It is doubtful whether this IMF-imposed integration into the world market always brings in its wake a healthy economic and social development. Protective duties and import controls, of which today's industrial nations made liberal use in the 19th Century when building up their national industries, have no more place in this concept than a system of foreign-exchange management which attempts to use limited export earnings according to national priorities. In this concept, developing countries can all too easily be reduced to the status of raw materials-producing low-wage countries, for this, in the words of the economists, is their 'natural factor advantage'.

The central measure in the liberalisation of foreign trade relations is usually the devaluation of the national currency which, together with the reduction of imports, is designed to ensure that the deficit country can sell its export goods more cheaply and can therefore sell more. Yet it is highly doubtful whether devaluations lead to higher export earnings as inevitably as the IMF would wish. The question is: who is going to buy all the exports released by devaluations? The main obstacle to high export earnings in many countries is not a lack of efforts to export but a limited overall demand which cannot be increased. In such a situation — which is further aggravated by the world economic recession and the increasing protectionism of the industrial countries — all that is achieved is cut-throat competition among the developing countries which leads to a redistribution of sales chances (see Chapter 4).

The fundamental flaw in the IMF's philosophy of economic recovery, fixated as it is on a short-term improvement in the balance of payments, is that it is not compatible, indeed often conflicts, with a long-term development policy. The IMF always responds to the multiplicity of balance-of-payments deficits with the same prescription: the restriction of demand. This may eliminate a balance-of-payments deficit in the short term but it cannot produce development. What is needed for development is a policy appropriate to the specific causes of indebtedness of each country, a policy which strengthens the productive base. An element of such stabilisation policy could, for example, be to respond to reductions in the price of export goods with export diversification measures and to the increase in import prices with import-substituting production. But precisely such policies are strangled by the Fund's rigid austerity programmes which are primarily concerned with the short-term manipulation of economic data.

The IMF reacts to such criticisms by pointing out that its concern as an institution for monetary and financial questions is with balance-of-payments aid and not with development aid and that monetary stability is a precondition for development (Gold, 1979, p. 18). The IMF does, however, now acknowledge verbally that its stabilisation programmes must not prevent long-term structural change in the developing countries (Larosière, 1982, p. 6). This realisation has been included in the Executive Board's guidelines for standby arrangements. The Fund has also, verbally at least, moved away from the one-sided fixation of its therapy on deflation which has been described as a 'political economy of overkill' (Dell, 1982) because of the dangers of recession it brings with it. IMF officials today take every possible opportunity to stress that its policies include not only measures to control overall demand (deflation) but also measures to increase supply (Crockett, 1982, p. 13; Guitián, 1981a, p. 15). Since the beginning of the 1980s there have been tentative moves in this direction; but the influence of 'Reaganomics' (the monetarist economic policy of the Reagan administration) has at least partially reversed this trend and the philosophy of 'belt-tightening' still dominates in IMF programmes.

The realisation that its belt-tightening therapy was killing its clients rather than restoring them to health led the Fund to extend its credit agreements, which originally lasted only six months. Today these agreements normally run for a year and longer periods are by no means rare. The maximum validity — as in the case of the Extended Facility introduced in 1974, which offers not only higher drawing facilities but also longer repayment deadlines — is three years. Inadequate though these extensions are in view of the structural causes of developing countries' deficits, they do at least create a possibility of lessening the burdens of adjustment by a less rapid implementation of terms. They also give stabilisation policy if not a developmental orientation then at least a perspective which goes beyond the figures at the end of the next financial year.

The very fact that many developing countries have had to negotiate consecutive stabilisation programmes with the IMF over ten years and more[13] proves how ineffective the Fund's instruments are against balance-of-payments deficits whose deeper causes lie in the deformed structures of developing countries' economies. Realising that balance-of-payments problems could in many cases only be remedied in the long term, the World Bank introduced 'Structural Adjustment Loans' in 1980. Although not formally tied to an IMF agreement, this new type of loan — with which the World Bank has ventured away from its previous domain of project-oriented development finance — has in fact so far always been granted in close chronological connection with an IMF loan. Countries which commit themselves to a radical programme of economic reforms supervised by the World Bank and designed to achieve a long-term improvement in the balance of payments can qualify for a Structural Adjustment Loan. The nature of these Structural Adjustment Programmes and their influence on development is discussed in Chapter 4.

The IMF uses a system of phasing or staggered payment of loans for all drawings in the upper Credit Tranches — to ensure that the borrower country not only promises to take but actually does take the IMF's medicine. Only when certain performance criteria are met is the next instalment of the loan paid. These performance criteria are a few economic targets which, in the view of the IMF, indicate whether a stabilisation programme is successful or not. They usually consist of quarterly upper limits for the volume of domestic credit with special restrictions for the state sector and restrictions on the money supply and publicly-guaranteed foreign debt. Qualitative performance criteria may also be included, such as an undertaking not to introduce or to intensify payment restrictions. Control clauses which are left blank when the agreement is signed are also *de facto* performance criteria. They enable the Fund to adjust or fix targets according to economic data during the validity of the stabilisation programme.

If the borrower fails to meet one or more of the performance criteria, its drawing rights expire. 'Consultations' are then held in the course of which the Executive Board may regard the infringement as an exception and allow the next loan instalment or it may insist on negotiations for a new agreement (Crockett, 1982, p. 15). The stereotyped application of the same quantitative performance criteria — regarded as the core of every stabilisation programme[14] — strikingly illustrates the basic monetarist pattern of the IMF's uniform therapy. The purpose is to improve the balance of payments by reducing the money supply in the economy (and controlling the volume of credit) and thus to cut overall expenditure.

The argument often advanced in favour of performance criteria, which have been part of the IMF repertoire since the 1950s, is that they are easily calculable, readily available, objective data by means of which the economic development of a country can be effectively influenced (Daniel, 1981. pp. 32 f.). Apart from the economic implications of these exclusively monetary targets, the frequent (unintentional) infringements show how weak are the foundations on which these supposedly scientific data are based. Critics agree that the economic performance criteria set for developing countries are to a large extent arbitrary, haphazard and speculative (Dell, 1982, p. 610; Jeker, 1980, p. 47).

To force through its therapy, the IMF often insists that aid-seeking countries meet preconditions before a loan agreement is signed. In many cases, the IMF insists on devaluation as an advance concession (Williamson, 1982, pp. 36 f.). The greater the IMF's doubts about whether the measures it considers necessary will actually be implemented after the agreement is signed, the more exhaustive the list of preconditions[15] (Crockett, 1982, p. 15). In the case of notoriously corrupt regimes which have lost their international credibility and creditworthiness, the IMF often insists that important parts of the stabilisation programmes be implemented in advance — only then does it release the loan funds and give its 'stamp of approval'.[16]

The Fund attaches great importance to its supposedly non-political character, arguing that the principle of non-discrimination ensures that all countries are treated equally in the granting and conditionality of loans. According to the Fund its loans policy is determined solely by economic and technical considerations (Gold, 1983). The Fund's practice gives the lie to this claim. There are numerous examples to show that reform-oriented governments have been given terms which were incompatible with their political survival (but which, if not accepted, led to the refusal of the loan), whereas conservative-authoritarian and sometimes even fascist regimes in whose stability the West was interested for economic or geo-strategic reasons, have been granted comparatively weakly-conditioned loans. The USA has again and again succeeded in using the loans policy of the IMF (usually in conjunction with the loan-granting policy of the World Bank) for its own foreign policy ends.

Chile under President Allende was refused a standby arrangement after the country had been plunged into difficulties by a US destabilisation policy. The Fund would only permit Chile a far smaller loan from the Compensatory Financing Facility — a loan against which it could find no economic-technical argument. In contrast, the IMF was rapidly able to reach agreement on a standby arrangement with the fascist Pinochet regime (Morrell/Biddle, 1983, p. 7). Whereas socialist Vietnam received no loan when it invaded neighbouring Cambodia, South Africa, which had just brutally crushed the Soweto uprising, was given an IMF loan of US $464 million in 1976 — a sum almost equal to the increase in its military expenditure in the same year (Morrell/Gisselquist, 1978).

In November 1982, the IMF again granted South Africa a loan, this time totalling US $1.1 thousand million, even though the UN General Assembly had just voted by 121 votes to 3, with 3 abstentions, against IMF aid for the apartheid regime. The demand by Third World Executive Directors that

IMF aid should be coupled with the condition that the government should abandon its racist system of apartheid was not accepted — although even IMF economists have identified the racist 'structural blocking of the labour market', along with the drop in the price of gold and diamonds, as one of the major causes of the crisis. The USA forced the unusually weakly-conditioned loan through with the help of Canada and most West European countries who, though they frequently voiced reservations, ended up supporting the US line. The USA and its allies won the day with 53% of the total vote. The IMF thus became the last international organisation which supports the apartheid regime (Morrell, 1983; FT, 25 January 1983; WA, 13 June 1983, pp. 1391 f.).[17]

With the votes of the Third World, the USA in July 1981 forced through a Compensatory Financing Facility credit for El Salvador, even though in the opinion of the IMF management the country did not meet the requirements and West European directors spoke openly of a violation of IMF rules. US Executive Director Erb declared the export projections of the IMF economist to be simply incorrect and assured himself of the support of directors from developing countries who in view of their countries' needs were anxious to create a precedent for a liberal policy of loan-granting. A year later El Salvador was given not only a further loan from the Compensatory Financing Facility but also a standby credit which caused a sensation because of its generous terms. In it, three subjects which are normally part of an IMF stabilisation programme were completely omitted: interest rates, subsidies and prices of agricultural goods. There is no doubt that the loan-granting modalities of the IMF reflected the USA's interest in supporting a regime in El Salvador which it regarded as a caretaker for US interests, a regime which was at that time under pressure from a left-wing guerilla movement (Morrell/Biddle, 1983, pp. 2 ff.). [18]

Human rights violations by the Somoza regime caused the Carter administration in the USA to object to IMF loans for Nicaragua in 1978. In 1979 this policy was abandoned. As late as May 1979, nine weeks before Somoza's overthrow, the Nicaraguan regime received an IMF credit, most of which disappeared into the pockets of the Somoza clan. The new Sandinista government, despite great need, had to do without IMF loans because the Fund's terms were incompatible with a government policy which aimed to achieve growth and redistribute income (Morrell/Biddle, 1983, p. 11).

In 1981, a three-year loan which the IMF management had promised the Caribbean island of Grenada was reduced, following US pressure, to a one-year loan and to one-third of the original sum (LARR, 8 May 1981). The arguments for the granting or refusal of a loan are always economic and technical; but the real motives here were more or less openly political. In the case of Grenada, the USA's political objection was to the building of an airport which it feared could be used as a stopover point for the transportation of Cuban troops to Angola. US Secretary of State Haig declared in 1981 that the socialist government of Grenada would not receive a penny of indirect international aid, at which the US Executive Director in the IMF immediately objected to the planned loan. He argued that the excessive expenditure on the airport was the main reason for the country's economic difficulties and that this had not been sufficiently taken into account in the stabilisation plan (Rossiter, 1983).

To sum up: with the conditions it attaches to loan agreements, the IMF intervenes massively in the economic, social and political structures of deficit countries. These countries are dependent on the Fund's 'seal of approval' because their creditworthiness on international financial markets can only be restored if they have agreed a stabilisation programme with the IMF. The IMF's universal medicine, based on the three cornerstones of market economy, deflation and world-market integration can, if successful, bring about a short-term improvement in the balance of payments. But it does not open up development options; indeed in the worst case it prevents them. The IMF's stabilisation concept reflects the creditors' over-riding interest in the restoration of a country's ability to service its debts; similarly, the interests of Western industrial nations, above all of the USA, are paramount in the Fund's loan-granting practice. Despite all the assurances about equal treatment for member countries, some members are more equal than others. The practice of granting loans is often based on political calculations — indeed the conditions themselves, as will be seen, are sometimes political in nature.

How IMF Loan Agreements Come About

The periodical 'consultations' which every IMF member is required to attend generally form the starting point for negotiations on a loan agreement. A 'mission' or team of IMF experts then discusses with leading officials the economic development of the country and states the measures the Fund believes to be appropriate in view of the country's balance-of-payments and debt situation. The possible terms of an IMF loan may also be discussed during these visits. The request to start negotiations on a loan agreement must come from the country itself. It is usually addressed to the Executive Director responsible, who then passes it on to the Managing Director of the IMF. The request and the negotiations themselves, which are conducted by officials of the regional departments responsible (who also hold the consultations), are strictly confidential. The only information available in most cases is that an IMF mission is visiting the country.

Before this stage is reached, the mission produces a so-called briefing paper, a document which summarises the country's economic situation, indicates possible stabilisation measures and states the probable amount of the IMF loan. The IMF gets the rest of the information it needs by sending a questionnaire to the government's officials. The briefing paper is discussed with other IMF departments and amended correspondingly and finally presented to the IMF Managing Director. If necessary, the Managing Director will then call a meeting with the head of the mission and other heads of department to establish the position of the Fund on politically sensitive aspects of the projected stabilisation measures. With the approval of the Managing Director the document then becomes the mission's official instructions.

On the surface there is no difference between negotiations for a loan and routine consultations. A mission consisting of four to six economists and a secretary visits the member country for two to three weeks. The team of economists generally consists of the head of the delegation, usually a senior official in the relevant regional department, two specialists in the country concerned, a member of the department of payment and trade relations and officials from other IMF departments — depending on which aspects of economic policy are to be given special scrutiny. In recent years an increasing number of missions has included a representative of the World Bank.

The first part of the visit is devoted to data-gathering. IMF representatives get a picture of the current economic situation by visiting ministries and the central bank. Here they have the advantage of already knowing the leading civil servants and the local situation from their previous routine visits. The withholding of information is almost impossible as the team knows reliable sources of information. Besides, price increases and the black market value of the national currency can be found out easily enough by visiting shops in the capital.

The second part of the visit consists of bargaining and negotiation on the conditions of the loan agreement. The IMF team states the conditions which, in its view, a stabilisation programme must include, while as a rule the government tries to tone these down by pointing to their social, political or economic impact. The preconditions which a country may have to meet to qualify for a loan are also stated here. If, as often happens, the government cannot or will not accept the Fund's minimum conditions in this war of nerves, the mission leaves the country — only for the whole procedure to start again later.

If an agreement is reached, the next step is the formulation of the letter of intent. The form of this letter, addressed to the Managing Director of the IMF and generally signed by the finance minister and central bank governor of the aid-seeking country, varies from case to case, but it — or the accompanying enclosures — always contains a formal request to draw a certain sum and a detailed description of the stabilisation measures to which the government commits itself. The letter invariably contains quantitative economic targets (performance criteria) and the government concerned is required to inform Washington quarterly about the actual figures achieved so that the Fund can check whether the agreement is being kept.

Back in Washington, the chief of mission produces the so-called 48-hour report, a two-page paper summarising the negotiations for the Managing Director. Together with the draft of the letter of intent this is then sent round the various IMF departments, which for legal or technical reasons may suggest minor alterations. The IMF staff then produce a comprehensive report for the Executive Board, containing a detailed analysis of the country's economic situation and describing the hoped-for effects of the stabilisation measures. Together with the now-signed letter of intent the report is discussed in the Executive Board within four weeks and the loan request is presented for a decision. By this stage all the hurdles have been cleared — the Executive Board almost always follows the Fund management's recommendations. A report on the discussion in the Executive Board — which may perhaps influence how the IMF follows the implementation of the stabilisation measures — is then sent to the loan-seeking country. The loan agreement is in force, the first instalment of the loan can be paid (Crockett, 1982; Brau, 1981; Sidhom, 1979).

Back to Creditworthiness: the IMF's Mediating Role in Debt-Rescheduling

The IMF's importance as an international financial policeman is not confined to the disciplining of debtor countries through stabilisation programmes. Private and public, bilateral and multilateral donors regard IMF agreements as a signal to provide a debtor country with finance again, to grant it refinancing loans or to agree to an extension of payment deadlines by rescheduling. It is the catalysing effect of IMF agreements which gives the Fund its real power as the loans negotiated after an IMF agreement are far greater than the IMF loan itself.

The practice of rescheduling shows, however, that the role of the IMF is not confined to that of a catalyst. Even though the degree of IMF involvement may vary from case to case, there is no doubt that the 'honest broker' between debtors and creditors — a term the IMF is fond of applying to itself (IMF, 1981, p. 26) — has considerable influence on the modalities of rescheduling arrangements. It is its competence in judging the economic efficiency of deficit countries — a competence attributed to it by creditors and resignedly accepted by debtors — which assures the IMF of this influence.

Up to 1980, rescheduling arrangements were still regarded as exceptions in the management of debt, but they are now well on the way to becoming the rule. In 1973, two countries were forced to eat humble pie and ask their creditors for rescheduling arrangements. Eleven years later, in 1984, the corresponding figure was 26 countries. The total of rescheduled debts rose spectacularly from about US $300 million in 1973 to over US $100 thousand million in 1984 (see Appendix 1). IMF and refinancing loans are no longer enough for rescheduling candidates: their economies need a breathing space in the repayment of debt if their ability to service debts is not to suffer in the long term. The repayment deadlines for a part or for all of their debts have to be extended.

To ensure that the relief granted by one creditor is not used to meet obligations to others, creditors almost always insist upon multilateral negotiations. Two international forums for negotiating rescheduling agreements have emerged. In the Paris Club, an informal association of Western industrial nations, state and state-guaranteed loans are rescheduled.[19] If, as is increasingly the case, debts to private banks play an important part in the debt crisis, the debtor country has to negotiate with a committee of the main creditor banks — often known as the London or New York Club. IMF and World Bank loans have never been the subject of rescheduling arrangements, the duty to meet them on time being regarded as sacrosanct.[20]

The Paris Club has the longest tradition, going back to a meeting of Western industrial nations in Paris in 1956 at which trade and payment relations with Argentina were coordinated and the suppliers' credits granted to that country were rescheduled. Although the Paris Club has had a secretariat since 1974 and its work is carried out by officials of the French Treasury, the creditor countries still try to retain the informal character of this committee. Its meetings are held *ad hoc* and it has neither a fixed number of members nor statutes governing procedure (World Bank, 1984, p. xix). The purpose is to give the impression to the outside world that rescheduling arrangements are absolute exceptions in international financial relations and do not create precedents for other debtors — claims which have ceased to be valid since 1982/3 at the latest, when one debtor country after another turned up at the *Avenue Kléber* seeking rescheduling arrangements.

Not all rescheduling negotiations for public loans come under the aegis of the Paris Club. These negotiations have taken place in other cities such as London and The Hague; but the participants and the procedure in such meetings have been identical — except for the chairmanship — to those of the Paris Club. This also applies to rescheduling within the framework of aid consortia which, in the case of India, Pakistan and Bangladesh, was directed by the World Bank or, in the case of Turkey, by the OECD — negotiations which brought not only extensions of repayment deadlines but also promises of development loans.

Two conditions must be met for a meeting of the Paris Club to be called. Countries must have fallen into or be about to fall into arrears of payment and as a rule the debtor country must be willing to accept an IMF stabilisation programme. The French Treasury, at the request of the debtors, then invites representatives of the main creditor countries to a meeting in Paris.[21] Representatives of the OECD and UNCTAD have observer status, as do the IMF and the World Bank, who have been present at all such meetings except one since the Brazilian rescheduling negotiations of 1961.[22] By tradition the chairman of the Paris Club is the director of the French Treasury or one of his two deputies.

Rescheduling arrangements follow an invariable pattern: during a 'period of consolidation', which usually lasts a year, the sums due[23] are completely or partially (usually 80 or 90%) staggered. In the following three to four years, 'normal' debt-servicing payments must be made and the rescheduled sum must then be paid off over the next seven to nine years[24] (IMF, 1983). The precise conditions are set down in an agreed minute which provides the framework for bilateral negotiations between debtors and creditors. They are above all concerned with the amount of interest payable on the rescheduled debt. This interest is almost invariably at the market rate, because creditors insist relentlessly on the principle that rescheduling arrangements must be kept strictly separate from development aid payments. This means that the principle that applies in rescheduling arrangements today is the same as that which the Ghanaian Finance Minister Mensah aptly summed up in 1970: relieving debts by increasing them (see p. 120).

The IMF plays a key role in rescheduling agreements. Even the calling of a meeting depends on an arrangement between the debtor and the Fund; since 1966 rescheduling arrangements in the Paris Club are tied in principle to an IMF agreement. This tying may take various forms: it may range from the general condition laid down in the rescheduling agreement to carry out an IMF stabilisation programme to the commitment to meet the performance criteria stated in the IMF agreement and repeated in the rescheduling minutes. (The exception that proves the rule is Mozambique: the creditors were satisfied by the country's mere accession to the Fund in 1984 and by the promise of the Machel government to start negotiations for a standby arrangement immediately.) Not until these are met — these words are to be found in a rescheduling agreement with an unnamed country (IMF, 1981) — can bilateral agreements be signed and the rescheduling arrangement come into force.

The IMF plays a decisive role in negotiations on rescheduling conditions. The debt situation of the country concerned is discussed on the basis of documents prepared by the IMF; its representatives provide information on the balance of payments; the assessment of a country's capacity to service its debts is based on the IMF's analyses.[25] The repayment burdens which a given economy can be expected to bear in coming years are decided on the basis of the IMF's analysis. Creditors have no choice but to accept the more or less clearly stated recommendations of the Fund because the IMF has already, in the previously agreed stabilisation programme, taken into account the impact of the promised rescheduling conditions on the balance of payments and the debt structure.[26] Creditors cannot therefore capsize the IMF agreement to which they have tied the rescheduling by insisting on rescheduling modalities which conflict with the assumptions of the IMF agreement (IMF, 1981, p. 27; Hardy, 1982, p. 32).

Finally, the IMF also plays an important role in the implementation of rescheduling agreements. In these agreements the IMF is almost always assigned the task of keeping creditors informed about the economic situation of the debtor country, in particular about payments to other creditors and about the level of debt. As a rule, the IMF also informs all other creditors about the agreements negotiated with individual creditors.[27] Furthermore, it has a decisive influence on the application of the 'goodwill' clauses included in many agreements. These clauses promise new rescheduling negotiations at the end of the consolidation period if it should turn out that the economic capacity of the economy is not sufficient to pay the interest and repayment instalments then due.

A study of the agreements negotiated in the Paris Club with the assistance of the IMF shows how strongly the modalities are oriented towards the creditors' interest in rapid and profitable repayments of loans. The breathing space allowed to debtors is short, almost always too short to set economic growth in motion — growth which would make it easier to meet future debt-servicing requirements. When, after a short pause, the original debt — augmented by high moratorium interest rates and the consolidated debt — has to be serviced again, the result in many cases is a new foreign-exchange shortage which forces the debtor country to put in another application for rescheduling to the Paris Club. All concerned are fully aware of this; yet creditors as a rule prefer short-term reliefs to long-term solutions of debt crises. The economic prospects of the debtor could after all improve dramatically in the long term.

It would certainly be wrong to blame the IMF entirely for the fact that in rescheduling agreements the short-term interest of creditors in maximum repayment almost always takes precedence over the debtor's interest in the creation or maintenance of long-term development options. Given the inability of a debtor to pay, the negotiating position of the creditor is so strong that it is bound to impose its interests in rescheduling arrangements. Nonetheless, the IMF must bear part of the responsibility. Given its prominent position in the negotiating process — its expertise is almost indispensable for the creditors — it could easily persuade creditors to grant reliefs which would leave the debtor country scope to pursue growth-oriented economic policies — instead of obliging it to spend years trying to earn enough foreign exchange solely to service its debts.

Only when there is a risk that the global and geo-strategic interests of the West in the political and economic stability of a debtor country could be endangered by too-tough rescheduling terms are the creditors prepared to pay more attention to the development perspectives of Third World countries. In the case of Indonesia in 1970, creditors agreed to a favourably-conditioned long-term rescheduling of the country's overall debt in order to support the pro-Western Suharto regime and ensure continuing Western influence in South-East Asia. Through the mediation of German banker Hermann Josef Abs, an agreement was reached staggering the Indonesian debt over thirty years without moratorium interest. Over and above this the creditors agreed to a clause allowing for a further delay in debt repayments in the event of balance-of-payments difficulties. Ghana, which was experiencing similar difficulties in the same year, had far tougher terms imposed on it, even though here — as in Indonesia — the socialist regime had been replaced by a pro-Western government in 1966. Obviously Ghana did not have the same geo-political significance as Indonesia (see Chapter 3). In June 1980, creditors granted Pakistan's request for rescheduling negotiations — though there was no likelihood of delays in payment — and finally granted the country favourable conditions. The reason for the change in the creditors' attitude was the Soviet invasion of Afghanistan, which had increased Pakistan's geo-strategic importance. To strengthen NATO's south-east flank politically and economically, Turkey was granted comparatively favourable rescheduling terms in 1959 and in 1980. Development requirements, as these examples illustrate, are generally only taken into consideration when they coincide with the political interests of creditors and above all the USA.

When in the mid-1970s the proportion of private bank loans in the foreign debt of many developing countries shot up, it became increasingly difficult to cope with debt crises by extending repayment deadlines for state and state-guaranteed loans. An effective form of crisis management could only be achieved if private banks also granted reliefs. At first the banks showed little inclination to reschedule debts. In previous years, only short-term trade loans had been rescheduled. To avoid creating precedents for insolvency, banks preferred refinancing loans whenever relief in the repayment of medium-term loans became unavoidable: the debtor country was expected to meet its debt-servicing requirements on schedule. It came to be realised only slowly that rescheduling arrangements were necessary to bring financial relations between banks and debtors back into line. Now rescheduling negotiations on private debts in the London or New York Club have become routine for the major international banks, though in the early days these negotiations sometimes dragged on for up to five years. The total of rescheduled bank loans now far exceeds that of public loans (see Appendix 1).

The procedure and method of rescheduling are similar to those of the Paris Club. Representatives of the debtor country have to appear before a steering committee of the banks in which the main creditors are represented and empowered to act on behalf of the other creditors. In many cases coordination among the banks — 611 banks were involved in the rescheduling of the Mexican debt in 1983 — proves far more complicated than negotiations with the debtors who are completely at the creditors' mercy. The banks try to ensure that their divergent interests are protected in the agreement — interests which differ according to the nationality of the banks and the amount and structure of their claims.

As a rule only repayments of principal are rescheduled.[28] Debtors are expected to repay interest as originally agreed. Typical conditions for bank loans are a two- to three-month moratorium for 80–100% of sums due in a 'consolidation period' usually lasting twelve months. After the moratorium expires, the staggered sums then have to be repaid over a four- to six-year period. The moratorium interest rates are tough: generally between 1.75 and 2.25% over LIBOR. Private creditors suffer even fewer losses as a result of rescheduling arrangements than public creditors (Hardy, 1982, p. 30). The banks even earn on the ritual of rescheduling itself — whenever a rescheduling agreement is signed they pocket up to 1.5% of the amount rescheduled. In the case of Mexico in 1983 the banks were content with a mere 1% commission, which meant that the considerable sum of US $225 million fell due when the agreement was signed (LAWR, 20 May 1983).

The IMF also plays a key role in negotiations with private creditors in London or New York, which in most cases run parallel to the discussions in the Paris Club. Like public creditors, banks almost always insist on the conclusion of a loan agreement with the IMF before agreeing to a rescheduling arrangement. Only the IMF's 'stamp of approval' provides a guarantee that the debtor country will make sufficient efforts to meet its future debt repayments on time.[29] In the preparation of rescheduling negotiations, and above all the working out and presentation of statistical material, the Fund provides debtor countries with advice. In many cases, however, debtor countries have had to enlist the help of international investment firms to bring their debt statistics, which in many cases were in a hopeless mess, up to date.

Representatives of the IMF, with few exceptions (Poland and Nicaragua are two) regularly take part in negotiations on rescheduling conditions. They are sometimes also present (with the knowledge of debtors) at discussions among creditors from which debtors are excluded. Officially their function is confined to explaining the stabilisation programme, assessing the country's economic prospects and answering technical questions, but in fact — as the IMF acknowledges in the case of a country whose name it does not mention — it plays 'a more active role' (IMF, 1981, p. 38). The IMF representatives leave no doubt about how high the rescheduling sum must be and what additional sums the banks have to raise if the stabilisation programme is to succeed and the country's ability to repay is to be maintained.

Only in the case of major rescheduling arrangements for Latin American countries in the recent past has the Fund effectively insisted on a constant inflow of funds to debtor countries — an inflow which frequently did not occur after previous rescheduling arrangements. The injections of finance mobilised by the IMF, the BIS and various governments in concerted action were linked to promises by major banks to continue providing the country concerned with loans. In the case of Mexico and Brazil the IMF openly put pressure on the banks, stating that IMF funds would only flow once they fully undertook to continue supplying the debtor country with loans (World Bank, 1984, p. xvi). This was to prevent banks withdrawing from transactions with the debtor because of the increased risk and thus provoking a crisis which could endanger the world financial system.

To sum up: rescheduling arrangements through creditor clubs isolate debtors and enable creditors to coordinate their strategy — a process which is further facilitated by IMF services. The Fund's expertise enables the creditors to act in their collective self-interest — to extract from debtors the precise sum in debt-servicing which the economy can afford without destroying the country's debt-servicing capacity. It may be an accident that the most favourable rescheduling agreements have been achieved at negotiations where the IMF was either not present or played only a marginal role. The Sandinista government of Nicaragua in 1980 successfully insisted on holding rescheduling negotiations with the creditor banks without a previous IMF agreement and without IMF involvement. The New York investment bank Leslie, Weinert and Yohai, which conducted negotiations on behalf of the government, achieved favourable rescheduling conditions: staggering of debts over twelve years with five and a half years free of payments, a moratorium interest rate of only 0.5% over LIBOR (the maximum charged being 7%) and exemption from payment of commission fees (LAWR, 20 May 1981, pp. 8f.). In contrast, a study of the rescheduling agreements in which the IMF has played a leading part shows little evidence of the IMF being the 'honest broker' between creditors and debtors which it professes to be. The Fund pays far more attention to creditors' interest in rapid and profitable repayment than to the development options of the debtor country. 'Bailiff' would therefore be an apter term to describe the role of the IMF in rescheduling arrangements.

Notes

1. The national quota was at first to equal three-quarters of the annual average of imports and exports in the three pre-war years and would be adjusted periodically. If a country took up more than 25% of its 'Bancor' quota in loans, it was to be entitled to devalue. If a country called on more than a half of its loan quota, the clearing union would be entitled to require the country to deposit reserves and to devalue. If a country took up more than 75% of its quota for two years, then all its transfers would have to go through the clearing union.
2. The Keynes and the White plans as well as other plans discussed at Bretton Woods are printed in Horsefield, 1969, Vol. III.
3. Switzerland has several times granted the IMF substantial loans and is associated with the 'General Arrangements to Borrow' (GAB), a safety-net for the IMF formed by ten industrial countries and designed to protect the organisation against illiquidity in the case of larger loans.
4. The US quota was originally 31%. It would have been easy for the USA to force through a formula at Bretton Woods that would have given it an even greater lead in the quota distribution, but it was reluctant to shoulder the additional financial burden this would have entailed. (The quota has to be paid into the Fund.) (Horsefield, 1969, Vol. I, p. 95.)
5. All important decisions are prepared in the Interim Committee of 22 members, 11 from the industrial and 11 from the developing countries, which meets twice a year.
6. The IMF may now permit the payment of part of the quota in the national currency.
7. To date this applies only to buffer stocks for tin, cocoa, sugar and rubber.

8. These gold reserves exist because member countries formerly had to undertake to pay a part of their quota in gold. Following the decision to demonetise gold, a sixth of reserves were returned to member countries and a further sixth was sold at gold auctions and paid into the Trust Fund.

9. 1 SDR = 1.04 US dollars (August, 1985).

10. Developing countries therefore strongly support further SDR allocations, whereas the industrial countries are more sceptical about such liquidity-creation because of the dangers of inflation (see Chapter 4).

11. A Barclays Bank publication puts this laconically: 'in response to a sovereign risk loan application, the banks have, in effect, reduced their replies to three categories: yes; yes after an IMF loan has been negotiated; or no.' (*Barclays Review*, May 1981.)

12. Some letters of intent have been published officially, others have been leaked. A list of the agreements published up to 1969 is given in Gold, 1970, pp. 269 f. The Tanzanian government's letter of intent for the 1980 standby arrangement is printed in Gerster, 1982, pp. 252–65.

13. For example, Bolivia, Chile, Colombia, Guyana, Haiti, Honduras, Liberia, Panama, Peru, the Philippines, and Turkey (see Appendix 2).

14. In the words of IMF executive director de Larosière (1982, p. 7), 'the importance of performance criteria as signposts cannot be overstressed.'

15. As preconditions are never put into writing and are not implemented during the period of an IMF agreement, they are far more difficult to identify than conditions written in the letter of intent.

16. Examples of this are the loan agreements with Ghana in 1979, Zaire in 1978/9 and 1983 and Haiti in 1982.

17. Of this loan US $689 million was from the Compensatory Financing Facility and US $394 million from a standby arrangement.
As some directors pointed out at an executive meeting, it is highly doubtful whether South Africa needed the loan economically. With a projected trade balance surplus of US $1.6 thousand million for 1983 and a debt service ratio of 7.9% — expected to drop to 7% in 1983 — South Africa was creditworthy enough to meet its requirements without any difficulty whatever on the international capital markets. The South African regime was primarily interested in the aura of international approval which goes with IMF loans and would thus demonstrate to critics and sceptics at home and abroad how ineffective UN boycott calls are. In the event only a part of the loan was drawn and this was repaid before the deadline (Morrell, 1983; Nfa, 24 June 1983).

18. Much to the annoyance of the Reagan administration, the IMF refused the El Salvador regime a loan at the beginning of 1983 because its monetary policy was 'too lax' (FT, 5 May 1983).

19. As a rule these are private suppliers' credits insured by the export credit insurance of the supplier country.

20. In 1984 and 1985, some developing countries fell into arrears on their IMF debts — e.g. Zambia, Sudan and Liberia. Vietnam and Guyana, being behind on their repayments and turning deaf ears to the IMF's demands for payment, were immediately declared 'ineligible' for IMF loans by the Executive Board in December 1984 and May 1985 respectively (*South*, July 1985, p. 32, and August 1985, pp. 70ff).

21. The number of countries represented is generally between 13 and 16. They have at various times included Israel, South Africa and OPEC countries

who were in a clear creditor position towards certain countries (NZZ, 23 November 1983).

22. The exception is Poland, which when rescheduling negotiations began had not yet rejoined the IMF.

23. As a rule only loans running for over a year have been rescheduled.

24. The data on deadlines refer to Paris Club rescheduling arrangements since the 1980s. In reschedulings before this period, consolidation periods were frequently longer; but to make up for this, repayment deadlines were shorter and the proportion of the rescheduled sum to total debts was somewhat lower (IMF, 1981, p. 23). Exceptions prove the rule here.

25. To assess long-term development prospects and needs the Paris Club uses the expertise of the World Bank.

26. The IMF believes that there is no point in starting rescheduling negotiations before agreement in principle with the IMF because 'the creditors would not have the benefit of the detailed analysis of the debtor country's economy that is regularly undertaken as part of an arrangement with the Fund.' They would then be less likely to find an appropriate form of relief and would have no guarantee that the country would sign an agreement with the IMF (IMF, 1981, p. 27).

27. This is to check on the observance of the 'most favoured nation clause' in every rescheduling agreement which states that no creditor must be granted more favourable repayment terms than any other creditor.

28. The first exception was Nicaragua in 1980. Banks were forced to accept that civil war had virtually bankrupted the country (Bogdanowicz-Bindert, 1983, p. 832). More recently, rescheduling with major debtors also included interest payments.

29. The case of Peru shows how heavily the banks depend on the IMF to discipline debtor countries. In 1976, banks granted Peru a balance-of-payments loan of US $400 million tied to terms very similar to those of a typical IMF programme. It soon turned out that the banks had neither the expertise nor the means to supervise the implementation of the conditions. When it became clear that Peru was not meeting the performance criteria, payment of the second half of the loan was cancelled and the government told to apply to the IMF (Huff, 1982, p. 54; Belliveau, 1976).

3. Routes to Debt-Crises and IMF Crisis Management — Six Case Studies

Brazil — Austerity Policies: Walking the Tightrope

At the end of 1984 Brazil's foreign debt totalled $103 thousand million — a colossal burden which had accumulated after two decades of forced industrialisation, a policy initiated by the technocratic military government which took power in the coup of 31 March 1964. The provisional end of the military regime's economic policy of all-out industrial growth came when Brazil was forced to go cap in hand to the IMF in 1982/3 and to conclude rescheduling agreements with public and private creditors. Thus Brazil had returned to the starting point of its 'indebted industrialisation' of twenty years ago — though of course at a far higher level of development. Again a Brazilian government faced the difficult task of forcing through IMF-style stabilisation measures in order to restore the country's solvency and creditworthiness while at the same time trying to prevent the restrictive wage and social policies from provoking a rebellion. The country's first tentative moves towards democratisation for several years were suddenly jeopardised.

At the beginning of 1964 the position of the populist Goulart government, which had initiated a policy of land reform, and of income redistribution in favour of wage earners became untenable: the smouldering economic crisis, galloping inflation, a law restricting profit transfers by transnational corporations, the nationalisation of a subsidiary of the American corporation ITT and increasing disagreements on foreign policy with the USA had undermined the country's creditworthiness at a time when it was threatened with bankruptcy. US AID and the World Bank had imposed a credit boycott on Brazil. The measures which the USA and the IMF considered necessary for the stabilisation of the Brazilian economy simply could not be implemented by a democratically elected government wishing to be re-elected. While the Goulart government was considering the possibilities of a debt moratorium, the leaders of the Brazilian army staged a successful coup — with the tacit approval of the USA (Hayter, 1971, p. 135; Skidmore, 1973, p. 20; Payer, 1975, p. 57; Brummel, 1980, pp. 49 ff.).

All previous Brazilian governments since the Second World War had again and again 'vacillated between half-hearted attempts at stabilisation and ambitious development programmes' (Wogart, 1974, p. 12), but had abandoned deflationary policies as soon as their recessive effects on production and employment provoked political resistance.[1] The military dictatorship, however, soon reached agreement with the IMF on a stabilisation programme. It then forced through reductions in real wages[2] and credit restrictions, liberalised the profit transfers of transnational corporations and created a favourable investment climate for foreign capital by guaranteeing political stability by the repression of all opposition (Brummel, 1980, pp. 98f.).

From 1968 onwards, the deflation therapy was replaced by growth policies designed to bring about industrial expansion. The Brazilian military's industrialisation strategy aimed to achieve rapid development of the consumer-goods, investment-goods and arms industries — a development which, they hoped, would soon put Brazil into the industrial nation category. The strategy was based on a 'division of labour between the state and foreign corporations' (Esser, 1979, p. 86). While the economic activity of the state was concentrated primarily on the development of infrastructure, of the basic and arms industries, the subsidiaries of transnational corporations concentrated on the production of consumer durables and, at a later stage, increasingly on the production of investment goods. The authoritarian-repressive state regulated the distribution of income administratively — low wages for workers in order to keep the production costs of Brazilian industry competitive and high income for the upper- and middle-classes, in order to open up a capacious domestic market for industry.

The industrialisation strategy was, however, too debt-ridden from the outset. The capital-intensive import substitution industry remained dependent on the constant import of high-quality investment goods and of semi-manufactured goods which could not be produced in Brazil. Agriculture was to a large extent unmodernised and could not guarantee self-sufficiency in food — demand could only be met by expensive imports. The transnational corporations were also a considerable burden on the Brazilian balance of payments because they transferred huge sums of foreign exchange from Brazil by means of arbitrary price-fixing for imports and exports and profit transfers to parent companies.[3] The slow pace at which domestic energy resources were tapped and the almost total orientation of transport towards road traffic also proved to be grave developmental errors. It meant that economic growth was dependent from the beginning on oil imports and on the level of world market prices for oil. The financing needed for imports of investment goods, semi-manufactured goods, energy and food pushed Brazil's foreign debt up from $4.1 thousand million in 1968 to $13.4 thousand million in 1973 (Altvater, 1983, p. 22) — not yet a disaster in terms of development, because the ratio of foreign debt to GDP remained almost constant.[4]

As the growth of the economy depended heavily on oil imports, the oil price shock of 1973/4 hit Brazil hard. And as the industrial countries passed on their own increased energy costs by raising the prices of investment goods and at the same time, as a result of recession, cut their imports of Brazilian products, the country's balance of payments came under heavy pressure. Instead of adopting deflationary policies, the military government decided on an 'aggressive response to external shocks' (Cline, 1981), on a growth policy ready to risk inflation. These policies — accompanied in 1974 and 1977 by more restrictive financial measures — were designed to improve the balance-of-payments budget by boosting exports but above all by taking up foreign loans. Despite its economic problems — which they regarded as temporary — the international banks regarded Brazil as an attractive business partner and showered it with loans.

Brazil's foreign debt increased fourfold between 1973 and 1979 to reach $53.5 thousand million and the GDP debit more than doubled — from 16.4 to 36.5% (Altvater, 1983, p. 22). The rapid increase in foreign debt was largely caused by gigantic development projects, especially in the energy sector (for example the Itaipú dam and the Angra dos Reis atomic power complex), which were meant to make Brazil less dependent on oil imports but triggered off a huge demand for other imports. Vast tracts of land were used for the growth of sugar-cane from which alcohol was produced on a large scale as a substitute fuel for motor car engines (Rey, 1981). As a result, food prices increased and there was a growing demand for imports.

The beneficiaries of this industrialisation pattern were international banks, transnational corporations, the Brazilian military, the upper- and middle-classes. Its main victims were the many unskilled workers, the marginalised urban classes and smallholders.

The second oil-price shock (1979), the world economic crisis which followed it, the protectionism of the industrial nations and above all the enormous increase in the debt service burden as a result of US high-interest policies plunged the country into a debt crisis.[5] Brazil was caught up in a vicious circle in which it had to take up loans to pay its old debts and repay interest. There was less and less scope for the productive use of foreign capital, for earning the foreign exchange for debt-service repayments. Creditors began to worry about the capacity of their major customer to repay its debts, especially as the economic collapse of Brazil (and of Mexico) threatened the world monetary and financial system.

To avoid losing its creditworthiness altogether, the Brazilian government was obliged at the end of 1980 to abandon its expansionist economic policies and adopt deflationary measures to improve its balance of payments (Juruna, 1981, p. 14). At the turn of 1980 it looked as if Brazil would have to conclude a loan agreement with the IMF in order to regain its creditworthiness (*Euromoney*, October, 1980, pp. 89 ff.). But the government was reluctant to sign a formal agreement with the IMF because IMF-style stabilisation policies would drive the country into recession, undermine the government's support and endanger the process of democratisation.[6] In November 1980, the Brazilian government announced a stabilisation programme which to a large extent followed IMF lines but did not involve measures as drastic as the Fund would have imposed. By means of this programme the government succeeded in regaining the confidence of international banks in its economic policies — even without the IMF's seal of approval (LAWR, 21 November 1980). The stabilisation programme was effective — a balance of trade deficit of $2.8 thousand million in 1980 was transformed into a surplus of $1.2 thousand million in 1981 (*NZZ*, 5 January 1984). The rechannelling of resources into exports had a negative effect on the domestic market and was accompanied by increasing unemployment. But the efforts to increase exports could not prevent a further deterioration of the balance of payments or arrest the unstoppable drift towards an acute debt crisis.[7]

When the Mexico crisis alarmed the international world of finance in the late summer of 1982, Brazil was suddenly also regarded as no longer creditworthy. The inflow of loans which the country desperately needed to finance its balance-of-payments deficit was abruptly halved. Finance Minister Galveas continued to give public assurances that Brazil would not be applying to the IMF and that it had its problems under control (*Euromoney*, November 1982, p. 104), even though the major US banks had already told Central Bank President Langoni that no further loans would be forthcoming until Brazil had signed an agreement with the IMF (*Fortune*, 11 August 1983, p. 54).[8] The government had to accept this diktat and reach a rapid agreement with the Fund, because the country's foreign exchange reserves were dwindling as a result of the credit cutback. On 6 January 1983, it signed a letter of intent which left it with little room for manoeuvre with regard to the IMF. But it was not until the letter of intent was modified and the Brazilian *cruzeiro* devalued by 30% that the IMF Executive Board approved the $4.5 thousand million loan on 28 February (*IMF Survey*, 7 March 1983).

The terms of the three-year stabilisation programme connected with the credit agreement were completely in line with the traditional IMF medicine:[9] the balance-of-payments deficit was to be slashed in 1983 from $14.7 to about $7 thousand million (2% of GDP) and by 1985 was to be further reduced to about $4 thousand million (1% of GDP): the budget deficit — measured against GDP — was to be cut drastically from 16.9% in 1982 to 8.8% in 1983 and inflation was to be brought down from 100% at the end of 1982 to 85–90% at the end of 1983. To boost exports, cut imports, reduce state expenditure and increase state revenue, monthly devaluations of the *cruzeiro* were to be 1% higher than the rate of inflation. The domestic supply of credit was to be restricted, domestic interest rates increased, state subsidies for nationalised companies and services, for wheat, sugar and oil derivatives, for the export and agricultural sectors were to be cut. Export duties and import controls were to be removed. To make Brazil more attractive for foreign direct investment, the IMF insisted on the government introducing legislation to facilitate profit transfers by transnational corporations. As the IMF regarded the periodical adjustment of wages to inflation as the main cause of the inflation spiral it demanded the abandonment of wage indexation.

The IMF thereby made the reduction of real wages the central element in its stabilisation policy. The government had already moved towards the IMF objective of keeping wages significantly below the level of inflation in January 1983, when it decreed that wage-adjustments for the lower wage-earners were to be cut from 110% to 100% of the annual rate of inflation.[10] The standard of living of the poorer sections of the population deteriorated rapidly because as a result of devaluations prices rose twice as fast as the IMF demanded. While the Fund insisted all the more adamantly on an anti-inflation policy with strict wage restrictions, the government found it increasingly difficult to implement this wage policy. As unemployment increased rapidly and the marginalised urban classes who relied heavily on casual work found it more and more difficult to scrape a livelihood, riots and plunderings of supermarkets took place in several major cities in April 1983. Police and army units had to be brought in to restore order (*Veja*, 20 April 1983).[11] Tancredo Neves, at that time Governor of the state of Minas Gerais and in January 1985 elected President of Brazil, said that it was 'a serious sign of social injustice when a people loses respect for authority' (quoted from *Veja*, 13 April 1983, p. 24).

Although the government made every effort to comply scrupulously with IMF demands, the powerful resistance meant that it could not implement all its austerity measures at once. As a result, it failed the first performance criteria test in May 1983. It did manage to achieve a high export surplus, but failed to meet the targets for the reduction of the inflation rate, the credit supply and the budget deficit. The President of the Central Bank tried to persuade the IMF to tolerate a short-term overshooting of targets by pointing out the political dangers of the austerity programme. But the Fund would not relent and cancelled payment of the second tranche of the Extended Facility loan (*ICR*, February 1983, p. 54).

To qualify for a further inflow of IMF finance, the government stepped up its efforts to force through austerity measures at the expense of the lower classes. It cut subsidies for various goods and services, a measure which had been agreed with the IMF in January (*Veja*, 1 June 1983, pp. 108 f.). Overnight the price of petrol rose by 45%, electricity by 90% and wheat by 100% (NfA, 14 June 1983). Above all, the government responded to continuing IMF pressure to drastically reduce wages. In July 1983, it introduced a wage decree in parliament which restricted wage-indexation for all wage and salary earners to 80% of the rate of inflation. It had already removed from the 'shopping-basket' on which the rate of inflation was calculated a number of goods whose prices were rising above the average rate and it had also cut workers' real wages by arbitrarily changing the basis of calculation for periodical indexation.

In the middle of July 1983, oil- and metal-workers in state enterprises went on strike for several days in protest against the government's wage policies. The government declared these strikes illegal, dismissed several hundred workers and forced the strikers to return to work (*Folha de Sao Paulo*, 23 July 1983). A few days later, the trades unions called a one-day national strike but not all workers took part. Protest demonstrations were held in Rio de Janeiro, Sao Paulo and Porto Alegre (*Veja*, 27 July 1983).

Although popular pressure made rapid implementation of restrictive wage policies impossible, the IMF and the creditors made the resumption of loan-granting conditional upon precisely this point. In the meantime, the shortage of foreign exchange was beginning to make itself felt — in July 1983 Brazil was unable to repay a $400 million instalment on a $1.2 thousand million bridging loan granted by the BIS in January. The government coupled the repayment of the BIS loan with the resumption of IMF payments. Contrary to its own guidelines, the BIS did not declare Brazil insolvent because this would have amounted to a declaration of Brazil's bankruptcy and would have led to a collapse of major international banks. Instead, the BIS tacitly granted a delay in repayment (LAWR, 15 July 1983). The government's strategy of putting pressure on the BIS in order to force the IMF to relent did not work. On the contrary, the IMF's negotiating position was strengthened when Minister of Planning Neto had to request rescheduling negotiations within the Paris Club in August. As always, creditors made rescheduling conditional on Brazil reaching agreement with the IMF (FT, 23 August 1983).

While the IMF and the creditors remained inflexible, opposition within Brazil to rigid austerity policies was growing. On 1 September 1983, Central Bank Governor Langoni resigned because he did not wish to be responsible for the IMF programme, which could 'only be implemented at an extremely high price in social terms' (quoted from *Veja*, 7 September 1983, p. 96). The PMDB (*Partido do Movimento Democrático Brasileiro*), the opposition party, whose position had been strengthened in the parliamentary elections of 15 November 1982, produced an alternative economic plan in which it strictly opposed any agreement with the IMF and called instead for a debt moratorium with a three-year exemption from interest repayments (*Veja*, 24 August 1983, p. 21).[12] The IMF's policies became increasingly unpopular even with industrialists, angry at the favouring of transnational corporations while they themselves were threatened by bankruptcy and political instability.[13]

In September 1983, strikes and lootings increased.[14] The standard of living not only of the underprivileged, but also of the middle classes — the mainstay of the government — deteriorated rapidly (*Veja*, 26 October 1983, pp. 36 ff.). Now the Catholic Church also joined in the criticism of austerity policies. At a mass in Sao Paulo attended by 50,000 people, Cardinal Evaristo Arns strongly criticised the government's recession policies 'which have caused so much misery and deprived us of the right to determine our own fate' (quoted from SZ, 28 September 1983).

Criticism continued to be concentrated on wage policies — a precondition for the resumption of IMF payments — which the government was trying to force through in the face of resistance from the trade unions and the political opposition. It only succeeded at the third attempt, at the beginning of November 1983. Two bills had been rejected by parliament in September and October, with even government supporters voting against, although the government had tried desperately to persuade all members of parliament to follow its line. Protest demonstrations were held in the capital during the parliamentary debate in October. The virtual siege of the congress building led President Figueiredo to declare a temporary state of emergency in the city (*Veja*, 28 September 1983 and 26 October 1983). The fact that the wage decree was finally passed with the votes of the government parties in November was the result of massive government pressure on dissidents within its own parties and also to a toning down of the bill compared with its predecessors. Instead of the originally proposed 80% indexation for all wage-earners, the wage bill which was finally passed provided for an average indexation of 87% and 100% for low wage-earners — though alterations in the shopping-basket meant that even this 100% indexation was actually equivalent to a real wage reduction of about one-eighth per annum (*Veja*, 2 November and 16 November 1983).

Although the passing of the law led to further protest strikes (*Veja*, 16 November 1983), the government managed to keep resistance in check by using repressive measures. The IMF accepted this new law, accepted an amendment to the letter of intent of January of the same year and gave the go-ahead for payment of $1.2 thousand million of the Extended Facility Credit.[15] On the same day, the creditors in the Paris Club signed a rescheduling agreement of $3.8 thousand million with Brazil. A week later Brazil repaid the overdue BIS loan (NZZ, 24 and 25 November 1983 and 2 December 1983). As in the case of Mexico the previous year, the IMF had to prod the reluctant banks to produce a package totalling $6.5 thousand million. Together with public foreign loans, this added up to about $11 thousand million.[16] Only with the help of these funds was Brazil able to cover its balance-of-payments deficit and meet its debt repayment commitment. The loans from the IMF, the banks and public grantors were used exclusively to meet foreign debt repayment commitments.

The Brazilian crisis had for the time being been brought under control, thanks to the granting of the IMF's seal of approval, the rescheduling of public and private loans and new injections of finance — or rather brought under control as far as the world financial system was concerned. The interests of the creditors were guaranteed by a deflationary policy which shuffled the burdens of the crisis onto the lower and middle classes and enabled Brazil to service its foreign debts in an orderly fashion again. This deflationary policy, which helped to increase exports, drastically reduced imports from $19.4 to $15.3 thousand million in 1983 and plunged the country into recession. Whereas GDP fell by 3.9% in 1983, industrial production slumped by 9.5% (NZZ, 5 January 1984).[17] Numerous company bankruptcies and a drastic rise in unemployment and under-employment resulted. The process of marginalisation was sharply accelerated, increasing numbers of wage-earners — even members of the middle classes — lost their regular income and had to resort to parallel market activities or crime.[18]

The real income of those who stayed in work dropped considerably. Wage indexation even before the November Wage Act had not made up for inflation which, according to official sources, totalled 167% between January and October — the inflation rate for food was 310% (bfai-Mitteilungen, January 1984). The government reacted to lootings, strikes and protests by intensifying repression. At that time the process of democratisation was seriously in danger. In its attempts to walk the tightrope between the interests of the people and the claims of its creditors, the government — under pressure from the IMF — forced through the traditional IMF austerity policy against a broad opposition which included most social classes. Yet the Figueiredo regime was never able to meet the inflation targets set by the IMF. Despite the remarkable trade surplus ($13.1 thousand million in 1984) which impressed creditors as well as the Fund, Brazil again and again had to renegotiate the performance criteria of the stabilisation programme and to sign one letter of intent after another. It was a continual attempt to gain and retain the seal of approval for its creditworthiness to rescue the industrialisation model initiated in 1964 and threatened by the debt crisis. The newly sworn-in President Sarney who, instead of the suddenly deceased Tancredo, replaced a disillusioned Figueiredo in 1985 inherited a heavy burden. . .

Bibliography, Brazil

Altvater, Elmar (1983), Der Teufelskreis der Auslandsverschuldung — der Weltmarkt auf dem Weg in eine Kreditkrise? in *Prokla*, 52, September 1983, 3–40.

Brummel, Hans Jürgen (1980), *Die Grundlinien der brasilianischen Aussenpolitik (1964–1978) unter besonderer Berücksichtigung der Beziehungen zu Lateinamerika*, Frankfurt/M.

Cline, William (1981), Brazil's Aggressive Response to External Shocks, in Cline, William (ed.), *World Inflation and the Developing Countries*, Washington, D.C.

Esser, Klaus (1979), *Lateinamerika. Industrialisierungsstrategien und Entwicklung*, Frankfurt/M.

Fishlow, Albert (1973), Some Reflections on Post-1964 Brazilian Economic Policy, in Alfred Stepan (ed.), *Authoritarian Brazil*, New Haven/London, 69–118.

Frieden, Jeff (1981), Third World Indebted Industrialization: International Finance and State Capitalism in Mexico, Brazil, Algeria and South Korea, in *International Organization* 3, 407–31.

Hayter, Teresa (1971), *Aid as Imperialism*, Harmondsworth.

Juruna, Julia (1981), La dette extérieure, facteur de déstabilisation, in *Le Monde Diplomatique*, December, p. 14.

Payer, Cheryl (1975), Internationaler Währungsfonds und Dritte Welt, in Steve Weissman (ed.), Das trojanische Pferd. Die 'Auslandshilfe' der USA, Berlin, 48–58.

Rey, Romeo (1981), Der tödliche Wettlauf. Verschuldungsmisere der Dritten Welt am Beispiel Brasiliens, in *Frankfurter Rundschau*, 10 October 1981 (Wochenendbeilage).

Skidmore, Thomas (1967), *Politics in Brazil, 1930–1964*, New York.

Skidmore, Thomas, (1973), Politics and Economic Policy Making in Authoritarian Brazil 1937–71, in Alfred Stepan (ed.), *Authoritarian Brazil*, New Haven/London, 3–46.

Wogart, Jan Peter (1974), *Stabilisierungs- und Wachstumspolitik in Brasilien*, Stuttgart.

Würtele, Werner (1983), Brasilien, in Michael Ehrke et al. (eds.), *Lateinamerika*, 7, Hamburg, 135–52.

Portugal — A Typical IMF Programme as a Way Out of the Crisis?

Even by its own standards, only a few IMF stabilisation programmes can so far be regarded as successful — so it is no wonder that the IMF boasts about the few successes. It is particularly fond of quoting the success of its 1978 stabilisation programme for Portugal, a country on the threshold of industrialisation. 'Portugal's balance of payments shifted from a sizable deficit to surplus within two years, with assistance from and a stabilisation program agreed with the Fund', wrote IMF official Brian C. Stuart (1981, p. 25). Stuart's judgement underlines the fact that the development of the balance of payments is the sole criterion of success here.[19] Falling growth rates are included, in fact almost regarded as inevitable in this reckoning, unemployment and social misery are accepted as inevitable side effects. The economic, but above all the social and political costs of IMF successes are not considered, nor is the question of whether long-term stabilisation is achieved. The example of Portugal shows that after a short-term improvement in the balance of payments, the deficit rose dramatically from 1980 onwards and foreign debt doubled in the space of three years. In September 1983 Portugal had to reach another stabilisation agreement with the IMF to restore its creditworthiness.

25 April 1974: after almost 50 years of dictatorship the 'Armed Forces Movement' overthrew the fascist state set up by António de Salazar and inaugurated the 'flower revolution', the principles of which were decolonisation, democratisation and economic development. Democratic reconstruction was, however, ill-starred from the beginning. The state had accumulated substantial gold and foreign exchange reserves under Salazar and his successor Caetano, but at the cost of creating deep structural problems in industry and society (Silva, 1982; Almeida/Barreto, 1976; Baklanoff, 1979).

The economy was severely affected by the long-overdue break-up of Portugal's colonial empire, because it lost sales markets and cheap sources of raw materials. Half a million white settlers (almost 6% of Portugal's total population) returned to their mother country. The social deficits produced by and inherited from fascism were a serious obstacle to democratic reconstruction in the poorhouse of Europe. To combat these problems, the transitional governments of 1974/5, still fired with revolutionary spirit, introduced a series of reforms (Morrison, 1981): in south Portugal large-scale landholdings were transferred to the ownership of workers' co-operatives as part of agricultural reform; the large corporations and banks — all owned by a clan of the seven richest families — were nationalised; workers were given industrial, political and social rights, wage-earners were given a guaranteed minimum wage and social, health and educational facilities were extended and improved.

The drop in production which often goes hand in hand with a revolutionary upheaval, the flight of capital, structural deficiencies in the underdeveloped economy, the huge rise in the price of oil imports and the recession in the industrial countries which followed the oil-price explosion — all these factors led the deficit-financed reform policy into a cul-de-sac: unemployment and inflation reached unprecedented levels, increasing consumer demand led to rising imports, while at the same time income from exports and tourism as well as remittances from emigrant workers dropped. The balance-of-payments deficit became so large that foreign exchange reserves were exhausted and the Bank of Portugal had to sell or mortgage some of its substantial gold reserves. To finance the gaps the government had to seek further foreign loans.

Portugal now found it increasingly difficult to raise the loans it needed. Western lenders — governments and banks — thought that Portugal with its 'socialist pluralism' was already heading for communism and they saw NATO's southern flank in danger (Rees, 1975).[20] And one means of forcing Portugal to change course was to deprive it of the finance it needed (Eisfeld, 1982). By mid-1977, liberal and social democratic forces had gained the upper hand over revolutionary elements. Only then did a number of NATO states indicate their willingness to grant Portugal a loan of US $750 million — on the condition that Portugal concluded a standby credit arrangement (on strict terms) with the IMF (*Expresso*, 28 May 1977). The minority socialist government under Soares had already signed an agreement in April 1977 with the IMF with easier terms, to qualify for a US $300 million loan from the USA (*The Guardian*, 8 January 1977).[21] For the IMF loan the Fund accepted the measures the government had passed shortly before in its first economic package: 15% devaluation, an increase of the credit interest rate, a 15% ceiling on wage rises, price increases for state services and a reduction of state price controls in the form of cuts in subsidies for basic articles (*IMF Survey*, 2 May 1977).

These first austerity measures had not, as the socialist government hoped, restored Portugal's creditworthiness. The prospect of a US $750 million loan led the government to start further negotiations with the IMF. In August 1977 they led to a second economic package which contained monthly devaluations by 1% and a further increase in domestic interest-rates (*Expresso*, 17 September 1977). These measures, however, did not go far enough for the IMF; and by now even the IMF representatives realised that a more drastic austerity programme would lead to serious social and political tensions. So as a *precondition* for giving its seal of approval the IMF made a direct political condition which far exceeded its solely financial brief: that the government should reach a consensus with parties, employers' associations and trade unions on drastic economy measures (*O Tempo*, 3 November 1977). The IMF was clearly trying to bring about a change in the Portuguese balance of power. Soares tried to enlist the support of social groups for a 'social pact' but they rejected this proposal as well as the 1978 austerity budget. In December 1977 the government had no choice but to resign. The only alternative was a coalition between Socialists and Christian Democrats. The most important point in the coalition agreements was the resumption and conclusion of negotiations with the IMF. By May 1978 these goals had been achieved. Prime Minister Soares announced the agreement with the IMF in a television broadcast and warned the Portuguese people of 'hard times' ahead (FT, 11 May 1978).

The IMF's diagnosis of the cause of the crisis was: the 'wage explosion', overvalued currency and excessive money supply; the Fund's treatment was correspondingly simple. 'This programme is remarkable for its simplicity', observed the chief IMF negotiator (Schmitt, 1981, p. 1). Silva Lopes (1983, p. 141), Governor of the Portuguese Central Bank, described it as a 'typical stabilisation programme'.[22] A further drastic increase in interest-rates for loans and the severe limitation of credit meant that capital for private industry and the state now became scarcer and dearer. The programme set particularly restrictive ceilings for public sector borrowing. The purpose here was to reduce the state sector, which had become increasingly important since the wave of nationalisations in March 1975 and to restore the primacy of private industry.

The limitation of the budget deficit to 6% — as against 7% in 1977 — meant substantial cuts in social expenditure, subsidies on basic goods, fertilisers and petrol and in subsidies to nationalised companies. To increase state revenue, the government raised income-tax by 10%, sales-tax by 30%, welfare contributions by 10% and prices for state services (gas, water, electricity and public transport) by up to 50%.

The IMF successfully insisted on a wage ceiling of 20% in 1978. Inflation in 1977 had been 27% and the increases in taxes, contributions and prices suggested that inflation in 1978 would scarcely be less. So the IMF was clearly aiming for a further reduction of real wages. A further devaluation of the *escudo* coupled with a 0.25% increase in the monthly rate of devaluation (to 1.25%) was intended to improve Portugal's competitiveness on world markets and to make Portugal more attractive for tourism. Imported goods became more expensive as a result of devaluation — which was meant to curb imports and make administrative import restrictions superfluous until the end of 1979. It was hoped that devaluation would reduce Portugal's balance-of-payments deficit from US $1.5 to 1 thousand million. As in every stabilisation programme, the government had to agree to regular 'consultations' with the IMF in which the implementation of these measures would be checked.

Shortly after the signing of the IMF agreement, the US $750 million loan was granted. The IMF seal of approval had restored Portugal's creditworthiness on international capital markets. Transnational corporations now began to invest more heavily in Portugal. The Fund had determined the economic policies of 1977 with the agreement of April 1977 and the measures in the second economic package of August 1977, and with the standby arrangement of May 1978 it also laid down the lines of economic and domestic policy in 1978 and 1979. Changes of government did not affect this, and austerity policies remained the guideline of the Liberal–Conservative presidential cabinet which took office when the Christian Democratic–Socialist coalition collapsed in July 1978. *The Banker* (October 1978, p. 47) referring to the powerful influence of the IMF, spoke of 'government by the IMF': 'Whatever happens on the political front . . . the country's future is inextricably linked to the economic program agreed with the International Monetary Fund.'

The IMF's deflationary policy led to an abrupt reduction in overall economic demand and a marked drop in economic growth. Imports in 1978 dropped below the level of 1977 in real terms. At the same time export returns, income from tourism and remittances by Portuguese emigrant workers rose rapidly, so that by the end of 1979 the balance-of-payments deficit was almost closed. In view of this positive development the government of Mota Pinto decided to resist IMF pressure and not to sign a further agreement (WSJ, 29 May 1979). The government was indirectly supported in this attitude by the international banks who in May 1979 — even without the IMF's stamp of approval — granted Portugal a US $300 million loan, thereby affirming its creditworthiness.

IMF representatives attributed the positive export trend to the improved competitiveness of Portuguese exports thanks to devaluation and the reduction of real wages (Schmitt, 1981, p. 11). The increase in exports was, however, above all a result of the positive world economic developments in 1978 and 1979 and even without the IMF programme Portugal's balance of payments would have improved considerably. The modest success of the first major devaluation in February 1977 showed that changes in the exchange-rate could only minimally improve the country's competitiveness; its export products (mainly textiles, cork, wine, fish, olive oil and wood) respond more to demand stimuli than to price stimuli because of the low level of manufacturing involved (Rodrigues, 1977). Hence, sales depend primarily on demand from major trading partners (the EEC countries and the USA).

The doubling of remittances by Portuguese workers abroad and of income from tourism can only be partially attributed to the IMF measures. Devaluation makes the rate of exchange from transfers abroad more favourable and increases in interest-rates make investment possibilities more lucrative — but these measures had only a limited impact on transfers by Portuguese emigrant workers. Until the first parliamentary elections in April 1976, many emigrants, worried by the uncertain political situation, had held back the remittances with which they normally supported their families in Portugal. These sums, which had been accumulating for some time, were all transferred at once and this played a major part in improving the balance of payments. Income from tourism dropped in 1974 and 1975 — a fact which can be explained by the recession in EEC countries and negative reports in Western media on the political course of the revolutionary governments. The number of tourists began rising again in 1976.

The IMF's crisis strategy was not fundamentally different from its development policies of the 1960s: overall economic growth and a sound balance of payments were to be achieved by increasing traditional export production on the basis of lower wages and a 'competitive' — devalued — currency. But the national and international conditions had now changed. The revolution had eliminated the political basis of the former state-guaranteed low-wage policies. The oil crisis and recession in industrial countries caused world trade to stagnate — and it was the steady growth of world trade up to 1974 which had favoured exports and remittances by emigrant workers. Decolonisation resulted in the loss of cheap raw materials sources and safe sales markets for companies which were uncompetitive in world markets. In 1974 the country faced structural problems which had been concealed under fascism and colonialism: inadequate domestic food production, a domestic market too under-developed for industry and excessive economic dependence on foreign technologies, investment-goods imports and loans.

The IMF's stabilisation was built on shaky foundations: from 1980 the export dynamism of the years 1978 and 79 slackened and imports rose over-proportionally, with the result that new deficits in the balance of payments opened up. Portugal today is further than ever from the goal stated in the letter of intent: 'to create a solid basis for long-term development by a substantial stabilisation effect' (*Económia*, 2/1978, p. 307). While other West European countries were increasing their growth rates, the deflationary policies in Portugal cut the rate of economic growth from 6.9% in 1976 to 3.3% in 1978. Reduced sales opportunities and more expensive loans severely affected small and medium-sized industrial and handicrafts companies. In 1978, 1,194 companies went bankrupt as against 610 in 1976 (Banco de Portugal, 1981). The only companies to remain relatively crisis-proof were those with high self-financing capacities and the subsidiaries of transnational corporations with access to the financial resources of their parent companies. The beneficiaries of devaluation and low-wage policies were export-oriented companies (both Portuguese and foreign); the foreign trade crisis reflected in the balance-of-payments deficit shifted to domestically-oriented industry, which was hit by the drop in demand. Their investment activity tailed off and this in turn took its toll on the labour market. The return of 500,000 Portuguese citizens from the former African colonies had already boosted unemployment figures, and the official unemployment rate rose from 6.7% in 1976 to 8.4% in 1978. Realistic unofficial estimates put the rate as high as 15% (*The Banker*, October 1978, p. 48).

The inflation spiral — which had been started off by a sudden rise of wages before the IMF era — slowed down only slightly. Instead of falling to the levels the IMF expected, the inflation rate rose from 18% in 1976 to 27% in 1977 and then remained at a high level: 22% in 1978 and 24% in 1979.[23] From 1977 onwards inflation was fuelled mainly by IMF-imposed devaluations as the price of imports continued to rise (Stallings, 1982, p. 95). Inflation made further devaluations necessary. The core of the inflation problem — a level of domestic production which could not cope with demand — was not tackled at all (Mateus, 1981).

Wage-rise ceilings remained significantly lower than the inflation rate and this led to a continual loss of purchasing power for wage and salary earners. There was an average reduction of real wages of 7.1% in 1977, 3.2% in 1978 and 3% in 1979. These reductions cancelled out the gains in purchasing power made in 1974 and 1975 and restored the former redistribution of social wealth: the wage quota (wages expressed as a percentage of national product) dropped from 63% in 1975 to 48% — equal to the pre-revolutionary level — in 1979. Wage and salary-earners in towns and cities, the unemployed, pensioners and agricultural workers — all groups which have to spend a considerable proportion of their income on basic products — were especially hard hit by the above-average increases in hitherto state-controlled prices for basic foodstuffs and public services.

These groups were also affected by the rise in petrol prices, which made the transport system — mainly buses and lorries — more expensive. Cuts in fertiliser subsidies, rises in petrol prices and interest-rates were also a blow to small farmers, as the price of agricultural products lagged far behind expenditure. The economy measures stopped the extension of the social, educational and health system which had only begun in 1974/5 and also entailed cuts in state house building and infrastructure improvement schemes.

The negative social effects of the IMF programme were limited in comparison with other countries, where they have led to widespread impoverishment and violent 'IMF riots'. This was because the system of social security that had been built up by then cushioned at least the greatest hardships and because the government did not stick rigidly to IMF terms either in the cutting of state expenditure or in the restriction of the credit supply (Lopes, 1983, p. 158).[24]

The fact that the short-term stabilisation of the balance of payments 'was achieved with a minimum cost in terms of economic growth' (Stuart, 1981, p. 26) was less the achievement of the IMF than of the pressure of legitimation which the government faced — if it wanted to be re-elected it had to do something about unemployment and could not completely give in to the IMF's deflationary policies.

The year 1977 not only brought the end of expansionist economic policies but also paved the way for political and social restoration. The IMF's policies objectively supported those social groups, classes and parties with an interest in dismantling nationalisation, agricultural reform, progressive labour legislation and other achievements of the revolution. The leader of the employers' association CIP backed the agreements with the IMF despite the deflationary effects he feared this would have (*Expresso*, 22 April 1978). He did so because capitalists hoped that the IMF package would bring about social and political change. State economic policy would again support private initiative and abolish 'investment-inhibiting' laws.

Employers and big landowners in the farmers' association pinned their hopes all the more on the IMF as a vehicle of social and political change because their power to push through their interests had been reduced considerably since the expropriation and nationalisation wave of 1975. Their calculations proved correct: during the negotiations with the IMF the socialist minority government, together with the two conservative parties, the PSD and the CDS, passed laws in parliament which limited the state sector, pushed back agricultural reform, lessened the impact of labour legislation for the benefit of workers and improved opportunities for direct investment by both Portuguese and transnational companies.

The conservative forces, with the help of the IMF, also scotched the hesitant attempts at an alternative stabilisation policy. In mid-1977, the Ministry of Planning put forward a 'Medium Term Economic Plan' which had the backing of the left wing of the government.[25] The plan aimed 'to show a way out of the current crisis' and to present 'a model for a new social and economic development of the country' (Plano, 1977, p. 138). This plan blamed the country's permanent economic structural crisis for its balance-of-payments difficulties. Instead of an IMF-style remedy — rapid stabilisation of the balance of payments at high economic and social cost — the plan proposed the elimination of structural defects and the satisfaction of the basic needs of the people. Based on the constitutional postulate of comprehensive state planning and economic activity, the plan advocated an expansionist adjustment policy geared to basic needs, with special emphasis on job creation programmes and the mobilisation of domestic resources for import substitution. But the wing of the government which wanted to follow the IMF line won the day by August 1977, when the second economic package was passed.[26]

The IMF-style economic crisis management intensified political and social polarisation and prevented the re-election of the socialists. In the parliamentary elections of December 1979, the Socialist Party (PS) lost votes to the Communists and the Conservatives. The liberal–conservative Democratic Alliance (AD) took office and sped up the process of restoration. The PS's loss of votes is hardly surprising considering that its austerity policies had severely affected its traditional voters from the working-classes and the middle-classes. The PS had kept next to none of the social-reformist election promises of 1976.[27] The Portuguese example demonstrates that economic policies approved by the IMF can undermine the basis of reform-oriented parties and governments because the solution to the crisis is achieved at the expense of their electoral clientele (Brandao de Brito/Vitorino, 1980).

The socialist transitional governments and Soares cabinets must undoubtedly bear part of the responsibility for the economic crisis which led to IMF intervention and the complete failure of the model of 'socialist pluralism'. A development-oriented stabilisation policy which recognised and accepted the financial costs of a democratic fresh start, ought, however, to have allowed Portugal a longer period of adjustment.[28] The Fund's officials were not interested in these requirements: the IMF's abrupt stabilisation measures increased social and political polarisation, blocked social and political reconstruction and helped to lay the foundations for the later change of government and the process of social restoration. The IMF programme led the country into recession, could not cope with the problem of inflation and merely shifted the economic crisis from the export industry to domestically-oriented industry, which was hit by the slackening of the domestic economy. The IMF-imposed economic policy was not combined with even a medium-term development concept and could not achieve a lasting stabilisation which would have solved the permanent structural crisis and opened up long-term development perspectives. Instead the Fund relied on the old growth model based on export-orientation and low wages — a model which had been used since the Salazar regime of the sixties.

This resuscitated development strategy did not save the 'little Hong Kong' of Europe[29] from new balance of payments crises. In 1982 the balance of payments deficit was US $3.2 thousand million, the largest in the country's history; foreign indebtedness rose from US $5.8 thousand million in 1978 to US $13.5 thousand million in 1982 and of these US $4 thousand million were short-term debts. The debt-service ratio rose to 27.5% in 1982 (*IMF Survey*, 24 October 1983). Balance-of-payments deficits and increasing debt-servicing charges began to put a question mark against Portugal's creditworthiness on the Eurodollar market (*The Banker*, April 1983, p. 75), so that in September 1983 Portugal was forced to sign another agreement with the IMF.[30] The model of successful stabilisation again had a 'painful therapy' as Soares, Prime Minister in the centre-left coalition since June 1983, put it (*O Jornal*, 12 August 1983). The IMF insisted on a halving of the deficits in the state budget and balance of payments, on drastic reductions in loans for the public sector, interest-rate increases, financial support for exports, radical cuts in subsidies for basic goods, a ceiling on wages below the rate of inflation, tax increases and large-scale dismissals in state enterprises. It also insisted that private enterprise should be allowed into areas which till then had been exclusively state-run (such as banks, insurance, cement and fertiliser production). At the IMF's insistence, the government had already devalued the *escudo* by 12% in June.

The austerity programme succeeded in boosting exports and reducing imports. As a result the current account deficit decreased rapidly from $1.6 thousand million (1983) to $472 million (1984), remaining remarkably below the IMF target of $1.2 thousand million. The improvement in external accounts restored Portugal's creditworthiness and qualified the country for a $500 million loan of an international bank consortium in March 1985. The other side of the coin was a slump in domestic demand by 7% and a GDP decrease of 1.5%. Inflation soared to nearly 30%, real wages dropped substantially and the official unemployment rate shot up from 8.3% to 10.3% (FT, 18 January and 2 April 1985).

In other words: while externally oriented economic activities expanded, the domestic market shrank, which meant that the weight of austerity had again to be borne by the wage-earners and the socially weak. Representatives of the Church and the trade unions accused the government of an economic policy producing social injustice and hunger (*Expresso* 16 June 1984 and 15 December 1984).[31] As early as October 1983 people suffering from the massive cuts in their standard of living gathered in a bid protest rally in Lisbon (*O Jornal*, 10 October 1983).[32] Without leading to a social upheaval protesting, especially by the trade unions, did not cease . . .

Bibliography, Portugal

Almeida, Carlos and Barreto, António (1976), *Capitalismo e Emigracao em Portugal*, Lisboa.

Baklanoff, Eric (1979), The Political Economy of Portugal's Old Regime: Growth and Change Preceding the 1974 Revolution, in: *World Development*, Vol. 7, 799–811.

Banco de Portugal (1981), *Relatório Annual 1980*, Lisboa.

Bogdanowicz-Bindert, Christine (1983), Portugal, Turkey and Peru: Three Successful Stabilization Programmes under the Auspices of the IMF, in: *World Development*, Vol. 11, 65–70.

Brandao de Brito, José M. and Vitorino, António (1980), O FMI e as eleicoes intercalares, in: *Economia e Socialismo*, 46/47, 22–33.

Eisfeld, Rainer (1982), 'Nelkenrevolution' und Aussenpolitik: Das Scheitern des sozialistischen Pluralismus in Portugal nach 1974, in *Leviathan*, 4.

ILO (International Labour Organization) (1979), *Employment and Basic Needs in Portugal*, Geneva.

Lopes, José Silva (1983), IMF Conditionality in the Stand-by Arrangement with Portugal of 1978, in *Estudos de Economia*, III, 2, 141–66.

Mateus, Augusto (1981), Politica ecónomica, dinâmica de inflacao e reparticao do rendimento em Portugal (1974–1979), in *Estudos de Economia*, I, 3, 319–54.

Morrison, Rodney J. (1981), *Revolutionary Change in an Open Economy*, Boston.

North Atlantic Assembly (1981), *Portugal's Economic Situation and Aid Requirements*, Brussels.

Plano 1977, *Plano de Medio Prazo 1977–80*, Ministério do Plano, Lisboa.

PS 1979, Partido Socialista, 3° Congresso Nacional, Lisboa.

Rees, David (1975), Southern Europe: NATO's Crumbling Flank, in *Conflict Studies No. 60*, (British Institute for the Study of Conflict), London.

Rodrigues, António (1977), Desvalorizacao do escudo — seu significado e consequências, in *Economia e Socialismo*, 16, 3–30.

Schmitt, Hans-Otto (1981), *Economic Stabilization and Growth in Portugal*, Washington.

Silva, Manuela (1982), Crescimento económico e probreza em Portugal

(1950–1974), in *Análise Social*, 72-73-74, 1077–86.

Stallings, Barbara (1982), The IMF in Europe: Inflation Fighting in Britain, Italy and Portugal, in R. Medly (ed.), *The Politics of Inflation: A Comparative Analysis*, New York, 77–103.

Stuart, Brian. (1981) Stabilisation Policies in Portugal 1974–1978, in *Finance and Development*, 3, 25–9.

Sudan — Debt Crisis as a Result of Development Gigantomania

With a foreign debt of more than $9 thousand million (FT, 29 March 1985), Sudan is one of the most heavily indebted states in Africa. In 1982 the ratio of the debt-service requirement to export earnings was 115%. Sudan earned less foreign exchange than it needed to meet its interest and principal repayments. The country has been a permanent client of the IMF since 1979. In 1983 it signed its fifth rescheduling agreement in four years.

The reasons why this poverty-stricken Third World country accumulated such a huge debt were political rather than economic. Sudan has neither the potential for large-scale export industrialisation nor is it rich in minerals. Its main exports for decades have been cotton, peanuts and gum arabic, none of which are high-earning products. It was primarily political interests which led Western donors to shower the Sudan with development aid money and commercial loans.

For the USA and the European Community the Sudan — in its important geo-political situation between the 'socialist' states of Ethiopia and Libya — has proved an increasingly pro-Western, strictly anti-communist bastion. After the Middle East war of 1973, Sudan became more attractive for Arab creditor states (Saudi Arabia, Kuwait, the Gulf Emirates and Egypt) when its government under President Nimeiri claimed that its seven-year plan could make it 'the bread basket of the Arab world'. The hope was that the land and water resources of the Sudan could be so developed with the aid of Arab petro-dollars and Western technology that its production of wheat, sugar, peanuts and cattle would meet a substantial part of the Arab 'brother countries' food import requirements, which would in turn make them less dependent on imports from the West (Tetzlaff/Wohlmuth, 1980).

The ambitious plan completely failed and ended in a debt fiasco, of which the main cause — in view of the limited administrative, infrastructural and financial capacity of the country — was over-ambitious investment. The path to crisis was marked by growing current account deficits financed by foreign loans and caused by an import boom which could not be made up for by export earnings because of a drop in cotton production[33]. The rapid rise in import costs was caused primarily by the disproportionately high increase in oil and sugar consumption[34] which in turn has to be explained in terms of the development strategy and consumption patterns of the Sudanese state class. The modernisation of agriculture (the introduction of machinery such as diesel pumps and tractors), the establishment of technology-intensive industrial companies and the spectacular increase in the number of private cars — in itself a strain on foreign exchange — meant that increasing amounts of expensive oil had to be imported. Sugar had developed into a basic good of which the government had to guarantee sufficient supplies (at reasonable prices) for the urban masses if it wanted to avoid provoking riots which could threaten its political survival.

The Sudan's balance of payments was also strained by the policy of import-substitution industrialisation pursued by the state-class — a policy financed by the creaming off of agricultural surplus production in the form of lower state purchase prices and by the taking up of loans abroad. As a result of its industrialisation efforts the country not only had to spend more on oil imports but also on investment goods and food imports. As there is a shortage of private entrepreneurs willing to invest in the Sudan, industrialisation became a joint project of the state, foreign investors and international financiers. Between 1973/4 and 1977/8 about US $3 thousand million flowed into the country in industrial investment (Wiemann, 1982, p. 107).[35]

The state economic sector was simply not capable of carrying out its function as the motor of industrialisation — it did not have the staff, the finance or the infrastructure to do so. Bureaucratic inefficiency, over-staffing, lack of spare parts and electricity failures meant that state industrial enterprises in most cases worked at only 30–50% capacity[36] and the resulting high losses had to be covered by taking up loans from local banks.[37]

Sugar production is a spectacular example of state misplanning. After independence, five sugar factories and plantations were set up in Sudan. In 1962 the first of these, Guneid, started production, followed by New Halfa three years later, Sennar in 1976, Hagar Assalaya in 1979 and finally Kenana in 1980. All these factories got into debt and — except for the Kenana factory which was still being built — had to be rehabilitated at high cost.[38] The debacle in the sugar sector was less because of the poor management of individual factories — the government replaced the supposedly inefficient Sudanese managers by foreign managers on the 'recommendation' of the IMF — than the failure of the bureaucratic-ministerial running of the economy as a whole. If companies are not provided with the necessary foreign exchange to maintain or to renew machines, production is bound to drop and unit costs are bound to rise in the medium term. The costs have to be borne by the state. The pressure of the balance of payments as a result of the follow-on costs of private investments and state mismanagement could have been far worse if the Nimeiri regime had actually succeeded in carrying out investments of $6.8 thousand million outlined in its six-year plan from 1977/8 to 1982/3. The money for this plan was to be provided mainly by Arab financiers but also by transnational corporations and Western banks. They were to be encouraged to invest by an investment promotion act which would guarantee tax exemption and free transfer of profits. Although only part of the projects were carried out, the Sudanese Finance Minister estimated that the follow-on costs in 1982/3 were $425 million, a sum equal to 25% of imports or 50% of the current budget (Ghorfa, 1982, p.11).

The list of expensive projects which completely overtaxed the country's financial and administrative capacities is a long one. The following are examples of projects which exemplify development gigantomania rather than development:

● the Kenana sugar project (costs: $750 million)

● the Jonglei Canal in South Sudan by means of which the Nile marshes are to be drained and new irrigation possibilities opened up for Egypt and north Sudan (costs: over $1 thousand million)

● the planned oil pipeline from Kosti to Port Sudan, which will bring oil produced by the US Chevron corporation on to world markets (costs: $900 million)

● the planned oil refinery in Kosti ($1 thousand million)

● the planned Meroe hydro-electric dam ($600 million)

● the Rahad irrigation project for cotton and peanuts, partly financed by the World Bank ($346 million).

The example of the Kenana sugar factory near Kosti on the White Nile — in the firm's own words 'the largest integrated sugar-mill and sugar refinery in the world' — shows the disastrous effects one large-scale project financed with foreign loans can have on a country's economy if that project has to import all the initial products and machines necessary for production and if it is therefore susceptible to unpredictable price fluctuations on world markets. Kenana owes its existence to an idea which T. Rowland, Chairman of the Lonrho concern which is omnipresent in Africa, suggested to President Nimeiri in 1971. In June 1972, the Sudanese government signed a project agreement in which Lonrho was granted a number of extraordinary concessions by the state (extremely low land rents, free use of water, tax exemption, special rights in the use of the railway). But sugar production did not actually begin until 1980 (Glaubitt/Lagemann 1980, pp.183f; Oesterdiekhoff/Wohlmuth, 1983, pp.195 f).

Kenana is no ordinary development aid project, but a joint enterprise of the Sudanese state with private foreign capital without direct support from the World Bank or other public development agencies. Indirect support comes in the form of public development aid for infrastructure projects (railway, road and port construction) which are essential for the production and marketing of Kenana sugar. A third of the Kenana shares is owned by the Sudanese government, 32% by the Kuwaiti government and 11.4% by Saudi Arabia. The remaining 24% of shares are owned by transnational corporations and Arab development companies. The costs of the project, originally estimated at not more than $125 million, had risen to $750 million by February 1983.[39]

In economic terms, the Kenana project is dubious because it costs more in foreign exchange than it earns. On the debit side foreign exchange is required for:

— the servicing of loan debts totalling several hundred million dollars
— investments as part of the five-year development plan (1980/85) totalling $35–40 million
— annual running costs (for spare parts, marketing abroad, salaries for foreign experts and managers) totalling more than $30 million.[40]

On the basis of these figures, the company's annual foreign exchange costs for the next years can be estimated at more than $100 million. Against this must be set possible savings of sugar imports totalling $60 million in the most favourable case, assuming an import substitution rate of 300,000 tonnes and a world market price of $200 per tonne.

Whether the sugar factory, which is now being managed by the US corporation Arkel, will ever be able to operate profitably in micro- or macro-economic terms depends both on the development of the world market price for sugar and on the prices which the Sudanese state, as the factory's main customer, pays for sugar. To operate profitably, Kenana would have to produce at least 300,000 tonnes annually at a price of $300 per tonne.[41]

Although the production target was almost reached in 1983, Kenana is still in the red, because the world market price for sugar dropped from $600 per tonne at the time of project planning to $150 in 1978/9 and has remained low ever since. The main reason for this price drop was a drop in demand in the USA because of competition from the sugar substitute isoglucose.

In 1975, the Sudanese government agreed to take the first 150,000 tonnes of annual production at London world market prices — though bills were to be settled in Sudanese currency. The state was also granted a first-purchase option on production beyond this level. These purchases were to be paid for in foreign exchange (again at London stock exchange rates). As the world market price for sugar dropped to a low level, and on the other hand prices for oil and other imported initial products rose steeply, the factory would never on the basis of the agreement have been able to earn the foreign exchange necessary to meet the high debt-service requirement to cover the running costs payable in foreign exchange. At the beginning of 1983, the production costs at Kenana were 100% above the world market price for sugar.

The private Kenana company appealed to the government to raise its prices above the world market level and thus prevent losses. The government was obliged to comply with this request because investment costs of several hundred million dollars could not be simply written off — quite apart from the fact that the personal prestige of President Nimeiri was at stake. If Kenana cannot cover its costs, the Sudanese state pays the bill; if the state cannot pay then foreign creditors pay the bill. Sudan subsidises its fellow shareholders with foreign exchange. The actual amount by which company deficits are financed by the public budget depends on annual secret negotiations between the company management and the industry minister.[42] Today it is evident that the Sudan would have been better off not building Kenana and continuing to import sugar. *Arabia* (February 1983, p.26) complained that 'sugar from Kenana will be the most expensive in the world'. Kenana has thus become a 'white elephant'*par excellence* for Sudan: magnificent but not very effective, and expensive to maintain.

The actual cost of the Kenana project to Sudan can only be estimated. The project has produced indirect political, social and ecological costs which together destabilised the Nimeiri regime, which increasingly resorted to repression to stay in power. At the end of 1981, the debt crisis partly caused by the Kenana project left the Sudanese government with no alternative but to accept an IMF austerity programme. It then cancelled subsidies not only for flour and petrol but also for sugar — a subsidy which kept down the cost of domestically-produced and imported sugar for the Sudanese consumer. The resultant sharp price rises (in the case of sugar 60%) led to protests in the course of which the police shot dead at least 26 demonstrators (*Sudanow*, March 1982, pp. 8f.).[43]

The construction of the Jonglei canal — another foreign-exchange consuming large-scale project which is indirectly connected with Kenana — could produce disastrous ecological results. The 32,400 hectare sugar plantation of Kenana uses up two million litres of water per minute for irrigation — one reason for the drain on and shortage of Nile water in northern Sudan and in Egypt. This in turn has led to plans to implement the old Jonglei canal plan, a dubious project. Experts feared that the planned drainage of the Nile marshes in south Sudan ('Sudd') could lead to a huge environmental disaster. Ecologists warned that the reduced inflow of Nile water into the marshes could cause the ground water level to sink even to the Sahel level, which could mean the desert advancing as far as the Congo basin in a few years. It was also feared that climatic changes could occur throughout the region. Experts predicted less rainfall, a drop in agricultural production and the spread of hunger (Erdmann, 1983).

Even before the completion of the canal — an event which is uncertain — there are already signs that the people who live in the marshes (400,000 to 1,000,000) are being deprived of their livelihood — because the water is literally being drained from beneath their feet. It is therefore no surprise that the Anya-Anya-II guerilla movement which is fighting the Khartoum regime has recruited strong support from the Dinka tribe which was driven from the canal area. Not only will the loans taken up to finance the construction of the canal put a strain on the country's balance of payments for years to come but high, indeed incalculable, costs are incurred for the uncertain prospect of extending export production and import substitution in North Sudan and in Egypt. Huge investments will be required merely to contain the ecological damage — not to mention the additional expenditure on the apparatus of repression with which the resistance of the south Sudanese against the Khartoum regime is to be broken. The Jonglei canal, like other large-scale projects, would bring more costs than benefits and further increase the country's debt.

The Kenana sugar factory and the Jonglei canal are merely two examples of a whole series of projects which are the main cause of the Sudanese crisis: gigantic development projects which financially and administratively overtax the state, cause serious ecological damage and culturally alienate the people, and over a long period use up more foreign exchange than they can earn in export production or save in import substitution. Nor are they likely to contribute to the development of national productive forces. The country is financially ruined[44] yet there is no evidence that the new military government which ousted Nimeiri in April 1985 will abandon the world market oriented development strategy favoured by the Sudanese state class and its foreign advisors. Although the Sudan has proved a bottomless pit, Western creditors will be prepared to invest in the country because they can be confident that the new regime will remain a loyal and anti-communist ally of the West.

Bibliography, Sudan

Bank of Sudan (1982), Economic Research Department: *The Signals of Crisis in the Sudan's Balance of Payments 1970/71–1980/81*, Khartoum

Erdmann, Gero A., (1983), Sudan: Der Jonglei-Kanal — das grosste Kanalbauprojekt der Welt, in *Blätter des izew*, No. 111, August. 41–44

Ghorfa (1982), Zeitschrift der Arabisch-Deutschen Vereinigung für Handel und Industrie, Bonn, Vol. 3 No.2

Glaubitt, Klaus/Lagemann, Bernhard, (1980), *Arabische Integrationsexperimente. Der Sudan als Bewährungsfeld arabischer Produktions-und Entwicklungsintegration*, Tübingen and Basel

Nyot Kok, Peter, (1983), Open Door: Closed Fists. A General Survey of the Evolution of Official Policies Towards Private Foreign Investment in the Sudan (1956–1977), in: Peter Oesterdiekhoff/Karl Wohlmuth (eds.), *The Development Perspectives of the Sudan*, Munich etc.

Oesterdiekhoff, Peter/Wohlmuth, Karl (eds.), (1983), *The Development Perspectives of the Democratic Republic of Sudan. The Limits of the Breadbasket Strategy*, Munich, Cologne and London

Sudan Development Corporation (1981), *Annual Report and Statement of Accounts*. For the Year ended 21st December 1980, Khartoum

Tetzlaff, Rainer/Wohlmuth, Karl, (1980) (eds.), *Der Sudan. Probleme und Perspektiven der Entwicklung eines weltmarktabhangigen Agrarstaates*, Frankfurt/Main

Tetzlaff, Rainer, (1984), Kenana — The Biggest and Most Costly Sugar Plant in the Third World, in: *Africa Review of German-African Relations*, Bonn, Vol.XXV, No. 2-3.

Wiemann, Jürgen, (1982), Der Sudan: Entwicklungsvoraussetzungen und Entwicklungsstrategie, in: Deutsches Institut für Entwicklungspolitik (eds.), *Arme Länder Afrikas, Strukturprobleme und krisenhafte Entwicklung*, Berlin (West)

Zaire: The Work of the Cleptocrats and the Impotence of the IMF

In the summer of 1979, Erwin Blumenthal, a financial specialist who had for many years been Director of the German Bundesbank's Foreign Department, left the Zairean capital of Kinshasa a disillusioned man — a month and a half before the official end of his mission. Blumenthal had been working in Kinshasa on behalf of the IMF since August 1978 and had attempted, with Prussian methods, to bring order to Zaire's state finances and in particular to its foreign exchange budget. The utterly corrupt Mobutu regime had lost all creditworthiness and finally been obliged to bow to the pressure of its international creditors. It had been forced to accept international control over the Central Bank, the Finance Ministry and the Customs and Excise Department. As *de jure* deputy governor of the Central Bank, Blumenthal had wide decision-making powers and was the *de facto* director of the *Banque du Zaire*.

After leaving Zaire, Blumenthal wrote a report which was published by the *Comité Zaire*, a Zairean opposition group, in Belgium in 1982. Two of the key sentences in this report are: 'Mobutu and his government regard the idea of repaying their debts as a joke ... To date the IMF's efforts to stabilise and improve the economic situation of Zaire have not been crowned with success.' (Blumenthal, 1982, pp. 6 f.)

In these short sentences, Blumenthal summarises the situation in Zaire. In terms of its resources (copper, cobalt, huge reserves of hydro-electric power, wood, fertile land most of which has hardly been used for agriculture) Zaire is one of the richest countries in Africa; yet this vast country with its per capita income in 1980 of US $220 (*World Development Report 1982*, p.118) is one of the twenty poorest states on earth. Zaire's state-class has acquired the dubious reputation of being by far the most corrupt and extravagant in Africa. Its unscrupulous self-enrichment, its life-style *à la* Louis XIV and its gigantic industrial projects, which are strategically important for the survival of the regime but damaging in development terms, prevent the country's wealth being used for the benefit of the vast majority of the Zairean population. To protect their kind of 'development path' against the demands of the underprivileged, the state-class resorts to brutal repression.

The corruption and economic mismanagement in Zaire is evident on all sides and has led to the *de facto* recolonisation of important national institutions. The same phenomena can be observed in many parts of

Africa, where corruption and mismanagement prevent the countries concerned from fully realising their development potential.[45] There are words in many African languages for this form of corruption, although there is no precise equivalent for their meaning in English. In Ghana, the word is *kalabule*, in Zaire it is *matabiche*. In every case, such words describe unofficial extra payments for all kinds of services — payments which bolster the income of rich and poor alike and are not infrequently the bulk of their overall income. Corrupt state-classes can feather their nests by this means, yet the same practices also guarantee the livelihood of many minor civil and public servants. Indeed, the system even has a social function. Foreign investors, creditors and advisers exploit this system to the full. Through bribes and dubious advisory activities many countries are talked into accepting 'development projects' which contribute nothing whatever to sound economic and social development.

Dramatic deteriorations in the terms of trade, oil-price and interest shocks — all external factors — are frequently not the causes but merely the catalysts of debt crises. They reveal the real causes, which are covered up in periods of relative prosperity. What happened in Zaire could also happen in other African countries: Western creditors and the IMF have tried, so far in vain, to impose capitalist rationalism in Mobutu's empire, by means of draconian stabilisation programmes and direct control of key state institutions. Yet by skilful manoeuvring the Mobutu clan has again and again managed to hoodwink them. Mobutu and his clan do not enjoy the universal admiration of Western politicians, businessmen and bankers, but there is obviously no pro-Western alternative to them in Zaire. Given Zaire's great strategic importance for the USA, it can always count on financial and — as the case of Shaba in 1977 and 1978 showed — also, if necessary, military support from the West.[46]

General (now Marshal) Mobutu, who came to power in the CIA-backed coup in 1965, can at least claim the historic achievement of leading Zaire (which till 1960 was a Belgian colony and till 1971 the Democratic Republic of the Congo) out of the economic and political chaos of the first years of independence. The crucial year for the Mobutu regime was 1967, which saw a constitutional reform which strengthened his personal power, a monetary reform in which the Congolese franc was replaced by the *zaire* and a stabilisation programme, in conjunction with the IMF which inaugurated an almost eight-year period of relative economic and political stability, reinforced by the high world market prices for copper, Zaire's main export. All these factors aroused expectations of a promising future. The *zaire* developed into a hard convertible currency and Zaire's economy achieved impressive growth rates.

This was also the phase in Zaire's history in which the state-class emerged and consolidated its position. This class, mainly urban and petit-bourgeois in origin, increased its power by gaining control over state revenue, steadily expanding the state sector, integrating the army into an alliance of power and interests and neutralising, if not brutally repressing, the opposition (Nour, 1982; Schmitz, 1983; Wood, 1981). The Mobutu clan, a small circle of friends and advisors — including the army leadership, the guarantor of the regime — form the core of the state-class. And around this inner core of a few hundred people is an outer core of 2–3,000 people, out of a total population of 31 million.

By the precipitate introduction of 'Zaireanisation' (1973) and 'radicalisation' (nationalisation, in 1974) the state-class tried to establish a sound economic base, which, though it did not involve them directly in production, enabled them to take over political, legal, administrative and income-distributive control of almost the entire Zairean economy. Qualified foreign workers were replaced by poorly trained, inexperienced but politically loyal Zaireans who in many cases did not bother about using capacity, storage, buying spare parts and sales organisation but often operated on the principle 'turnover equals pure profit'. The result was numerous bankruptcies and the breakdown of the economy.

The Zairean state-class has had no incentive to accumulate capital by its own, independent efforts. It drained the country dry in a parasitic, consuming style, investing exclusively in the modern sector, where capital utilisation could be improved or where prestige was to be gained by large investments — prestige which kept up the illusion of national greatness, even in the eyes of the underprivileged.

Unlike the governments of industrial states, the Zairean state-class did not attempt to achieve a balance between unequal sectors of the economy, for instance by specific measures to improve neglected areas such as the run-down agricultural sector or the extremely poor transport system. State economic and financial policies were primarily designed to increase the state-class's share of social surplus produce at the expense of the powerless mass of the population. A large proportion of the wealth this class appropriated had been transferred to foreign exchange accounts in Europe or the USA or wasted on luxury consumption. The investment and consumption habits of the ruling class and particularly of the Mobutu clan have been the main reason for Zaire's economic decline (Gould, 1980).

Zairean 'cleptocracy' (Nour, 1982, Gould, 1980) or rule by a corrupt, self-enriching state-class was based on:

● a chronically over-valued currency which offered a permanent incentive to convert worthless national currency into foreign exchange and to smuggle goods and currency

● a wide-ranging system of corruption in which import licences were granted in return for bribes

● control of state enterprises and key state institutions such as the Central Bank (the supreme monetary institution), the Finance Ministry and the Customs Department

● access to the profits of the major foreign-exchange earning enterprise

GECAMINES through the state marketing company SOZACOM (*Société Zairoise de Commercialisation des Minerais*) which in turn has been under the direct control of the President's Office

● the possibility of paying foreign exchange earned in Belgium for the sale of copper and cobalt directly into Belgian instead of Zairean accounts — a procedure which has been impossible to check and opened the door to self-enrichment

● price discrimination against the agricultural sector by mainly state-run marketing organisations which were constantly transferring resources from the country to the town, where the state-class then had an opportunity to appropriate them

● the possibility of directly protecting their own interests in international negotiations on economic, development or military cooperation.

The amount of foreign exchange which Mobutu and his clan transferred abroad for their private purposes cannot be precisely assessed because the financial institutions concerned insist on their obligation to maintain secrecy. Estimates put the amount at between US $4 and 6 thousand million. Mobutu himself, with a private fortune of anything up to $4 thousand million, is one of the richest men in the world (Nguza, 1982, pp.126 ff; *Africa Now*, 3/1982, p.12 and 11/1982, p.33). These sums are as high as the level of Zaire's foreign debt, which was US $5.2 thousand million at the beginning of 1982 (OGEDEP, 1981, p.31). If all the money which the Zairean cleptocracy has salted away into foreign accounts were transferred back to Zaire, the country could pay off its foreign debts overnight.

And there would probably still be a vast amount left. In November 1980, thirteen members of the powerless and uninfluential Zairean parliament bravely told the government that even a quarter of the sums criminally transferred abroad would be enough to wipe out the country's foreign liabilities. The thirteen were immediately arrested on the grounds of subversive activities, incitement to rebellion and insulting the President (NZZ, 22 April 1981).

Mobutu owns hotels, castles, mansions and luxury apartments in Belgium, France, England, Australia, the USA and Africa.[47] Gbadolite, the town where he was born, has been rebuilt in Versailles style. Through Zaireanisation Mobutu took possession of 14 companies, which he plundered to boost his personal income (Nguza, 1982, p.130). Whenever it suited him, he got round the country's laws by smuggling diamonds, gold and copper. Through the state enterprise SOZACOM, which until 1984 marketed copper and cobalt exports, the President has been able to buy French helicopters, Italian military jets and Chinese army equipment on a barter basis — completely unchecked and unhindered (Blumenthal, 1982, p. 18).

Transport aeroplanes which the USA delivered to Zaire as part of a military aid programme were 'requisitioned' to smuggle cobalt for

Mobutu. Food supplies from the USA, including supplies from the US Food for Peace programme (PL 480), have disappeared mysteriously, never to be seen again (ACR 1979/80, p.460). Of the gross takings from the world title fight in boxing held in Kinshasa in 1974, 40% went straight into Mobutu's private coffers. A CIA member accused Mobutu of putting US $1.4 million of CIA money to support the Angolan FNLA in its fight against the MPLA straight into his own pocket (Kabwit, 1979, p.398).

Up to 20% of the budget has been used by Mobutu, his clan and the political apparatus immediately subordinate to them (Nour, 1982, p.496). According to Blumenthal, the Presidential Office made no distinction between official and personal expenditure. Even when the Head of State made a private visit abroad or his wife went to Paris to buy expensive clothes, it had all been at the state's expense. To protect the cleptocracy at home, the military apparatus had to be expanded. According to the US Arms Control and Disarmament Agency (ACDA) Zaire spent one-eighth of its budget between 1971 and 1980 on the army.

In 1975, the cleptocratic development 'model' in Zaire collapsed. The slump in copper prices, the drastic price increase in the price of oil, investment goods and food imports, the collapse in demand for Zaire's main exports caused by world recession and the closure of the Benguela railway through Angola because of war exhausted foreign exchange reserves and ruined the national budget. Giant projects such as the Inga dam scheme, the high-voltage power line between Inga and Shaba and the *Voix du Zaire* TV station — projects which together cost US $2.5 thousand million — now proved to have been serious acts of misplanning. The errors of building the Kinshasa motorway, purchasing expensive French Mirage fighter-jets and building the completely unproductive steel works in Maluku now came home to roost. Above all else, the damage caused by economic mismanagement, corruption, smuggling and self-enrichment now became clear.

In the course of 1975 Zaire found itself practically unable to pay its debts. The international private banks, which in the first half of the 70s had made the astonishing error of classifying Zaire as a good risk and were partly responsible for the rise in its foreign debts from $86 million in 1967 to $2,000 million in 1974, now held back. The Mobutu regime was obliged to ask for IMF aid. There now followed two typical IMF stabilisation programmes (March 1976, April 1977) a 42% devaluation (March 1976), debt-rescheduling agreements within the framework of the Club of Paris (June 1976, July and December 1977), an informal debt-rescheduling agreement with the private banks (November 1976), the announcement of a three-year stabilisation plan — the Mobutu plan — in November 1977 and the introduction of reprivatisation measures in response to IMF pressure. But these measures led neither to a stabilisation of the shattered economy nor to the restoration of Zaire's creditworthiness (Wood, 1981; Rép. du Zaire, 1981).

The IMF stabilisation programes of 1976 and 1977 were doomed to failure not only because they were directed at economic structures which scarcely exist in an under-developed, structurally heterogeneous economy such as Zaire's. The crucial factor which contributed to this failure was that the main cause of the malaise — the cleptocratic behaviour of the Zairean state-class — was not sufficiently taken into account and is indeed hardly mentioned in the IMF's analyses even today (IMF 1979; IMF 1981; IMF 1982). The creditor states, however, quickly realised this mistake. Following long, tough negotiations, and only after the Mobutu regime's survival in the second Shaba crisis had been assured by direct military intervention by Belgium, France and the USA, they forced Mobutu to submit key Zairean institutions to international control. In mid-June 1978 the first of three conferences between the creditor countries, the World Bank and the IMF took place in Brussels, where Mobutu *de facto* transferred sovereignty over the Central Bank, the Finance Ministry and the Customs Department to the IMF and to Belgian experts. But the creditor countries were not prepared to risk becoming involved in a new Zaire adventure without a draconian stabilisation programme (*NYT,* 14 June 1978; *NZZ,* 16 and 17 June 1978). The standby arrangement was not finally signed until 27 August 1979 — after Erwin Blumenthal had left Zaire.

Blumenthal took up his post in the *Banque du Zaire* on 17 August 1978, with a brief to prevent the state-class having unlimited access to the country's currency reserves. In his period of office the *zaire* was devalued four times, on 1, 7 and 27 November 1978 and on 2 January 1979 and the official exchange-rate of the *zaire* was cut by half (Rép. du Zaire, 1981, p.62). At the end of 1978 he blocked *Banque du Zaire* loans and foreign exchange transfers to Litho Moboti, the real head of the Mobutu clan, and to about 50 Zairean companies, most of them belonging to the Mobutu clan (AC, 3 January 1979). It is said that Blumenthal showed Litho Moboti the door when he turned up as usual at the bank to collect his foreign exchange 'pocket money'.

In conjunction with the World Bank, the IMF also attempted to gain control over the proceeds of GECAMINES exports, taking them out of the hands of the President's Office. A World Bank delegation which visited Zaire in September 1978 had got wind of the shady dealings and obliged Mobutu to give a personal promise that he would pay back the embezzled and stolen sums. He found the necessary capital (where else?) at GECAMINES (AC, 17 January 1979; Blumenthal, 1982, pp. 17ff.).

When checking Central Bank accounts, an IMF team came upon special accounts abroad of which there was no record in Kinshasa's book-keeping and to which only the governor of the Central Bank and the President had access. Blumenthal closed these accounts, which had been opened at Belgian, French, Swiss, West German, British and American banks; in doing so he brought the relatively small sum of US $5 million back into the Central Bank's official accounting system. Blumenthal arrived in Brussels on 1 August 1979 only to discover that precisely $5 million had been transferred from the Belgian SOZACOM account to Mobutu's private account (Blumenthal, 1982, pp.22 ff,).

Relations between the IMF and Zaire resembled a game of cat and mouse. Again and again, the most powerful international organisation tried to force Zaire onto the path of economic and financial virtue by means of tough stabilisation measures and direct control of state institutions. In turn the cleptocratic state-class seized every possible opportunity to frustrate these efforts and fend off restrictions on their access to the Zairean surplus product. Mobutu, despite occasional disagreements with the USA and Belgium, played his pro-Western, anti-communist card skilfully, in the certain knowledge that the USA, Belgium and France would not leave the country in the lurch if economic and military problems arose which could endanger the regime's survival.

After Blumenthal's departure the *zaire* was again devalued by 25% and a draconian IMF stabilisation programme was introduced. Zaire could only manage to meet the conditions of this programme by a further devaluation of 30% and signing a new letter of intent. These measures, together with a debt-rescheduling agreement within the framework of the Club of Paris (December 1979) and the private banks in the Club of London (April 1980), gave the Zairean economy breathing space — but did not bring stabilisation.

It is all the more astonishing, therefore, that in June 1981 an Extended Arrangement for 912 million SDRs was signed. Its main conditions were: 40% devaluation (the IMF had originally called for 60%), continuation of IMF controls and a drastic reduction of the budget deficit. A few days later, another debt-rescheduling agreement was signed within the framework of the Club of Paris. However, the Mobutu regime made no move to stick to the deficit limits for the national budget agreed with the IMF. To lessen the potentially serious consequences of the stabilisation programme, the Zaire government decided on an across-the-board increase in public and civil servants' salaries of 15%. The state-class was not prepared to accept a redistribution of income to its disadvantage, and the IMF did nothing to force through such measures. Although the agreed budget deficit limit for 1981 had been passed as early as August, the IMF paid the second tranche of the loan in November, after heavy lobbying on Zaire's behalf by the USA.

In February 1982, the IMF forced through the reprivatisation of 38 companies, but the new round of negotiations on a stabilisation programme failed to reach any agreement. In April 1982, the IMF Executive Directors decided to suspend the Extended Fund Facility loan — after a total of 175 million SDRs had already been paid out. Only a few weeks previously, however, the IMF had granted the Mobutu regime a Compensatory Financing loan of 106.9 million SDRs. This was not only to compensate for loss of export revenue (the statutory purpose of compensatory financing) but also to make up for the loss of the blocked Extended Fund Facility loan.[48]

Up to now, no cases of IMF money being absorbed directly into the Zairean financial jungle have become known. But indirectly every transfer by the Fund to the *Banque du Zaire* has been financial aid for the private purposes of the cleptocrats. The bizarre turns that confrontations between the IMF and state-classes can take seem to be infinite, as the case of the Haitian cleptocracy shows. Here, Jean-Claude Duvalier ('Baby Doc'), the ruler and plunderer of the Caribbean state, succeeded in transferring no less than US $20 million of a total IMF credit tranche of US $22 million into his own pocket in the space of a few days (Longchamps et al., 1983).

The IMF stabilisation programme in Zaire — as in other developing countries — could not work because it was attempting to influence economic structures which had scarcely developed in the country. They did, however, contain measures — such as devaluation and increases in producer prices in the agricultural sector — which were indispensable and necessary for development, measures which had to be forced through in the face of bitter resistance from the state-class.[49] Administrative control of key state institutions by an organisation that works on the principles of capitalist rationalism also appears to be a logically necessary step, though it can be criticised as a form of colonial thinking and action. But the IMF failed because, despite massive intervention, it merely tinkered with symptoms and did not attempt to change structures which were unproductive in development terms. It left intact the huge fortune which the Mobutu clan had amassed by theft, and the burdens of the stabilisation programme had to be borne by the already reeling underprivileged masses.

After almost two years of muddling through without the IMF seal of approval, the Mobutu regime and the Fund agreed on a new, tough stabilisation programme in September 1983 — a programme which included a 77.5% devaluation and considerable cuts in the budget. At the end of 1983 agreement was reached between Zaire and the creditors of the Club of Paris — and it was only then that the IMF gave the all-clear for payment of a 15-month 228 million SDRs standby arrangement which was followed by another 162 million SDR standby arrangement in April 1985 and by further Paris Club rescheduling in May 1985 (FT, 9 July 1985, Survey on Zaire).

The new IMF programme effected some stabilisation of the economy and largely drained the parallel market, yet it caused even more social hardship to the poor and shook the political stability of the Mobutu regime which in 1984 had to face a coup attempt and another Shaba uprising — turning the screws in a counter-move. The harsh austerity measures were relentlessly carried out on the back of the have-nots, but the privileges of the state-class were again left nearly untouched (although SOZACOM, a major source of Mobutu's self-enrichment policies was dissolved in 1984 due to heavy pressure of the Fund). All in all, the IMF failed to make a breakthrough in its struggle against the system of corruption.

The IMF does not have the power, in a sovereign state such as Zaire, to control all the key positions and loopholes which enable the state-class to carry on its cleptocratic practices. Although the behaviour and the interests of this class go against all the rules of capitalist rationalism, the USA is not interested in using sanctions to seriously weaken their position because this class has up to now always guaranteed that Zaire's foreign policy would be pro-West and anti-Soviet. The USA's specific interests in Zaire have led it to exert influence on the IMF to make huge loans available to fill the financial gaps opened by the state-class. Zaire illustrates the way in which IMF policies towards debtor countries are co-determined by the global strategic interests of the world's leading capitalist power.

Zaire, Bibliography:

Blumenthal, Erwin (1982). Le Rapport Blumenthal, *Info Zaire,* October, No. 36.

Gould, David (1980), *Bureaucratic Corruption and Underdevelopment in the Third World: The Case of Zaire,* New York.

IMF (International Monetary Fund) (1979), *Zaire — Stand-By Arrangement,* Washington, EBS/79/126.

—— (1981), *Zaire — Extended Arrangement,* EBS/81/497.

—— (1982), *Zaire — Recent Economic Developments,* SM/82/3.

Kabwit, Ghislain (1979), The Roots of the Continuing Crisis, in *Journal of Modern African Studies,* 3, 381-407.

Longchamps, Fritz, et al. (1983), Les incroyables démélés du F.M.I. avec un régime corrumpu, in *Le Monde Diplomatique,* May, 21-2.

Nguza Karl i Bond (1982), *Mobutu ou l'incarnation du Mal Zairois,* London.

OGEDEP (Office de Gestion de la Dette Publique) (1982). *Rapport Annuel 1981,* Kinshasa (Zaire).

Nour, Salua (1982), Zaire in *Handbuch der Dritten Welt,* 4, edited by Dieter Nohlen and Franz Nuscheler, Hamburg, 468-521.

Rép. du Zaire (1981), *Note d'information,* Kinshasa.

Schmitz, Erich (1983), Stabilisierende und destabilisierende Faktoren eines Systems im wirtschaftlichen Niedergang. Der Fall Zaire, in *Afrika spectrum,* 1, 49-70.

Wood, Anthony (1981), The Funding of the Permanent Crisis: a Study of IMF Intervention in Zaire, in J. Caballero et al., *International Monetary Fund Policies in the Third World: Case Studies of Turkey, Zaire and Peru,* University of East Anglia, Development Studies, Occasional Paper No. 8.

Jamaica — Destabilisation of a Reform-Oriented Government in the USA's Back yard

'Manley has been voted out — but do the voters really want the IMF?' asked a leading article in the Jamaican *Sunday Sun* on 2 November 1980. In the parliamentary election of 30 October 1980, the conservative Jamaica Labour Party (JLP), led by Edward Seaga, won a landslide victory over the social democratic People's National Party (PNP) led by Michael Manley. The election campaign had been like a civil war, with several hundred people killed. The *Jamaica Daily News,* then sympathetic to the PNP, said that the election would be a choice between 'imperialism and anti-imperialism' (30 October 1980) and the question was whether the country should pursue its economic policies with or without the aid of the IMF. The opposition, for example the *Daily Gleaner* which was sympathetic to the JLP warned — and to good effect — of the 'communist threat' to Jamaica. By this it meant social reforms, nationalisation measures and the Manley government's foreign policy, with its commitment to Jamaican independence and the non-aligned movement and its support for a new international economic order. The JLP was particularly critical of the Manley government's relatively good relations with Cuba, the bogeyman of the United States.

In 1976, an alliance of reactionary forces had tried in vain to unseat the PNP. The Jamaican bourgeoisie and the Jamaican middle classes, which had originally supported Manley, Jamaican employers' associations, the *Daily Gleaner* and the JLP formed an anti-Socialist alliance of interests with the American bauxite corporations in Jamaica, the American media and the CIA. Their objective was to lead the country back to a free market economy and a firm pro-West course. In 1976, the US government and US banks stopped all loans to the Manley administration. Investment strikes, media campaigns, sabotage and violence were intended to lead to economic and political chaos. It was hoped that this would discredit the PNP government in its voters' eyes and enable the JLP to take over power. The plan misfired. The underprivileged majority of the population had tasted the benefits of Manley's social policies and, despite the serious economic and financial crisis, they confirmed the PNP in office on 15 December 1976 (Keith/Girling, 1978, pp.27 ff.).

The Manley government certainly deserved part of the blame for the country's economic problems. Foreign loans had not been adequately used for productive investment, and the foreign exchange needed to service the country's debts was not earned. A large proportion of foreign loans was used to finance social reforms and measures to develop the domestic economy — the basic principles of the productive use of foreign capital were carelessly ignored. The foreign exchange required to pay off interest and principal had to be drawn from Central Bank reserves. In 1976, the government was confronted with an acute shortage of foreign exchange. Manley had also scared off foreign creditors and investors with exaggerated anti-capitalist rhetoric, which further aggravated his difficulties, because they now held back their funds just when Jamaica needed them most.

An agreement with the IMF on a stabilisation programme was now necessary to restore the country's creditworthiness. In the years 1977 to 1980 the Fund, which had been called in by the Jamaican government, showed itself to be sympathetic to the American aim of destroying the Manley government. The IMF's economic stabilisation measures put most of the burdens on the shoulders of the underprivileged, politically destabilising a reform-oriented government which the USA disliked.

Although leading representatives of the IMF never tire of stressing the apolitical nature of the organisation and its exclusive concern with monetary and financial policy, a number of examples illustrate that the political power and strategic interests of the USA heavily influence the IMF's loan allocation policies — especially when the countries concerned are in the USA's back-yard.[50] The interests of the USA and the IMF are far from identical, yet in many cases they can be brought into line, as the example of Jamaica illustrates.

After its victory in the 1976 election, the Manley government, which had previously almost finalised an agreement with the IMF, thought it could afford to break off these negotiations and pursue an alternative economic policy.[51] It could not, however, solve the problem of the acute shortage of foreign exchange. Without the IMF's seal of approval it could not obtain the necessary foreign loans. On 22 April 1977, the government was forced to go back to the IMF with its tail between its legs. As a precondition for a loan the IMF insisted on a devaluation, but the government was able to force a compromise which took into account both the need to spare the underprivileged, above all the urban proletariat and the small farmers, and to improve the international competitiveness of Jamaican industry. Contrary to its 'pure' doctrine, the IMF accepted a multiple exchange-rate as a temporary measure. The unchanged basic rate was to apply to government transactions, bauxite exports and imports of basic foods, medicines, fertilisers and oil, whereas the special rate, devalued by 37.5%, was intended to stimulate exports and discriminate against non-essential imports.

To minimise the political damage which a typical IMF programme would cause, the Manley government in the course of negotiations skilfully used its influence on the governments of Canada, Great Britain and the USA, where the Carter government in its early phase was still relatively sympathetic to the problems of the Third World. Thus Jamaica achieved a compromise which toned down the usual IMF conditions. The programme contained restrictive money supply and budgetary policies, but no devaluation and no wage guidelines. On 11 August 1977, the IMF granted Jamaica a standby credit of 64 million SDRs.

The IMF had formally put its seal of approval on Jamaica's credit-worthiness; but potential foreign creditors, especially banks, considered the stabilisation programme inadequate. The inflow of foreign capital to Jamaica on which the IMF had counted was in fact no more than a trickle, so that as early as December 1977 the Manley government failed to meet the IMF's performance criteria. The Fund refused to re-negotiate the stabilisation programme. The PNP had duped the IMF in October by devaluing the special rate of the Jamaican dollar by 2.5% but not complying with IMF demands that it should also take steps to unify the exchange-rate.

Both parties realised that in view of Jamaica's deep economic and financial crisis a one-year stabilisation programme was simply too short and at the beginning of 1978 they opened discussions on the conditions for a three-year extended arrangement. As in 1977, the problems of devaluation and wage policies now came to the fore. The Fund now took a far tougher line and on 14 January 1978 it imposed the precondition of an average devaluation of 10%, which brought the basic rate closer to the special rate of exchange.

The government was required to accept monthly mini-devaluations based on the difference between Jamaica's inflation rate and that of its most important trade partners. Exchange-rate policies were thus closely linked to wage policies. The IMF regarded the improvement in the real income of Jamaican wage-earners as the main reason for the high rate of inflation, which in turn eroded the stability of the Jamaican dollar. To achieve a balance here, the monthly exchange-rate adjustments were to be linked to the wage rises permitted by the government. If the government wanted to keep the rate of devaluation low, it had to impose a restrictive incomes policy against the wishes of the trades unions. If the government granted wage-earners higher increases this would lead the IMF to insist on a higher rate of devaluation. Heavier devaluations would bring about price rises, and this in turn would bring the trades unions into the arena again. Thus the government was faced with a choice between two evils. Unlike the IMF the government did not regard inflation as primarily home-made, rightly pointing out that the sharp rise in import prices was a crucial inflationary factor.

So at first the negotiations made no headway. The IMF knew that time was on its side, because a failure to reach agreement weakened the government's negotiating position. The bourgeois wing in the PNP, which pragmatically advocated agreement with the IMF, now outnumbered the party left, who rejected an agreement with the Fund because an IMF package would hit the poor hardest of all. In March 1978 Manley dismissed Finance Minister Coore, who was politically responsible for the failure of the previous year's programme, and appointed Eric Bell, a financial expert sympathetic to the IMF, as his successor. There was now some progress in the negotiations but an agreement still could not be reached.

In the meantime the government came under ever greater pressure. Public and private investors and creditors from abroad kept an extremely low profile, and arrears of payments on foreign debts amounted to US $80 million by the beginning of May 1978. Production and employment were hit by lack of spare parts and raw materials, which could not be imported in large enough quantities because of the acute shortage of foreign exchange. Social tensions now increased considerably. On 17 April a protest demonstration in Kingston escalated into a violent street battle. The trade unions announced that they would resist wage-guidelines combined with further devaluations and the Jamaican bourgeoisie was alarmed at the probable effects of a drastically deflationary stabilisation programme such as that envisaged by the IMF. Manley's attempts to get an alternative economic policy off the ground with the help of the Jamaican left failed. There was no way of solving the acute shortage of foreign exchange without an agreement with the IMF, and this realisation finally sank in.

At a meeting in March, the international private banks, who were primarily interested in ensuring that Jamaica repaid its debts, told the IMF chief negotiator that they considered a draconian stabilisation programme to be necessary (Bernal, 1980, p. 55). The Fund now began to tighten the screws even more. Instead of being spread over three years, the emphasis was now to be placed on the first year of the three-year programme. On 10 May 1978, as part of its shock therapy, the IMF imposed a weighted devaluation of 25% on top of the mini-devaluations which were meant to amount to 15% per year. The different rates of exchange were also to be brought into line. The Fund also successfully insisted that the government should substantially raise indirect taxes on oil, alcohol, beer and cigarettes, that it should reduce price controls and introduce a wages guideline of 15%. In the private sector, the Fund insisted on a 20% profit margin. Throughout the economy there was to be a redistribution of resources from the public to the private sector. The Fund remained inflexible on the question of the highly controversial monthly crawling-peg devaluations, yet the Manley government had no choice but to accept the programme. The time factor on which the IMF negotiators had relied throughout the discussions now worked decisively in their favour.

This stabilisation programme, which the IMF imposed with crucial backing from the USA and American banks, led to the political destabilisation of the Manley government over the next two years. Admittedly there was a short-term improvement in the balance of payments. The budget deficit was also reduced by cutting back domestic credit and reducing the money supply by wage controls and increased revenue from additional indirect taxes. Despite this, no lasting economic stabilisation was achieved because there was clearly a tacit agreement among potential public and private creditors as well as domestic and foreign investors that nothing should be done to get the Jamaican economy back on its feet until there had been a change of government. This policy of inaction was based on the calculation that the economic crisis would drastically lower the standard of living of the poor who would blame the Manley government for this deterioration and elect the pro-Western JLP in its place.

The IMF programme did succeed in opening up the Jamaican economy for world markets. The main beneficiaries were the transnational corporations, who saw their production costs reduced, and the international banks, who now had guarantees that Jamaica would be able to service its debts. Even the Jamaican bourgeoisie, who had hoped that the IMF intervention would increase the inflow of badly-needed foreign exchange and reduce state intervention, was primarily affected by the deflationary impact of the programme because production input — raw materials, spare parts and machines — rose in price as a result of devaluation and also because most people's ability to buy Jamaican products was now severely restricted.

For three-quarters of the population, the IMF programme meant that the daily struggle for existence became even harder. The real wage index, which

from 1971–76 had risen from 100 to 132.5, dropped to 105 in 1978 and to 92.4
— well under the level of 1971 — in 1979. Devaluation, indirect taxes, cuts in
food subsidies and the introduction of wage guidelines all severely reduced
the standard of living of the underprivileged. The inflation rate, which in
January 1978 was 16.1%, had soared to 49.4% by December. In 1979, the
annual average inflation amounted to 30.9% (World Bank, 1982, p.253). The
price increases for basic articles such as chicken (plus 74%), salt-fish (plus
285%), milk (plus 83%), flour (plus 214%) and imported oil (plus 71%) were
by December 1978 far higher than the average inflation rate of 49.4%.[52] In a
survey by Carl Stone (1980, p.242), a Jamaican social scientist, carried out in
June 1978, 51% of those questioned said they were having increasing
difficulties in just getting by. Unemployment rose sharply: from 22.4% in
1976 to 24.2% in 1978 to 29.5% in 1980 (ECLA, 1982, p. 561). The black market
expanded rapidly; the smuggling of goods and foreign exchange and
trafficking in *ganja* (a drug) flourished. Yet the typical 'IMF riots' which
occurred in other countries in similar circumstances did not happen in
Jamaica. One reason for this was the government's influence over the
National Workers Union, traditionally sympathetic to the PNP. The
patience and ability to improvise of many Jamaicans — qualities inherited
from centuries of slavery — were perhaps even more important factors
here.

Manley's social policies, a cornerstone of his reforms, suffered a severe
setback as a result of the IMF programme. The employment and training
scheme for young people — constructive means of stemming the high rate
of juvenile delinquency — shrunk to a fifth of its original size. Major
hospitals were sometimes forced to close because of lack of medicine,
medical staff and maintenance personnel but also because of strikes. The
deterioration in medical services meant that in 1978 diseases such as gastro-
enteritis, typhoid fever, measles and gonorrhea reached record levels.

Graffiti such as 'The Poor Can't Take No More!' were now seen more and
more frequently on house walls, especially in Kingston. According to an
opinion poll (Stone, 1980, p. 64), 60% of farmers, 68% of workers and 45% of
the middle classes would have emigrated if they had been able to afford it.
And those who could afford it did so in huge numbers. In 1976, 9,000
Jamaicans emigrated to the USA. In 1978 and again in 1979, that number
rose to 19,000 — most of them highly qualified personnel: managers,
technicians, skilled workers, doctors.

The most significant political result of all this was that the IMF
programme slowly but surely eroded Manley's political base. The poor
blamed the government for the social imbalance in its programmes. The
opposition, the JLP, which itself supported IMF-style stabilisation
measures, skilfully exploited the government's awkward situation, blaming
Manley and his followers for the economic crisis and denouncing the
acceptance of IMF terms as a sell-out. Opposition leader Seaga, who later,
as Prime Minister, himself had to sign an agreement with the IMF, quite
rightly (but demagogically) argued that the combination of indirect taxes

and devaluation brought intolerable social hardships in its train, and he called on the Manley government either to re-negotiate the agreement with the IMF or to resign. Seaga's deputy Shearer, who was also the leader of the Bustamente Industrial Trade Union which has close ties with the JLP, slammed the agreement in parliament and called for re-negotiation of the conditions (*Jamaica Hansard* Vol. 3, No. 4, 1977/8, pp. 33 ff.). The anti-social effects of the IMF programme and the skilful JLP propaganda led to a serious drop in the PNP's popularity — a drop from which it had not sufficiently recovered by 1980. In the December 1976 election, the PNP won 57% of the vote. According to an opinion poll in June 1978, only 28% of those asked said they would vote PNP. And in the election in October 1980, 41% voted for the PNP (Girvan/Bernal, 1982, p. 46).

The stabilisation programme very nearly foundered on the performance criteria in the first of its three years. Jamaica was only able to meet the targets because the IMF agreed to expected income from the bauxite trade being brought forward and because the Fund chose to turn a blind eye to the negative budgetary developments. But for the second year beginning in mid-1979, the Manley government had to re-negotiate with the IMF. The Fund now imposed even tougher conditions. It was prepared to grant a 130 million SDRs loan from the Supplementary Financing Facility on top of the 200 million SDRs loan from the Extended Fund Facility granted in 1978; but in return it insisted on a social contract in which the government, the opposition, the trades unions and the employers associations would agree to the stabilisation measures. Opposition leader Seaga rejected such an agreement. He was not prepared to make any concession unless there was a political change of course in which the government moved closer to the JLP's position (*Daily Gleaner,* 4 July and 11 April 1979).

Although no social contract was reached, the IMF acknowledged the government's efforts and consented to the agreement running for another year. Having made this massive intervention in Jamaican domestic policy, the IMF dropped its insistence on monthly mini-devaluations. The government's request for a relaxation of the wage guidelines which were eroding real income was rejected. Indeed the IMF even forced through a reduction of the maximum annual wage increase from 15 to 10%.

The government now expected an upswing, yet no economic recovery came. In the middle of 1979 severe storms which ruined crops, soaring oil prices and high interest-rates throughout the world put a cross through all the government's calculations. Lenders continued to hold back — all the more so because Manley, in view of the hopelessness of the economic and social situation and the likelihood of defeat in the forthcoming election, veered further to the left. D.K. Duncan, a left-wing member of the PNP who had had to resign as General Secretary of the party in 1977, was again appointed to his former post. In the foreign policy field, Manley's attacks on the USA and the IMF were fiercer than ever before. The USA, which in 1977 had still been relatively well-disposed to Jamaica, now saw the Manley government as an ally of Cuba — and it was not prepared to tolerate another rebel in its own back-yard.

In October 1979, Finance Minister Bell informed the IMF that the stabilisation programme would probably fail by December and requested a re-negotiation of the original targets (*Jamaica Daily News,* 31 December 1979). An internal IMF paper took such imponderables as storms, oil prices and interest-rates into account, but at the same time it criticised the Manley government's domestic and foreign policies on the grounds that they discouraged potential investment. The IMF's goal was nothing less than a complete reversal of Jamaican domestic and foreign policy, because this would be the only way the country's creditworthiness could be restored (IMF, 1979). And of course it was also exactly what the USA wanted.

As expected, Jamaica failed to meet the performance criteria in December 1979 and the IMF and the Manley government started negotiations on the conditions for a renewal of the agreement. The Fund insisted on conditions unacceptable to a government which faced an election in 1981. These conditions were: a 15 to 25% devaluation, the ceiling for wage increases to remain at 10% and above all a 150 million Jamaican dollar cut in state expenditure which could only be achieved by 11,000 dismissals from the civil and public services. Protest demonstrations and strikes, domestic polarisation and violent crime reached unprecedented levels. Manley had no choice but to call the early general election in 1980 which the opposition had demanded.

The idea of resuscitating the three-year stabilisation programme and the credit arrangement that went with it was now abandoned. Yet at the same time the government requested a one-year standby arrangement, because it could not obtain foreign exchange without the IMF's seal of approval. In February 1980, the negotiations again started to make progress. The Fund mitigated its demands for cuts in state expenditure and by the middle of March the agreement was ready to be signed.

In the meantime a government commission had worked out an alternative stabilisation programme aimed at reducing social hardship. The Commission recommended that the government should break with the IMF as soon as an appropriate opportunity arose. Finance Minister Bell predicted that Jamaica would fail to meet the IMF performance targets as early as September 1980, a month before the planned elections. On 24 March 1980, the cabinet formally decided to break off negotiations with the IMF. Bell, who was sympathetic to the IMF, resigned and was replaced by a left winger, Hugh Small, who in April 1980 tried in vain to obtain the loans which the country so urgently needed. The international banks with whom he held discussions in New York referred him to the IMF. Yet during the annual conference of the Inter-American Development Bank in Rio de Janeiro, Small persuaded the banks to accept the validity of a debt-rescheduling agreement of June 1979, even without an IMF stabilisation programme. It was generally assumed by these bankers that there would be a change of government and a marked improvement in the investment climate in the near future.

The Jamaican economy did not collapse as the IMF had prophesied, thanks to higher-than-expected foreign exchange earnings from bauxite trading and to bridging loans totalling US $85 million from countries such as Libya, Iraq and the Netherlands. It no longer seemed so certain that the PNP would lose the elections. Opinion polls showed that its anti-IMF campaign was bringing it support. JLP gangs probably equipped by the CIA ran amok in Kingston and created a climate of fear which the JLP turned to its own account for propaganda purposes. It promised 'deliverance' from economic and social ills, from 'Communism' and chaos, from terror and violence, from the 'disastrous' rule of the Manley government.

The IMF and USA now completely abandoned Manley and prepared for the election of a new conservative government in Jamaica. Although the IMF is not authorised to conduct negotiations with anyone but government representatives, it received opposition leader Seaga for informal discussions at its Washington headquarters on 22 June 1980 — the same day on which a coup attempt, possibly inspired by the CIA, failed (LAWR, 11 July 1980).

The Manley government tried to exploit this intervention by the IMF in the election campaign and, together with the government of Trinidad and Tobago, it sent a protest note to IMF director de Larosière (FT, 14 and 28 October 1980). But the IMF programme of 1978/9 had so seriously undermined Manley's position that he could not gain the number of votes required for an election victory.

Jamaica, Bibliography

Bernal, Richard (1980), *Transnational Commercial Banks, the International Monetary Fund and Capitalist Crisis in Jamaica 1972-1980*, Kingston (Jam.).

ECLA (Economic Commission for Latin America) (1982), Jamaica in *Economic Survey of Latin America 1980*, Santiago de Chile, 543-95.

Girvan, Norman; Bernal, Richard and Hughes, Wesley (1980), The IMF and the Third World: the Case of Jamaica 1974-1980, in: *Development Dialogue, 1980: 2*, 113-55.

Girvan, Norman and Bernal, Richard (1982), The IMF and the Foreclosure of Development Options, in *Monthly Review*, February, 34-48.

IMF (International Monetary Fund) (1979), Confidential Memo to Managing Director and Confidential Briefing, 14 November 1979.

Keith, Sherry and Girling, Robert (1978), Caribbean Conflict: Jamaica & the US, in *NACLA* 3/1978, 3-36.

Manley, Michael (1982), *Jamaica, Struggle in the Periphery*, London.

Sharpley, Jennifer (1981), *Economic Management and the IMF in Jamaica 1972-1980*, Bergen (Norway).

Stone, Carl (1980), *Democracy and Clientelism in Jamaica*, New Brunswick (USA).

World Bank (1982), Jamaica: Development Issues and Economic Prospects, *World Bank Report No. 3782-JM*, 29 January 1982.

Stand-by Agreement with the International Monetary Fund 1977; Extended Fund Facility Arrangements with the International Monetary Fund 1978 u. 1979, Ministry Papers No.28, August 1977; No.34 July 1978 and No.26 June 1979.

Ghana — The IMF as an 'Honest Broker' between Debtors and Creditors in Debt-rescheduling Agreements

An ambitious but inefficient industrialisation programme introduced by the dictator Nkrumah and the dramatic collapse of world market prices for cocoa, its main source of foreign exchange, plunged Ghana into a serious economic and debt crisis in the mid-60s. In February 1966, the military took advantage of the crisis to stage a coup against the government, which claimed to be socialist. By this time Ghana's once substantial foreign exchange reserves (US $550 million) were exhausted and it had debts totalling $700 million. The most urgent problem for the junta, which described itself as the National Liberation Council (NLC), was how to deal with its short-term debts. Over $100 million in repayments were due in 1966, and some suppliers were already beginning to refuse to take Ghanaian orders because of overdue liabilities. The crux of the debt problem was the extremely high proportion of medium-term loans and the unfavourable repayment structure which resulted: over 80% of debts were medium-term suppliers' credits and 64% were due for repayment in the next five years.

The pro-Western junta, anxious to get the country out of its economic catastrophe but lacking any economic expertise of its own, unhesitatingly entrusted Ghana's economic fate to the economic directives of the IMF. Only nine weeks after the coup a standby arrangement was ready to be signed, in which the new government accepted all the IMF demands which the Nkrumah government had previously rejected. The IMF agreement of May 1966 was followed by three further standby arrangements until the end of NLC rule in 1969. These agreements gave the IMF and its sister-organisation the World Bank a decisive influence on Ghana's economic and financial policies. IMF and World Bank representatives took an active part in budget discussions, produced in conjunction with the government a graduated 'Stabilisation and Consolidation' plan for the economy and played a leading part in drawing up an import and export plan (Libby, 1976a, pp.65 ff).But the stabilisation of the economy and restoration of the country's ability to service its debts could not be achieved by these measures alone. An agreement with its creditors had to be reached in order to ease the crushing burden of repayments, to restore the country's creditworthiness and to secure additional financial aid. In April 1966, after it had been in office two months, the NLC, after IMF mediation, persuaded foreign import companies with long-overdue claims against Ghana to continue or resume deliveries to the country. A collapse of imports, which in view of the supply crisis could have posed a serious political danger to the government, was thus averted. Companies were prepared to do this not only because the NLC indicated that it was about to sign an agreement with the IMF but also because immediately after the coup and at the IMF's insistence, the government had unequivocally declared that it would honour all debts contracted in the Nkrumah era (FT, 12 April 1966; 6 May 1966).

In making this declaration, the NLC was primarily concerned to restore the confidence of the West in the country and its creditworthiness. But this assurance — given before either the amount of the debt or the circumstances in which it was contracted had been carefully analysed — made the negotiating position of Ghana's creditors even stronger. At the time of the coup the NLC, and even more the IMF, were already fully aware of facts which were later proved conclusively: a large number of the projects financed with medium-term loans were over-priced,[53] the services and goods supplied were frequently inadequate and in many cases corruption was involved. Repudiation of at least some of these debts would have been justified. It would have served as a warning to those unscrupulous exporters and their state export credit insurances which bore part of the responsibility for Ghana's debt crisis.

The new government's precipitate assurance that it would honour all debts meant that this chance was missed. Even later, when its foreign advisors strongly urged that the sum repaid to suppliers of goods on credit should be cut by 25–30%,[54] the NLC, in response to pressure from the IMF and the World Bank, persisted in acknowledging all debts, regardless of how they were contracted, to avoid putting Ghana's creditworthiness at risk. The IMF's interest in such a solution, which takes only the interests of the creditors into account, is evident: if the Fund had agreed to Ghana repudiating part of its debt, there was a danger that this would have affected other debtors' willingness to repay. Furthermore, the stamp of approval which the Fund had given by granting a standby arrangement would have been devalued.

With the signing of the IMF standby arrangement in May 1966 the way was now clear to ask creditor countries for more favourable repayment facilities. (When Ghana became insolvent, the claims of private suppliers were transferred to the respective national export credit insurances.) The conference between debtors and creditors was originally to have been held in Paris under the chairmanship of the IMF; but as Great Britain was the major creditor it was decided to hold the conference in London (FT, 26 May 1966). The creditors' reaction to Ghana's request for a postponement of repayments was reserved, but the IMF strongly supported its protégé (Hutchful, 1984, p. 12). IMF delegation chief Charles Merwin declared at the conference:

> Even if Ghana stops contracting new suppliers' credits and inflationary budget financing, restricts imports and opens the door to private capital, Ghana's balance of payments is such that there will not be enough foreign exchange to allow maintenance of contractual payments and to keep the economy running at a satisfactory rate. A rescheduling of Ghana's debts is essential to a reasonable rate of economic development of the country in the next few years.
> (Quoted from *The Economist*, 6 August 1966, p.551.)

The IMF and the NLC were together finally able to convince the creditors that for the time being Ghana simply could not meet its debt-service obligations. After Ghana had again assured them that it would pay all of its debts, they agreed to a moratorium until the autumn. It was agreed that Great Britain would then host a conference. The IMF, the World Bank and the Ghanaian authorities were to provide details of the — till then unknown — extent of the country's debts and assessments of probable developments of the balance of payments.

The conference between Ghana, its thirteen major creditors, the IMF and the World Bank was preceded by three preparatory meetings at junior levels and did not in fact take place until December 1966. Here a rescheduling agreement was reached on all suppliers' credits which had accumulated since the coup and all state-guaranteed repayments due by December 1968 (US $106 million). The conditions of the agreement were not fundamentally different from debt-rescheduling conditions of the Paris Club: in the so-called 'consolidation period' (June 1966 to December 1968) 20% of repayments due would be paid, 80% of repayments were postponed. After this, normal debt-servicing was to resume. After two and a half years (in July 1971) repayment of the consolidated debt would begin, over an eight-year period (ending in June 1979), with the amounts to be repaid increasing annually. The interest rate for the delayed repayment (moratorium rate) was to be negotiated separately with each creditor country. The average rate finally agreed was 6%, a rate usual for the market.

All concerned were aware that these conditions would, in the long term, overtax Ghana's ability to repay its debts. Nevertheless, the creditors refused to agree to a lasting solution of the debt problem, arguing that Ghana's economic situation might improve and the debt-service burden perhaps become more bearable. The only concession the creditors would make was to include a 'goodwill' clause in the agreement promising a new debt conference before the consolidation period ended.

This clause was applied in October 1968. A third IMF standby arrangement in May 1968, and an IMF report to creditors warning them that Ghana's debt-service obligations would strangle its economy, paved the way for a second rescheduling conference in London under the chairmanship of the United Kingdom. The agreement reached at this conference scarcely differed from the first rescheduling agreement. It stipulated that 20% of repayments would have to be made in a three-and-a-half year consolidation period from January 1969 to June 1972. After two years of normal debt-servicing, from July 1974 onwards, the rescheduled debts amounting to $79 million were to be repaid over a period of seven and a half years. As usual, the interest rate was to be fixed in bilateral negotiations between the parties, but an interest rate of between 5.5 and 6% was finally agreed on.

Because of its information lead, the IMF played a key role in the preparation and running of the conferences as well as the formulation and implementation of the agreements. With its analyses of Ghana's indebtedness and the development of its balance of payments, the IMF created the basis for the conferences. And through the agreements, the IMF's role as the creditors' informant on the debtor's debt-service payments and new foreign liabilities was officially recognised. Ghana's government had to authorise the Fund to provide the creditor countries with the necessary data and 'with such interpretation as might be necessary'.[55] Creditors were informed by the IMF about the moratorium interest rates which Ghana had agreed with other creditors, as well as what sums Ghana had repaid and to whom. By this means creditors were also kept up to date about Ghana's payments to its creditors in the socialist states.[56]

Both rescheduling agreements contained a clause committing the Ghanaian government to periodically re-examining its finance, trade and balance-of-payments policies in the framework of Article XIV consultations with the Fund. The first agreement specifically referred to the IMF stabilisation programme. Ghana's government had to repeat the promise already made in the letter of intent of May 1966 that it would only take up new medium-term suppliers' loans with the express approval of the IMF. It also had to promise to sign another agreement when the one-year IMF programme expired.

Though the IMF is fond of presenting itself as an 'honest broker' between debtors and creditors, a closer examination of its actions in the case of Ghana shows that it in fact functioned primarily as a debt-recoverer for the creditors. Its economic projections and analyses led to rescheduling agreements which imposed on the Ghanaian economy as high a debt-service burden as it was capable of bearing. With its superior expertise, the IMF presided over the conclusion of an agreement which clearly favoured creditors' interests. It is difficult to avoid the impression that Ghana was outmanoeuvred by the combined expertise of the IMF and the creditors. The *Financial Times* later wrote of the first rescheduling agreement: 'It was a most complicated formula and it is doubtful whether its full implications were realised by the Ghanaian negotiators at the time' (10 January 1973).

During the period of NLC rule, the IMF played a central role not only in debt-rescheduling but also in the mobilisation of development aid loans on favourable terms to back up its stabilisation programme. In April 1967 the Fund organised the first conference with potential Western aid givers (largely identical with Ghana's creditors), the World Bank, the United Nations Development Programme (UNDP) and the OECD. This was followed by three further conferences in the Ghanaian capital of Accra and in Paris, the last of which was held in May 1969. The conference had before it reports by the IMF and the Ghanaian government[57] analysing the export earnings, the debt-service burden and import requirements of the Ghanaian economy and also precisely quantifying the additional financial aid the country would need if the stabilisation programme were to succeed.

The IMF was able to report that Ghana was observing the conditions of the stabilisation programme and paying its debts according to the stipulations of the rescheduling agreements. These assurances meant that Ghana was granted the development aid loans it needed by the states at the conference. But the end result of this coordinated aid, the amount and conditions for which were negotiated bilaterally following the conference, was unimpressive. The payment of the loans regularly lagged behind the requirements defined at the conferences. If we take the debt-service repayments into account, we can see that the IMF crisis management restored the country's capacity to service its debts — but went no further. Economic growth capable of meeting the demands of a rapidly increasing population could not be achieved with such thin net capital inflow (see Table 3.1).

Table 3.1 Results of debt-rescheduling conferences and follow-up conferences during NLC rule in Ghana (in millions of dollars)

	1966	1967	1968	1969
1. Debt schedules as of February 1966 (i.e. unrescheduled)	53.2	86.8	92.4	64.4
2. Payments on basis of rescheduling agreements	16.8	14.0	42.0	28.8
3. Development aid[1] (disbursed)	11.2	20.2	47.9	52.6
4. Net transfer of resources (3 minus 2)	−5.6	6.2	5.9[2]	23.8[2]

1. Includes a US$ 17.3 million loan through the IMF Compensatory Financing Facility in December 1966.
2. The One-Year Development Plan of the Ghanaian government (Republic of Ghana, 1970, p. 6) quotes a net resource transfer of minus $5 million in the financial year 1968/9 (July–June).

Source: Calculations from Krassowski, 1974, p. 145.

In autumn 1969, following parliamentary elections, the military government transferred power to a civilian government under K.A. Busia. When the last standby arrangement expired in May 1970, the new government escaped from the straitjacket of an IMF agreement; but it now faced strong pressure from the people, who after three and a half years of enforced sacrifices and economic depression wanted an improvement. Prime Minister Busia therefore announced immediately after taking office that Ghana would negotiate a long-term settlement of the Nkrumah debts with its creditors (FT, 15 October 1969).

Public discussion now focused on the high burdens of debt-servicing and the tough conditions of the two rescheduling agreements. The government rightly criticised its creditors for imposing debt-service terms which jeopardised its existence as the country's democratically elected government; it also argued that these terms were an insurmountable obstacle to economic recovery. In particular, criticism was levelled at the high moratorium interest-rates (equivalent to commercial rates) which had pushed up the original burden of interest by more than a third or US $88 million (IMF, 1970, p. 24). This also explained why only four bilateral agreements with Western creditors and two agreements with socialist creditors on the lines of the second rescheduling agreement were reached.

The creditors showed little inclination to make further concessions to Ghana. They had already stated in the 1968 agreement (Article 13) that they regarded this rescheduling as final. However, Busia and other members of the government warned that Ghana would not be able to meet its obligations, which were due to reach a record level in 1972, and began thinking aloud about rejecting the debt. This prompted the creditors to agree to another debt conference to be held in the spring of 1970 (FAZ, BdW, 18 November 1969).

The creditors were playing for time. In several meetings, the Ghanaian government, which would have preferred bilateral negotiations, informed the club of its creditors about its balance-of-payments and growth projections. It soon became clear that Ghana required further concessions on debt repayment if any possibility of development was not to be nipped in the bud. Yet Great Britain, Ghana's major creditor, did not in fact hold the so desperately needed debt conference in London until July 1970.

The ten-man Ghanaian delegation proposed a solution which was feasible for Ghana and represented a final settlement of the debt problem: it consisted of rescheduling on IDA terms (retrospectively from 1 July 1969); the debt was to be repayable over 40 years with 10 years free of repayments and maximum interest of 2%. Ghana's proposals were on similar lines to the Indonesian rescheduling agreements, in which for the first time the creditors' principle that rescheduling and development aid had to be strictly separated was breached. Indonesia had persuaded its creditors to allow it to repay its debt (US $786 million) over a 30-year period with no extra interest costs.

But the Ghanaian delegation soon realised that its creditors did not attach the same geo-strategic and political importance to Ghana as to Indonesia, whose long-term stabilisation was crucial to its creditors. Again, no lasting solution of the debt problem was reached. After tough negotiations the creditors agreed to the rescheduling of half the payments due between mid-1970 and mid-1972. The agreement [58] provided for three possible ways of lightening Ghana's repayment load: a re-financing loan, postponement of repayments and additional aid payments. The measures would at all events contain a grant element of 61%.[59]

In return, the Ghanaian government, whose economic policies no longer bore the IMF stamp of approval, had to promise to boost exports, not to exceed its current expenditure levels, to improve taxation policies and to make more effective use of foreign exchange. The IMF and the World Bank were brought in to ensure that these conditions were met. Ghana's government had to promise that it would 'review' its economic, financial, trade and balance-of-payments policies periodically together with the two organisations. The 1970 agreement, like the two previous agreements, contained a clause authorising the IMF to inform each creditor about the conditions Ghana agreed with other creditors, the payments it made and about how its economy was developing. The results of IMF and World Bank studies were to be made available to the aid conferences which after the IMF stabilisation period were held under the auspices of the World Bank. The two organisations were further requested to produce documentation for the next debt conference, due to be held before the middle of 1972, when Ghana's debt burdens would become considerably heavier.

Ghana regarded the agreement as a starting point for further negotiations on a reduction of the moratorium interest rates from those set at the reschedulings of 1966 and 1968. The creditors took a different view. Their willingness to make further concessions was exhausted, especially as the World Bank had informed aid-dispensing and creditor countries that Ghana was not complying with the conditions of the latest rescheduling: government measures to combat the alarming drop in its foreign exchange were inadequate, the World Bank said, adding that it would either have to introduce higher import duties or else devalue. However, the Ghanaian government did not want to abandon its expansionist course and refused to apply these measures. The aid-giving countries also refused to make any promises of substantial aid and negotiations on an implementation agreement for the 1970 agreement with Great Britain broke down. Great Britain's reactions played a crucial role for other creditors and strongly influenced their attitude towards Ghana (Libby, 1976, p. 73).

Seven months later, the Busia government, under the pressure of falling cocoa prices and increasing balance-of-payments difficulties, had to submit to Great Britain's inflexible attitude. Reluctantly it accepted the high moratorium interest-rates of the first two rescheduling agreements and in return it was given a refinancing loan on favourable conditions for half of the repayments due between mid-1970 and mid-1972. Ghana's Minister of Finance Mensah over-rode the proprieties of the signing ceremony to make a number of highly undiplomatic remarks. He said that the ceremony was one of the 'most uncongenial' he had ever attended. Not only did the agreement tend 'to sanctify . . . the principle of relieving debts by increasing them' but embodied a 'particularly harsh application of that principle' (quoted from FT, 21 August 1971).

An acute shortage of foreign exchange caused by falling cocoa prices and high imports in the following months forced Ghana to go cap in hand again to Great Britain. The Ghanaian government asked the former colonial power to call the debt conference envisaged in the 1970 agreement and to grant longer-term credits to help Ghana over its current difficulties. But the

British government refused, saying that improved debt repayment facilities and promises of aid would only be given after Ghana had reached a stabilisation agreement with the IMF.

The Ghanaian government had no choice but to come to an arrangement with the IMF. By December 1971 the agreement, which marked an end of expansionist policies in all areas of economic policy, was ready for signature. But it was never signed. When the government complied with the IMF demands for a 48% devaluation, the armed forces took advantage of the people's anger at the huge price increases and staged a coup.

The new government now adopted a confrontation course in relation to the IMF and its creditors. To ensure the loyalty of the population, the junta, calling itself the National Redemption Council (NRC), reduced the level of devaluation. Bemused, the IMF had to agree to this first revaluation of a developing country's currency. As a leading Ghanaian civil servant put it: 'It has been conclusively proved that the political system of Ghana cannot support a devaluation of the order of 48.3%' (quoted from FT, 4 February 1972).

At the same time, Colonel Acheampong, Ghana's new strong man, declared that Ghana would not pay one-third of its medium-term debts and that it would only repay the other two-thirds on IDA conditions and without the moratorium interest-rates imposed in previous rescheduling agreements. He added that these sums would only be paid if creditors could prove that the loans were granted in the proper fashion and were used to finance viable projects. Short-term and long-term liabilities were not affected.

The creditors promptly reacted to the repudiation of the debt. They withdrew their export insurance guarantees and reduced development aid to a minimum. Thanks to rising cocoa prices on the world markets and an initially cautious, domestically-oriented development policy, the expected economic disaster was averted. Stabilisation did take place, without the IMF's stamp of approval and without financial aid from the industrialised countries of the West.

The NRC therefore was in no hurry to reach an agreement with its creditors. It waited for offers to be made and finally made the concession of accepting what in previous rescheduling negotiations had been a matter of course: collective negotiations coordinated by the IMF and the World Bank. In April 1973, the NRC accepted an offer by the creditors transmitted through the World Bank — an offer which showed a far greater willingness to make concessions than would ever have been conceivable under the Busia government.

A good year later, in May 1974, Ghana and its creditors finally reached an agreement in Rome [60] — an agreement which granted Ghana's major demand: after a ten-year delay in which moratorium interest of only 2.5% was to be paid, the medium-term debt would be repaid in 36 half-yearly instalments. A compromise was reached on the controversial question of moratorium interest-rates for the first two agreements: Ghana agreed to repay the interest which had accumulated before its debt repudiation and the interest for the period following this was waived. The agreement expressly allowed Ghana the right to refuse payments on credit contracts if the government could prove that they had come about through bribery and corruption — a clause which the government however did not apply.

The Rome agreement not only brought about a marked improvement in the balance of payments — with a grant element of 61% it was one of the most favourable rescheduling agreements ever achieved by a developing country.[61] It also enabled Ghana to resume normal trade relations and opened up new credit lines. The agreement bound the Ghanaian government to notify each creditor immediately of the implementation terms they had agreed with other creditors. There was no question of the IMF or the World Bank operating as the creditors' informants. It was clearly possible to get by without these two organisations.

But although Ghana was able to obtain more favourable rescheduling terms by refusing to pay its debts, it is doubtful whether this spectacular move paid off for the country in the long term. Ghana's creditworthiness was lastingly damaged by its violation of an almost sacrosanct principle of international financial relations. Even after the Rome agreement — though not only because of this — Ghana remained largely cut off from large foreign loans and direct investments. Nine years after the debt repudiation, Frimpong-Ansah (1981, p. 102), for many years Governor of the Bank of Ghana, complained that 'the incident has left its mark on Ghana's external relations . . . it has required a higher than average performance on our part to prove creditworthiness. Very high grades will for a long time be required of Ghana for average access to international capital.'

Bibliography, Ghana

Frimpong-Ansah, J.H., (1981), The Problems of Development and External Aid in Ghana, in *The Legon Observer,* 8 May, 98–106.

Hutchful, Eboe (1984), International Debt Renegotiation: Ghana's Experiences, in *Africa Development/Afrique Développement* (CODESRIA, Dakar) No.2, pp. 5–27.

International Monetary Fund (IMF) (1970), *Ghana — External Debt Service,* Washington, 19 October 1970 (SM/70/222)

International Monetary Fund (IMF) (1981), *External Indebtedness of Developing Countries,* Washington, May (Occasional Paper no. 3).

Klein, Thomas M. (1973), Economic aid by rescheduling, in *Finance and Development,* Vol.10, No.3, 17–20,pp. 34–5.

Krassowski, Andrej (1974), *Development and Debt Trap: Economic Planning and External Borrowing in Ghana,* London.

Libby, Ronald T. (1976), External Co-optation of a Less Developed Country's Policy Making: The Case of Ghana 1969–72, in *World Politics,* October, 67–89.

Libby, Ronald T. (1976a), The International Monetary Fund's 'Rehabilitation' of Ghana (1966–69), in *The African Review* (Dar es Salaam), 6, 4, 65–76.

Republic of Ghana (1970), *One-year Development Plan,* Accra-Tema.

Sederberg, Peter C. (1972), National Expenditure as an Indicator of Political Change in Ghana, in *Journal of Developing Areas*, 7, 1, 37–56.

Notes

1. From September 1954 to April 1955, a first stabilisation programme was carried out, though without any formal agreement with the IMF. In June 1958, Brazil signed a standby arrangement with the Fund. President Kubitschek, faced with a choice between an industrialisation programme or deflationary policies, broke off negotiations on a follow-on agreement in August 1959 because the IMF, in the president's words, was trying to force Brazil into 'national capitulation'. Finance Minister Lucas Lopes thereupon resigned. In May 1961 the Quadros government signed a standby arrangement with the Fund and a rescheduling agreement with its creditors. It was the fourth rescheduling of Brazil's debts after those of 1898, 1914 and 1931. The fifth followed in July 1964, shortly after the military coup (Skidmore, 1967, passim; Fishlow, 1973 pp. 70 f.; Brummel, 1980, pp. 43 and 46).

2. From 1964 to 1967 real wages dropped by 20–25% (Skidmore, 1973, p. 20).

3. Foreign corporations were responsible for up to a third of Brazil's foreign debt (Würtele, 1983, p. 142). It is extremely difficult to quantify exactly the costs and benefits of foreign direct investments for the Brazilian balance of payments — foreign exchange savings and earnings through import substitution and exports on the one hand, foreign exchange outflow through imports, arbitrary price fixing and profit transfer on the other.

4. On the credit side, the industrialisation policy made Brazil increasingly competitive on world markets; its export structure was also significantly diversified. Thanks to its increasing exports of manufactured products Brazil became less susceptible to price and quantity fluctuations in raw materials exports.

5. Brazilian economist Celso Furtado — who was Planning Minister before the 1964 coup — estimated that the world economic crisis and the burden of debt between 1979 and 1983 led to an increase in foreign debts of $40 thousand million (Veja, 30 March 1983). Short-term debts running for less than a year accounted for a substantial part of these debts. From 1979 to 1981 they rose from $3.6 to $12.9 thousand million, or from 6.8 to 17.4% of total debts. (Total foreign debts in 1981 equalled US $74.4 thousand million) (Altvater, 1983, p. 22).

6. Former Finance Minister Carlos Rischbieter warned against signing an agreement with the IMF: 'It would be terrible for Brazil to go to the IMF. It would be politically unacceptable' (Quoted from *Euromoney*, October 1980, p. 98).

7. These deficits were caused above all by the ever larger deficits of the services sector in which interest payments were by far the largest item.

8. As an agreement with the IMF would have been unpopular with the electorate because of the austerity measures it would involve, the government kept its first contacts with the IMF secret so as not to compromise the chances of the *Partido Democrático Social* — the government party — in the parliamentary election of 15 November 1982. Only a week after the election official talks with the IMF began (*O Estado de São Paulo*, 18 November 1982; FT, 22 November 1982).

9. The letters of intent are reprinted in: *Jornal do Brasil*, 7 January 1983, *O Estado de São Paulo*, 5 March 1983. The modification of the letter of intent was necessary because the provisional data on the budget deficit and rate of inflation for 1982 soon proved to be too optimistic.

10. Given the above average price rises for basic goods, even the 110% indexation was scarcely enough to maintain real wage levels.

11. In São Paulo alone, one person was killed, 127 injured and 566 arrested. Damage to property totalled two thousand million *cruzeiros* (*Veja*, 13 April 1983, p. 27).

12. See Celso Furtado (1984), *No to Recession and Unemployment*, London. The Brazilian government rejected the idea of a unilateral debt moratorium or even of a debtor countries' cartel to repudiate debts. Talks were held with other Latin American countries in an effort to work out a common negotiating position towards creditors and thus to arrive at better terms, but these talks proved fruitless.

13. At the beginning of 1980, only 5.2% of industrialists described Planning Minister Neto's work as bad or very bad. Four years later, this figure had shot up to 73.3% (*Veja*, 11 January 1984, p. 88).

14. In September alone, the Brazilian press recorded 227 lootings of supermarkets in which hundreds of people were involved. In Rio alone there were 84, in São Paulo 56 (*Veja*, 5 October 1983, p. 40).

15. The Fund also granted Brazil a Compensatory Financing credit of 64.5 million SDRs (*IMF Survey*, 6 December 1983).

16. It was not until February 1984 that all the 700 or so banks agreed to provide funds. A first tranche of $3 thousand million was paid in March 1984. In this credit package the banks granted Brazil a rescheduling of $5.5 thousand million.

17. In 1982, GDP had risen by 1.4% and industrial production by 1.2%.

18. It has been estimated that the second economy — legal and illegal transactions which are not registered or taxed by the state — now accounts for 20–40% of GDP (*Veja*, 19 October 1983, p. 116).

19. Other writers of the same provenance come to similar conclusions even today — e.g. Bogdanowicz-Bindert (1983, p. 70).

20. The countries now concerned about political developments in Portugal had under the Salazar dictatorship believed that 'the vital importance of Portugal's geo-strategic position adequately warranted its admission to the Alliance even at a time when its internal situation was characterised by a dictatorial and absolutist system of government which set it apart from democratic western systems.' (North Atlantic Assembly, 1981, p. 11.)

21. This very short term US-credit carried repayment terms so harsh that the Portuguese were compelled to dispose of 46.2 tonnes of the official gold holdings in September 1977 so as to meet their obligations. (ICR 1/78, 102.)

22. The agreement is published in Portuguese in *Economia* (Lisboa), 2/1978.

23. Only when the IMF programme ran out did the government cut the inflation rate to 17% by means of price controls (1980). But by 1981 the rate was 25%, in 1982 19% and in 1983 it reached 29%.

24. The Portuguese government did not have to worry about possible blocking of loan payment by the IMF on the grounds of failure to meet performance criteria — because it did not call on the US $70 million loan. The

government's sole concern had been to obtain the IMF stamp of approval.

25. The plan was worked out in close cooperation with a team of advisors from the International Labour Organisation (ILO) who put forward a basic needs-orientated development strategy for Portugal (ILO, 1979).

26. The liberal wing in the PS minority government had strengthened its position in the government re-shuffle of March 1977. Newly appointed Minister of Trade Mota Pinto had publicly declared that the Medium Term Economic Plan would only be passed 'over his dead body' (*Expresso*, 28 May 1977). Finance Minister M. Careira, Industry Ministry N. da Costa, Labour Minister M. Gonelha and Agriculture Minister A. Barreto threatened to resign if the plan was passed and implemented (*O Tempo*, 26 May 1977; *Expresso*, 25 June 1977). In November 1977 the government officially withdrew the plan. In September 1977 Manuela Silva, the Secretary of State in the Ministry of Planning responsible for the plan, resigned when it became clear that the government did not intend to pursue the plan.

27. Soares self-critically admitted this in his report to the PS Party Congress in March 1979 (PS, 1979, p. 27).

28. On purely economic grounds there would have been scope for this: Portugal's gold reserves and its comparatively low level of overall debt in 1976 ought to have been adequate guarantees of financial standing for loans to be granted.

29. From FAZ, BJW (13 July 1983) in an article on the textile and clothing industry — Portugal's main export industry — where wage levels are 20% of those in West Germany, just under half of those in Greece and 90% of those in Brazil. Wage costs in Portugal are only 10% higher than those in Hong Kong.

30. The letter of intent is printed in *Banco de Portugal*, boletim trimestral, 3/1983, pp. 5–11.

31. See e.g the dossier of trade union CGTP 'Poverty and Hunger in Portugal' (*Miséra e Fome em Portugal*, Lisboa, December 1984).

32. An opinion poll in September 1983, shortly after the new economy package was announced, proved highly critical of the Soares cabinet. Only 7% of those asked thought the work of the government to date had been 'good'; 41% thought it was 'average', and 46% said they thought it was 'bad' or 'very bad.'

33. Between 1970/71 and 1980/81, the Sudan's trade balance deficit increased thirtyfold from $33.3 million (imports $387.7, exports $354.4 million) to $1.078 million (imports $1.855.2, exports $777.2 million). The production of cotton-lint, its major export, fell during this period from 1,316,000 to 518,000 bales. This decline was caused by low state purchasing prices and unsuccessful diversification experiments with wheat and peanuts (Bank of Sudan, 1982).

34. Between 1970/71 and 1980/81 sugar imports — despite production in four Sudanese factories — rose from $25.0 to $183.6 million and oil imports from $24 to $430 million (Bank of Sudan, 1982).

35. Most of this was invested in 28 projects initiated or backed by the Sudan Development Corporation up to 1979/80, including 11 weaving mills and textile factories, 7 food-processing factories, 3 transport companies, 2 construction and cement companies and shareholdings in 5 banks (Sudan Development Corporation, 1981, p.12).

36. 'The textile industry with 22 factories, 7 of which are state-owned and

32,000 workers, is the main industry. Its productivity is about 30%.' (*Auslands-märkte*, Lausanne, 29 January 1982).

37. In December 1980 even the state cotton purchasing organisation, the Gezira Board — once the goose which laid the golden eggs — had debts totalling $202 million with local banks.

38. The total losses amounted to $33 million in Guneid and $6.7 million in New Halfa (for Kenana see below).

39. Information given to author R.T. in February 1983 by Dr Desai, Finance Director of Kenana.

40. About 60 experts and managers who had to be recruited from abroad receive high salaries, two-thirds of which are paid in foreign exchange (Tetzlaff, 1984).

41. Statement by the Kenana management to author R.T. in February 1983.

42. In 1983 this minister was Mohamed el Beshir el Wagie, previously Director-General of Kenana.

43. *Institutional Investor* (international edition, September 1983, pp.182ff), the magazine of the major US banks, praised the regime for its political courage: 'Despite unrest and bread riots, the rulers have continued to turn the screws.'

44. 'The Sudan is bankrupt, the victim of grandiose development plans which overtaxed its abilities' wrote the *Wall Street Journal* (6 May 1983). From the viewpoint of his own country, academic lawyer Nyot Kok wrote (1983, pp.262f.) that the Sudan had been 'perhaps too generous with its investment concessions and privileges.'

45. See cover story in *Jeune Afrique Economie* 3/1982: *Corruption — Connais pas.*

46. Zaire is strategically important because of its vast, in many cases untapped raw material resources and its position as a Central African bulwark against Soviet-Cuban ambitions.

47. In Belgium and France alone, the following are owned by Mobutu: 1) Chateau Frocourt, Eghezee-Namur, 2) Residence Josephine, Ave. De Tervuren 327, Woluwe, 3) Ave. du Prince d'Orange 49–51, Uccle, 4) Ave. Napoleon, Uccle, 5) Ave. Marechal Ney 51, Uccle, 6) Ginstlaan 10 a, Rode St. Genese, 7) Ave. Foch 20, Paris (*Africa Now*, 3/1982, p.13).

48. Our account of the more recent developments is based on press reports, 'grey literature', data published by the Zaire Finance Ministry and information gathered in discussions during a period of research in Zaire.

49. In 1972 Mobutu proclaimed that there would be no devaluation of the Zaire currency as long as he lived. In 1978, the Zaire government passed a resolution against any devaluation during the three-year stabilisation pro-gramme (MTM, 14 April 1978).

50. See also Chapter 2.

51. On negotiations and stabilisation programmes see especially: Stand-by Arrangement Jamaica-IMF, 1977; Extended Arrangements Jamaica-IMF 1978 and 1979; Girvan et al., 1980; Sharpley, 1981; Manley, 1982.

52. Authors' calculations based on: Statistisches Bundesamt, Wiesbaden, *Länderkurzbericht, Jamaica, 1982,* Stuttgart/Mainz, 1982, p.26.

53. Independent experts reckoned that the total of goods and services sup-plied to Ghana through suppliers' credits in the Nkrumah era amounted to only 70–75% of the actual value of the contracts (Krassowski, 1974, p.84; cf. IMF, 1970, p.3).

54. These were representatives of the Harvard Advisory Group who had come to Ghana through the mediation of the IMF and the World Bank (Sederberg, 1972, p.54).

55. Agreed Minute on the Repayment of the Medium Term Debt of the Government of Ghana and Others Resident in Ghana, London, 9 December 1966, Article 4; Agreed Minute . . . London, 22 December 1968, Article 4 (3).

56. Though not represented at the conference, the socialist countries also rescheduled Ghana's debt in bilateral negotiations — but at far lower rates of interest (2.5–3%).

57. Republic of Ghana, Ghana's Economy and Aid Requirements, Accra, 1967; 1968; 1969.

58. Agreed Minute of the Rearrangement of Medium Term Debt Repayments due from Ghana between July 1970 and June 1972, London, 12 July, 1970.

59. The grant element expresses the percentage difference between the actual value of the repayments and the original value. In general, and in this case, it is based on a discount rate of 10% in accordance with the DAC guidelines of the OECD. Klein (1973, p.19), gives an example of how this is calculated.

60. Agreed Minute on the Repayment of the Medium-Term Debt of the Government of Ghana and Others Resident in Ghana, Rome, 13 March 1974.

61. In the same year, Pakistan also achieved equally favourable rescheduling terms.

4. IMF Stabilisation Policies — A Concept of Crisis Management in Need of Reform

IMF Interventions – An Obstacle to Sound Economic and Social Development

In Portugal, the IMF's stabilisation programme improved certain macro-economic data for a few months, but could not prevent the country's next economic crisis. In Brazil, the draconian austerity measures dictated by the IMF almost ruined the first tentative movements towards democratisation. In Zaire, the IMF failed to make a breakthrough in its struggle against corruption. In Jamaica, the IMF's loans policies enabled the USA to get rid of a government of which it did not approve. And in Ghana it helped to impose debt-rescheduling terms which left the country no scope to finance its development.

In short, the IMF is not accomplishing its task as crisis-manager for the Third World. Its remedies are effective only in the short term, if at all; wherever the interests of debtors and creditors conflict, it unyieldingly defends the interests of the latter. The main victims of its savage treatment are the underprivileged sections of the population in the developing countries. Not infrequently, IMF stabilisation means political de-stabilisation.

IMF crisis management has come in for criticism ever since the stabilisation programmes were introduced. In the 1950s and 1960s a few experts attacked the Fund for the effects its policies had had in a number of Latin American countries – but this criticism mostly went unheard or was ignored.[1] Argentina in the years 1958–63 is a classic example of the economic, social and political consequences of the IMF recipe, a recipe which remains much the same today. Three years of economic policies under the auspices of the IMF did lead to a short-term improvement in the balance of payments and a slight economic recovery, but at the expense of higher unemployment, sinking real wages and a drastic increase in the cost of living – which hit wage-earners hardest of all and led to numerous strikes. In 1962, despite the IMF policies, a new economic crisis began to loom up and the government, fearing a loss of political support, countered with expansionist financial policies. The IMF responded by suspending its fourth standby credit. The government was then forced to re-negotiate with the IMF to re-establish Argentina's creditworthiness. But the government's efforts to walk the tightrope between satisfying the demands of the population and meeting the IMF's demands for austerity failed. In March 1962, the elected president was deposed in a military coup. Only three months later a new IMF agreement imposing severe austerity measures was signed (Eshag/Thorp, 1965).

The IMF did not come under criticism in wider circles until the second half of the 1970s, when it took on an increasingly important role as crisis manager in the Third World.[2] In view of the high social and political costs of drastic cures dictated by the IMF, it is hardly surprising that reform-oriented governments such as those of Tanzania and Jamaica — both with first-hand knowledge of the effects of IMF demands — strongly criticised the IMF. As early as 1977 Jamaican Prime Minister Manley stated: 'We cannot continue to be told that the price of balance-of-payments support through the IMF may involve measures that cause mass starvation.' And Tanzanian President Nyerere in 1980 put forward the provoking question: 'When did the IMF become an International Ministry of Finance? When did nations agree to surrender to it their power of decision making?'

In 1979 and 1980 Jamaica and Tanzania hosted international conferences at which economic experts and politicians reiterated Third World criticisms of the IMF and called for a reform of the organisation. In the final communiqués of these conferences — the Terra Nova Statement (named after the conference hotel in Kingston, Jamaica) and the Arusha Initiative (named after the conference town in Tanzania) — the legitimacy of the IMF as crisis manager for the Third World was radically questioned.[3] It was argued that most developing countries had played no part in its creation; that the Fund had become a neo-colonial instrument by which the industrial countries disciplined the Third World; that it did not do justice to the structural problems of the Third World; that it treated industrial and developing countries unequally, for example by passively accepting independent exchange-rate policies by the USA while at the same time forcing developing countries to devalue drastically. The IMF's economic philosophy was criticised as ideological because by erecting the principles of the market economy into a dogma they left no scope for alternative development strategies. IMF stabilisation programmes systematically favoured the traditional centres of power in the developing countries. They not only jeopardised political systems, they also reversed democratic processes.

These criticisms are valid and telling. L'Hériteau (1982) describes the IMF's adjustment programmes as a 'new gun-boat policy', yet even without adopting her standpoint it is clear that the Fund's stabilisation policies lean heavily towards creditor countries' interest in rapidly restoring debtor countries' repayment capacities. In doing so they ignore the sometimes devastating economic, social and political effects of their programmes. The IMF realises that its policy of 'adjustment' involves hardships, but it regards them as inevitable if economic health is to be restored (Nashashibi, 1983).[4]

IMF deflation policies, with devaluation and reduction of domestic credit as their cornerstones, are based on the Fund's almost invariable diagnosis of 'excessive home demand' which has to be reduced. The implementation of these policies often leads to economic recession in the debtor countries. A short-term stabilisation of the balance of payments may also occur, but the price for this is reduction in the use of domestic productive capacity, an increase in unemployment and a reduction in the growth rate — sometimes even a real reduction — of Gross Domestic Product (GDP). The IMF's stabilisation programme brought Chile a fall in per capita income of 12.7% in 1975, and had similar effects in Peru in 1977–8 (-3.9% and -4.6%), in Zambia in 1977–9 (-7.4%; -2.6%; -11.8%) and in Turkey in 1979–80 (-2.8% and -3.2%).[5] In other cases, such as Portugal in 1978, IMF policies halved economic growth even though the economy — in a favourable world economic climate — was more export-oriented.

The example of Argentina shows how severely IMF deflationary policies particularly reduce domestic economic activity. At the end of a five-year stabilisation period from 1958–63 the country's GDP was slightly lower than its original level (-2%); industrial production, which was largely oriented towards the domestic market, dropped, while exports rose by more than a third (Eshag/Thorp, 1965, pp. 23, 29). Fifteen years later (1976–8), two IMF programmes produced a similar trend: while exports achieved a significant growth rate of 15%, industrial production slumped — with only a slight change in the GDP — by 7.3%.[6]

The contraction of the domestic economy imposed by the IMF leads to numerous dismissals and increases unemployment. Many companies go bankrupt, not only because they are hit by the contraction of the domestic economy but also because the liberalisation of foreign trade deprives them of protection against far more powerful world competition. The number of company bankruptcies in Latin America in a period of IMF-dictated stabilisation rose even more than in Portugal (cf. p. 86); Chile was especially hard hit: in 1973, 25 Chilean companies went bankrupt, but by 1977, after IMF shock therapy had taken effect, the number of bankruptcies shot up to 224 (Rivera, 1981, p. 91).[7]

If IMF recipes almost invariably lead the domestic economy into recession, their effect on foreign trade is to integrate the economies of the developing countries increasingly into the world market. The possible growth of the export sector does not create enough jobs and companies to offset the damage done to the domestic economy. The devaluation of the national currency and the abolition or at least the liberalisation of controls on foreign trade are intended to set an export boom in motion and bring in additional foreign exchange; but these measures do not always achieve the desired effect. In theory, devaluation should lead to better sales prospects for manufactured products on the world markets, but narrow limits are set to any such increase in developing countries' exports by the comparatively low quality of the goods and the protectionism of the industrial countries.[8]

In the case of agricultural and mineral raw materials, which are the major exports of the developing countries, devaluation rarely creates chances for an export boom. A change in the national currency's rate of exchange has no impact on sales prospects because it does not affect the world market price for these exports, which is always quoted in dollars or pounds sterling on the international commodity markets. At best, devaluation increases the profit margin for domestic producers, thus giving them an incentive to increase supplies.[9] Yet there is no guarantee that this increased production will be sold, because the world raw-materials markets are dominated not by the sellers' supplies but by the buyers' demand. The developing countries' raw-materials' sales and hence their foreign exchange earnings are thus a function of economic development in the industrial countries.[10]

Though the purpose of devaluation is to improve the competitiveness of a raw-materials producing country, it can in fact often lead to a spiral of competitive devaluation among countries producing the same raw material. The result of these exchange-rate fluctuations is an over-supply of the raw material on the world market. This accelerates the slump in prices and reduces the foreign-exchange earnings of all producer countries. Developments on the copper markets provide a good example of this process: in 1975, the price of copper slumped spectacularly compared with the previous year and the major copper-producing countries — Chile, Zambia, Zaire and Peru — found themselves in such dire balance-of-payments difficulties that they had to ask the IMF for help. The Fund imposed hefty devaluations on all four countries. The result was over-production, which, in the next two years, forced the price in real terms below that of 1975, despite economic recovery in the industrial countries (Jeker, 1980, p. 43; Dell, 1982, p. 607).

Devaluation and the abolition of foreign trade controls are seen not only as means of increasing the inflow of foreign exchange from exports; they are also intended to make a developing country's economy more attractive to foreign creditors and investors. In practice, these goals are rarely achieved. What happened in Ghana from 1966 to 1969 (see pp. 117f) is likely to recur in other countries with comparably low development prospects. The decontrolling of profit transfer and the reduction of payments arrears lead to an outflow of foreign exchange which is not offset by direct foreign investment and promises of further credits. Not even the IMF's seal of approval can make these countries attractive for transnational corporations and international banks.

Even in cases where income from exports rises and a net inflow of foreign capital is achieved, the negative effects of IMF-dictated integration into world markets can still outweigh these benefits. Devaluation and other foreign trade liberalisation measures commit debtor countries even more heavily to their traditional pattern of exports, which in most cases consists of one or two raw materials. As the majority of developing countries are competitive only with these products, integration into the world market hinders the diversification of their export structures and heightens their susceptibility to the often spectacular slumps in raw material prices on world markets.[11]

The application of IMF therapies can even lead to a real fall of non-traditional exports, particularly if imported primary products' or capital goods' prices suddenly leap as a result of the change in the rate of exchange and production then stagnates or sinks — as in Jamaica in 1978. The IMF sees devaluation not only as a means of boosting exports but also of raising the price of imported consumer goods, thus reducing domestic demand as well as the balance-of-payments deficit. But as the import structure of most developing countries is relatively rigid, this assumption often proves incorrect. Luxury consumer goods, spare parts for national industries, oil, medicines and basic foods which cannot be produced at short notice at home continue to be imported — even though their prices, expressed in terms of the national currency, may have doubled. Thus devaluation leads to an erosion of purchasing power which can force down demand for home-produced goods (whose prices are further increased by reductions in subsidies and price liberalisation). IMF measures frequently lead not to a development of the domestic market but all too often to a contraction, an enforced restriction of demand and a reduction in supply.

Devaluation can also seriously affect the ability of domestic borrowers to service their foreign debts. To pay off loans in dollars and other hard currencies, they have to earn correspondingly more of the national currency to offset the drop in its value. To prevent the negative effects of abrupt and severe devaluation in particular, the IMF has recently permitted more crawling peg devaluations and has even allowed the introduction of multiple exchange-rates — though this of course goes against the pure theory. In the case of Mexico in 1982, a severely devalued rate of exchange was introduced for import and export calculations and, alongside this, a less-reduced rate for currency transactions in the servicing of debts. The object of this was to prevent domestic borrowers getting into difficulties because of devaluation (FT, 20 December 1982; NZZ, 27 December 1982).[12]

Despite the dangers to the domestic and export economy often connected with a drastic devaluation, it must be conceded that in certain conditions devaluations are not only economically justified but necessary for development. A heavily over-valued currency caused by a domestic inflation rate notably higher than that of the trade partners can lead to disastrous developments when, for example, imported foodstuffs or primary products become cheaper than comparable national products and domestic production drops as a result.[13] An over-valued currency may also be exploited by corrupt state-classes to line their pockets uninhibitedly at the expense of the country as a whole. One example — from Zaire — will serve to illustrate this: an importer acquires an import licence, often by bribes, by means of which he exchanges national currency (relatively worthless in real terms) for hard currency at the Central Bank. With this he then buys and imports goods — at least that is what the forged import papers and bribed customs authorities state. In fact, only part of the money is used to buy imports, the rest is deposited in the importer's bank account.

A variation on this theme is often played in Latin American countries, where it has made a major contribution to the disaster of national indebtedness: an alleged investor is given permission to take up a foreign currency loan to make the imports necessary for his investment. But there is no investment or import whatever; the money finds its way into an American or Swiss bank account or is invested in property abroad. The loan is duly repaid, in comparatively worthless national currency, to the Central Bank, which carries out the transaction; the bank in turn has to pay the creditor in foreign exchange from which the country itself has received no benefit whatever. This and similar practices are the rule rather than the exception in many places — a wide network of givers and takers of bribes profit from this system and damage the entire national economy. In such cases, devaluation is justifiable in development policy terms because it brings the official exchange-rate into line with its real value and reduces the incentives for such corrupt practices.

As a rule IMF stabilisation policies aim to achieve and do in fact achieve not only a contraction of the domestic economy and greater integration into world markets but also a substantial reduction of the role of the state sector, of state expenditure and of state influence on economic activity generally. The IMF uncompromisingly pursues a free market economy ideology which forces Third World governments to restrict public borrowing substantially, cut subsidies for basic goods, social services, transport and state enterprises, increase prices for state services, raise indirect taxes; to dismiss workers in the public sector; to limit public investment in favour of (hoped-for) private initiative and to pull down protective barriers aimed to protect national industries, especially manufacturing industries, from over-powerful foreign competitors. All these measures are imposed with the intention of pushing down inflation, cutting the balance-of-payments deficit and developing the economy through market mechanisms.

The IMF's medicine, in the short term at least, generally succeeds in reducing the balance-of-payments deficit in foreign trade. In domestic economies, it generally reduces budget deficits,[14] but only rarely does it manage to combat inflation in the long term. On the contrary, price increases within the Third World economy are often at first accelerated. Admittedly the reduction in the volume of domestic credit and the restrictive money supply and budgetary policies imposed by the IMF tend to reduce inflation; but the effect of these measures is not immediate and at best medium-term. In contrast, the reduction of subsidies, price liberalisation and devaluation and in some cases increases in indirect taxes lead to what can be very high price rises. In autumn 1982, the IMF instructed the Ecuadorean government to increase the price of petrol by 120% and the price of bread by 45% (FR, 23 October 1982) — measures which were fiercely opposed by the population.

Almost invariably, IMF measures start a spiral of inflation which affects all products, including many which were not directly involved. Shock therapies in particular — drastic subsidy cuts, wide-ranging price liberalisation and severe devaluation — start off a spiral of rising prices which immediately creates new imbalances — such as those the shock therapy was originally intended to combat. Although the Fund proclaims that the fight against inflation has top priority in its package of measures, many IMF programmes end up leaving the rate of inflation as high as it was in the beginning, with the national currency again under pressure to devalue. In Argentina, for example, the IMF stabilisation programmes from 1976 to 1978 and the IMF-approved neo-liberal economic and financial policies of the military dictatorship up to 1982 failed to get inflation under control — they merely succeeded in reducing inflation from 160.4% in 1977 to 87.6% in 1980. And they could not prevent it rising to 204.6% by 1982. In Uruguay, too, the rate of inflation remained persistently high; after five years of continuous IMF stabilisation the 'impressive' figure of 63.5% was achieved (*Lateinamerika*, 7, 1983, pp. 114 and 272). A comparative study of the success of IMF-style stabilisation policies in Latin America concluded that, with the exception of Chile, not one of the programmes examined had notably reduced inflation (Whitehead/Thorp, 1979, p. 273).[15] Latin America has as many permanent IMF customers as it has countries with chronic inflation — a devastating indictment of the Fund's anti-inflation policies.

The IMF ideology, which dismisses state intervention and state planning as evils and advocates the virtues of the privately organised free market economy does contain a rational core in that state enterprises and state bureaucracies in developing countries are often overstaffed and corrupt and their planning, administration and production are often inefficient and wasteful of foreign exchange. The logical consequence of this ideology is dismissals from the state sector and an attempt to re-privatise state enterprises. In Ghana, for example, 50,000 employees were dismissed from state service in the first year of the stabilisation period 1966–69 in compliance with IMF demands (Libby, 1976a, p. 86). In Argentina in the stabilisation period 1976–79 the number of those employed in public administration was cut by 11.5% and in state enterprises by 18.9% (*Lateinamerika*, 6, 1982, p. 152), with the inevitable result that the army of unemployed increased correspondingly, as there was no chance of finding alternative employment in the deflated economy.

The reduction of state influence on the economy does not, moreover, automatically lead to an increase in the private investment which was allegedly kept down by the state. Indeed, a cutback in state investment activity frequently leads to a reduction in overall economic activity[16] — either because there is no national bourgeoisie or entrepreneurial class to create coherent market economy structures or because the embryonic bourgeoisie is more interested in the consumption of luxury goods (imported from foreign countries) than in productive investment. Attempts to privatise state enterprises often run into difficulties not only because domestic private investors are reluctant to take on the risks of running ailing companies but also because the developing countries themselves do not possess the capital, expertise or managerial skills needed to run private businesses successfully.[17]

In many developing countries only the state is in a position to carry out the specific investments necessary for the development of the national economy and to provide an economic and social framework designed to coordinate agricultural and industrial production and distribution structures and to satisfy mass demand. Given the absence or weakness of national bourgeoisies, 'the state enterprise is a historical necessity' (Elsenhans, 1982a), because the private sector, in the free play of market forces, is generally not in a position to fulfil its economic role — the production of goods and services to meet the population's basic material requirements. Developing countries do not, as a rule, have functional equivalents which could take over the role of the state in economic activity. The IMF therapy of seeking greater efficiency simply by reducing the role of the state is wrong. And given the potentially explosive social and political consequences of mass dismissals, it is frequently disastrous.

The reduction of state influence on price structures and a cutback in state price controls — a policy which the IMF emphatically pursues — cannot in all cases be condemned. In many cases, low producer prices, especially for agricultural products, serve to provide the urban classes so vital for a regime's survival with cheap food — or else, in the case of export products such as cocoa, coffee or cotton, to keep the difference between world market prices and local prices as large as possible; the difference can then be siphoned off by the state. Many small farmers, in Africa in particular, have been so de-motivated by state price policies that they have stopped producing for the market and returned to subsistence farming. The overall economic consequences here have sometimes been disastrous, especially in Ghana and Zaire: production of food and agricultural exports slumped, the drop in food production had to be offset by expensive food imports, smuggling and blackmarketeering flourished. The balance of payments also suffered as a result, because the neglect of agriculture meant declining foreign exchange earnings while the expenditure of foreign exchange rose.

When in such cases the IMF insists on the abolition of state price controls, an increase in producer prices and a free market agricultural economy, this is certainly beneficial for the country's economic and social development. The agricultural sector, the cornerstone of all development, cannot be stimulated unless small farmers are given incentives. The IMF does not, however, appear to realise that price control policies are only one of a number of obstacles preventing a rise in agricultural production: land-ownership and marketing structures, rural infrastructure and transport often prove formidable obstacles to development because they are, as a rule, completely inadequate and — despite all the rhetoric from the governments of many developing countries — are not given adequate support.[18] Price incentives are valuable, but in isolation they are inadequate as a means of stimulating the agricultural economy. Socially, too, they are dangerous when combined with cuts in food subsidies, which push the standard of living of previously privileged urban classes below subsistence level.

Contraction of the domestic economy, increasing integration into world markets and reduction of state influence — these are all dry economic terms, but for many people they mean that the struggle for survival becomes even harder. The marginalised urban classes (poor, mostly unemployed, living in shanty towns) and wage- and salary-earning urban classes (working classes and wage-dependent middle classes) are especially hard hit by IMF measures. In Latin America, these classes form the majority of the population.

Both groups are severely affected by the deterioration and rise in price of public services imposed by the IMF in its efforts to cut budget deficits. Public transport becomes far more expensive and the quality of medical services and education often deteriorates. The lower the income of those affected, and the greater the dependence on social services, the more devastating the effects of IMF austerity programmes. This is also true of food, a major item in the expenditure of low-income earners; a cutback in state food subsidies generally means that food prices rise much faster than those of other consumer goods such as vacuum cleaners, refrigerators and television sets. In Chile, for example, the price of milk jumped by 400%, bread by 367%, potatoes by 850% and carrots by 1,589% in 1975, the year of the IMF shock therapy; the average rate of inflation for the entire year was 340% (Rivera, 1981, p. 77). In Turkey, the price of consumer durables increased by less than 100% between January 1980 and December 1981, whereas the price of bread rose by 140%, flour by 200%, rice by 202%, sugar by 400% and milk by 166% (Werle, 1983, p. 140).

The effects of cuts in subsidies and price rises are compounded when the IMF insists on keeping wage and salary rises below the rate of inflation, thus reducing real income. In 1978 and 79 the governments of Portugal and Jamaica respectively had to promise the IMF to implement such measures. In Brazil, too, the Fund vehemently insisted on cuts in real wages in 1983. IMF officials frankly admit that they see no 'alternative to a decline in the real wage if internal balance is to be restored' (Nashashibi, 1983, p. 16). They argue that 'real wage rates may have to fall and real profit rates increase so as to encourage increased foreign capital inflow and private domestic capital formation' (Johnson/Salop, 1980, p. 23). Wage- and salary-earners in Argentina, Chile and Turkey also had to swallow substantial cuts in real earnings: in Argentina 27% in 1958–9, in the public sector 50% in 1975–7 and in the industrial sector 18% in the same period. In Chile, where the IMF gave loans for the first two years of the Pinochet era, real wages dropped 30%. And in Turkey real wages fell as a result of IMF programmes by 54% between 1977 and 1980 (see Eshag/Thorp, 1965, p. 23; Foxley, 1981, p. 202; Werle, 1983, p. 54).

The IMF's package of measures, designed to stimulate private investment and bring in foreign capital, in fact leads to a redistribution of income in favour of the wealthy classes at the expense of the poor and property-less masses. Following an IMF standby arrangement for 1973–76 in Uruguay, the poorest 40% of the population's share in national income dropped from

17.9% to 15.7%, while that of the richest 20% rose from 43.5% to 46.7% (Foxley, 1981, p. 203). And in Chile under the Pinochet dictatorship and the impact of IMF stabilisation policies the share of the top 20% in overall consumption increased from 34.1% in 1972 to 51.0% in 1978, whereas the share of the poorest 60% was slashed from 42.1% to 28.1% (Rivera, 1981, p. 95).

Despite severe cuts in the standard of living, those who are earning wages and salaries are still comparatively well off, as IMF programmes generally lead to widespread dismissals in private industry and in public services, thus raising unemployment and underemployment. The number of people without a regular income, however low, increases. In Chile, for example, the official unemployment rate shot up from 4.8% to 14.5% between 1973 and 1975, and, in the capital Santiago, from 5.6 to 18.7% in the same period (Whitehead, 1979, p. 96). In Turkey the official unemployment rate rose from 13.1% in 1977 to 17.5% in 1981 (Werle, 1983, pp. 48, 145).[19] In Zambia during the IMF stabilisation programme in 1978–9 the number of people able to work increased by 112,000, but the number of wage-earners dropped by over 8,000 (*ARB*, 15 October–November 1980, p. 5706). The process of marginalisation, which is going on inexorably throughout the Third World, is further accelerated by the Fund's policies. The result is frequently a rise in criminality such as we have seen in the case of São Paulo. In Mexico City the poor are increasingly resorting to armed violence as a means of staving off death by starvation since the introduction of the stabilisation programme at the end of 1982 (NZZ, 11 January 1984).[20] In Peru, the austerity measures affected the living conditions of the slum dwellers so badly that more people died from malnutrition and disease (Gerster, 1982, pp. 71ff.).

Although agricultural workers are as seriously affected as the urban poor by IMF measures, the impact on the peasant classes is comparatively slight. Small farmers in particular — especially in Africa — often operate at mere subsistence level and, as they are hardly involved in the cash economy, remain largely unaffected by IMF therapies. IMF-dictated price liberalisation and the lifting of state controls on producer prices — which are often kept artificially low — provide an incentive to produce for the market, though the often disastrous marketing structures set strict limits to their ability to do so.[21] Farmers and tenant farmers already producing for the market benefit from these price incentives; yet at the same time they have to pay more for transport, fertilisers and seed. Whether on balance they end up as victims or beneficiaries of stabilisation programmes depends on the specific measures which the packages contain.

Small traders, small producers and craftsmen benefit from IMF-imposed price liberalisation measures; yet production often suffers as a result of restrictions on domestic credit and the rising costs of imported primary products. Contracting domestic demand leads to a drop in sales. As a rule, larger companies are better able to cope with this situation than small companies. More and more of the petit bourgeoisie are impoverished by bankruptcy, though some emerge even stronger from this cut-throat competition.

National bourgeoisies engaged in the import-substitution industry — such bourgeoisies have developed in Latin America and some Asian countries in particular — are not only affected by the contraction of domestic demand but also exposed to fiercer foreign competition. The result is a sharp drop in the income, sometimes even a proletarianisation of such classes, unless they can shift their activities to other areas at short notice. In Chile, which for many years swallowed the IMF's medicine in pure, undiluted form, large sections of the national bourgeoisie transferred their capital from the import-substitution to the export industry, the financial sector or the import trade (Calderón, 1981, pp. 36ff.).

The state-classes which — in Sub-Saharan Africa in particular — rule in place of a bourgeoisie are, in economic terms, only marginally affected by IMF programmes — by the rise in the price of imported goods and the restrictions on corrupt practices.[22] The main beneficiaries of IMF measures are export-oriented big landowners, wholesalers and sections of the bourgeoisie — they profit far more from the integration into the world market brought about by IMF programmes than they are harmed by deflation.

Transnational corporations involved in the export trade in developing countries benefit even more than the above-mentioned groups because, unlike purely national enterprises, they can get round credit restrictions by tapping the financial resources of their parent companies.[23] The liberalisation of payments systems facilitates profit transfers and devaluation enables them to buy up uncompetitive home companies cheaply. This can result in the denationalisation of the economy. In Brazil, transnational corporations, assisted by the IMF programmes from 1965 to 1967, gained control of a large section of the manufacturing sector.[24]

Thus IMF stabilisation policies often lead to a marked deterioration in the supply of the basic material needs of the poor, to a further redistribution of social wealth and power in favour of the propertied classes and to a power shift towards the export-oriented segments of the national ruling class and the transnational corporations. IMF-stabilised countries are increasingly afflicted by growing political tensions and social polarisation.

If cuts in food subsidies, mass dismissals and devaluation all take place overnight, the livelihood and in some cases the physical existence of the lower classes is threatened. This frequently leads to strikes and unrest lasting for weeks and these in turn are usually put down by police or army repression: those who rebel are social groups severely affected by IMF measures — workers, students, intellectuals, civil servants in key positions — who, unlike the marginalised masses, are capable of articulating their interests. In June 1981, workers in the Moroccan city of Casablanca went on strike to protest and demonstrate against cuts in real wages imposed by the IMF. The police and army intervened to crush the strike. Official statistics said 66 people were killed, but according to unofficial estimates more than

600 were killed and 2,000 arrested (AC, 16/1981). Two and a half years later, in January 1984, the same story: IMF-imposed increases in the cost of basic foods, gas, fuel, school and university fees, led to unrest in North Moroccan towns in the course of which the state authorities killed at least 140 people (FT, 23 and 24 January 1984). Only a few days previously, a 'bread revolt' in Tunisia triggered off by IMF-inspired measures led to 80 deaths according to official figures (over 140 according to unofficial estimates); about 1,000 people were arrested. Further estimates indicated that the damage caused in the course of the riot was several times what the government would have saved as a result of cutting subsidies (NZZ, 20 January 1984).

In January 1977, the Egyptian government was forced by popular protest to restore state subsidies for flour, sugar, tobacco and oil; 79 people were killed in the demonstrations (McCauley, 1979, pp. 171f.). The same happened in September 1984 when food riots left three people dead (NZZ, 3 October 1984). In Liberia in April 1979 the announcement of plans to increase the price of rice led to spontaneous riots; 41 people were killed and 548 injured (ARB, 15 April–15 May 1979, 5090). At the beginning of 1982 in Sudan, demonstrations protesting against the rise in sugar prices were brutally crushed, the police killed at least 26 students and pupils (Sudanow, March 1982, p. 9). Three years later a similar picture: IMF-imposed bread price increases provoked riots in which eight people were shot (FT, 1 April 1985).

In Latin America, too, IMF austerity programmes led to protests in which many people were killed. From 1977 to 1984, IMF austerity measures in Peru led to numerous demonstrations, strikes and riots in which dozens of people were killed by the police and army (McCauley, 1979, pp. 163ff; LAWR, 27 August 1982 and 18 March 1983; NZZ, 14 January 1984). In October 1982 and March 1983 and January 1985, general strikes were held in Ecuador, mainly in protest at the IMF-imposed increase in bread and petrol prices. In any case, the army intervened and several deaths and injuries resulted (FT, 25 March 1983 and 11 January 1985). Six people were killed in March 1982 in the Bolivian town of Cochabamba when the army crushed a peaceful demonstration against IMF-imposed austerity measures (*Lateinamerika*, 7, 1983, p. 130). At the beginning of 1984 and again in January 1985 price rises caused by an IMF-dictated devaluation led to riots in the Jamaican capital, Kingston, in which at least eleven people have been killed (FT, 17 January 1985).[25]

IMF stabilisation policies frequently lead to a serious weakening of support for the government.[26] IMF 'stabilisation' often means political and social destabilisation. Governments face a choice between refusing to cooperate with the IMF and thus losing their international creditworthiness (which would have serious social consequences) or using repression to force through IMF measures at the expense of the lower classes. Thus the IMF tends to favour conservative and authoritarian regimes; indeed it sometimes even brings them to power, when governments are reluctant to apply IMF remedies and the military then take over 'to save the country from economic chaos'.

With remarkable frequency, IMF interventions coincide with military coups; the military takeover in Argentina in March 1976 — as in 1962 — was closely connected with negotiations for an IMF standby credit. The civilian government of Isabel Perón could not force through the IMF demands because resistance, especially from the trades unions, was too strong. Yet the IMF insisted on its terms and refused to grant the urgently-needed loan. The army leadership then took advantage of the economic crisis and the government's weak position and took over power. It proceeded to crush popular resistance and soon reached an agreement with the IMF.[27] In Ghana, the Fund was indirectly responsible for bringing the Acheampong military regime to power. An IMF-dictated devaluation led to riots and protests and the military took advantage of the situation to overthrow the tottering Busia government (Libby, 1976, p. 86). Negotiations for IMF loans also played an important part in a number of other cases where civilian governments were overthrown by the military: in Brazil in 1964, in Chile and Uruguay in 1973, in Turkey in 1960, 1971 and 1980.[28] Brutal military regimes came to remarkably rapid agreement with the Fund on stabilisation programmes, crushing all resistance from the outset. The bloodthirsty dictatorships in South Korea and Chile are outstanding examples of this.[29]

'The IMF has overthrown more governments than the military' complained the veteran Costa Rican social democrat Pepe Figueres (*Der Spiegel*, 7, 1982, p. 120). This may seem an exaggeration, but it is true that IMF interventions frequently confront governments with crises which they find extremely difficult to overcome, and which in some cases they do not survive. Reform-oriented governments, of course, have particular difficulties with the IMF's therapies because IMF measures hit their potential voters extremely hard. When such governments, for the sake of their international creditworthiness, do finally accept IMF packages, they often pay the price in the next parliamentary election. In Jamaica, the Manley government was elected in 1972 and 1976 on a manifesto of social reform, thanks mainly to the votes of the middle- and lower-classes. It lost the 1980 election largely because it had to force through the IMF's draconian austerity programme against resistance from its own supporters. In Portugal, the election in December 1979 proved a debacle for the Socialist Party because the lower-classes resented Soares' imposition of IMF-dictated policies (see Chapter 3). In 1981, the Carazo government in Costa Rica, after long agonising, accepted IMF austerity measures. It was voted out of office the following year (*LAWR*, 26 June 1981).

It is not always governments that fall during or as a result of IMF negotiations. Quite frequently it is finance ministers and central bank governors who resign during negotiations with the IMF; or else they are dismissed as political scapegoats for IMF policies by governments anxious to preserve their popular support.[30]

The world's 'financial policeman' is an adept at manoeuvring governments whose declared economic philosophy conflicts with its own into impossible situations. If the government does not reach agreement with the IMF, it risks the loss of its international creditworthiness and an intensification of the economic crisis, which almost inevitably leads to a loss of legitimation; if it accepts IMF demands, its international credit-worthiness is restored — but at the expense of a contraction in the domestic economy and a social polarisation which may equally lead to a loss of legitimation. The IMF's intervention in national economic, financial and budgetary policies is in itself a violation of national sovereignty — and in many cases IMF intervention does not stop here: in 1978 and 1979, the Fund insisted that the governments of Portugal and Jamaica should reach a political consensus with trades unions, employers' associations and the parliamentary opposition on the implementation of the IMF package — a move which inevitably meant the abandonment of social reform in favour of conservative restoration. At the end of 1979, the IMF even raised the issue of Jamaica's foreign policies — viewed with suspicion by the USA — arguing that these policies reduced Jamaica's international creditworthi-ness (see Chapter 3).

In response to complaints that its stabilisation programmes have disastrous political and social effects, the Fund argues that the severity of its terms depends on the stage the crisis has reached. It goes on to point out that many governments are only prepared to enter into stabilisation agreements when their economies are completely ruined and radical measures are indispensable. Mistaken economic and financial policies would lead to governments losing support even without IMF intervention and would have drastic effects, perhaps even more drastic than IMF policies. It would, the IMF argues, be more appropriate therefore to talk of 'mismanagement coups' and 'deficit riots' than 'anti-IMF riots' (Nowzad, 1981, pp. 18ff.). The argument that even without IMF programmes the social and political costs of government policies would sooner or later be just as high, if not higher, cannot be easily dismissed. This cannot, however, justify the Fund's shock therapies, which almost inevitably lead to resistance, any more than it can make the IMF's terms appear more judicious or socially acceptable. Why, it may be asked, are the supposedly inevitable burdens of economic adjustment thrust on the shoulders of those classes least responsible for the crisis? Are the Fund's loan policies not also to blame if governments, justifiably alarmed at its harsh terms, often wait until the crisis has turned into a catastrophe before turning to the IMF as a last resort? Or if they break off negotiations with the IMF because they know they cannot 'sell' these terms to their electorates?

Despite all criticism of the social ignorance often demonstrated by the Fund's programmes, it must also be remembered that governments frequently use the IMF as a convenient scapegoat for their own anti-social policies; they blame the Fund for measures which they themselves implement but for which they do not wish to accept responsibility. In January 1977, a cut in food subsidies in Egypt provoked serious riots, for which the Sadat government blamed the IMF.[31] As usual in such cases, the

Fund did not reply and accepted the role of scapegoat. In fact, the IMF had merely insisted on reducing the budget deficit, a goal which could have been achieved by cutting the excessive defence budget or putting greater burdens on the middle- and upper-classes rather than cutting food subsidies (Gerster, 1982, p. 108; Ww, 18 September 1981, p. 11).

In judging the effects of IMF stabilisation programmes, it is possible to disregard their social and political consequences and concentrate entirely on the results of IMF studies, in which the macro-economic development of the countries concerned is the sole criterion of success. Even viewed from this perspective, the success of these policies is seen to be meagre. According to the IMF's own analyses, 60 of the 79 stabilisation programmes which took effect from 1963 to 1972 achieved their goals. Success, in this analysis, meant merely that governments achieved the goals stipulated as performance criteria in the loan terms (particularly a reduction of the expansion of domestic credit). If the success of IMF programmes is analysed not in terms of the means employed but of their impact on overall economic activity, an improvement of the balance of payments can be seen in two-thirds of all cases. Yet these improvements were by and large not statistically significant. It is also evident that in most cases the Fund did not achieve its primary objective of containing or reducing inflation and that economic growth slumped in 40% of all cases (Reichmann/Stillson, 1977).

A study of the effects of twenty-one programmes between 1973 and 1975 paints an even gloomier picture: only seven of these programmes could be described as successful in IMF terms, and 'even then only with some qualifications' (Reichmann, 1978, p. 41). Political resistance to these measures was so strong that the IMF therapy could only be fully applied in a few cases. Fourteen countries reached or exceeded the balance-of-payments position promised by the Fund, but of these only three actually applied the economic measures demanded by the Fund. 'The performance in relation to price targets was, in general, not successful' (Reichmann, 1978, p. 41). Only in nine cases was the rate of inflation reduced. Over a third of the programmes failed to achieve the growth targets set by the Fund. A more recent study which looked at 23 standby arrangements in 1978 and 1979 came to scarcely more positive conclusions: only half the countries concerned reached the targets for balance of payments, growth and inflation. The Fund had to console itself with the fact that the variables, in the majority of cases, had moved in the desired direction (Finch, 1981).

The ignorance which IMF programmes display about the social and political effects they produce flagrantly contradicts the IMF's statutory mandate 'to promote and maintain a high level of employment and real income and to contribute to the productive potential of all its members' (Article I.2); but above all it conflicts with the IMF Executive's guidelines on the granting of standby credits, in force since 1979. These guidelines stipulate that the Fund should 'take due account of national social and political goals, the economic priorities and situation of members and the causes of their balance of payments problems' (IMF Survey, 19 March 1979, p. 82).

Nor does the Fund, as a rule, meet the requirement laid down by its Director-General de Larosière that stabilisation programmes should be compatible with the development options of the debtor countries (Larosière, 1982, p. 6). Policies which deflate the economy, causing domestic capacity to go to waste; which aim to influence economic structures by applying free market principles, though these cycles do not exist in most developing countries; which attempt to achieve world market integration by forcing up export production, without reflecting on the possible dangers; policies which plunge large sections of the population deeper into misery, intensify social polarisation and, at best, prop up the social status quo; which strain the resilience of democratic systems of government and have to enter into unholy alliances with repressive military regimes; such policies do not constitute a basis for economic and social development, development being defined as

> the independent development of productive forces to supply the entire society with vital material goods and services within the framework of a social and political order which provides equality of opportunity for all its members and allows them to take part in political decisions and share in their jointly-produced material wealth (Nohlen/Nuscheler, 1982, p. 62).

The IMF's policies do undoubtedly have a positive effect on certain overall economic data; indeed on occasions its conditions make good sense in terms of development policy — but this does not invalidate the general criticisms. Terms which trigger off riots and coups do not deserve the name of 'stabilisation'. When even international creditors regard social and political stability as key elements in their loan policies, it remains incomprehensible why the IMF still rigidly adheres to a distinction between politics and economics and refuses to recognise that economic measures can produce social and political consequences which show the improvement of the balance of payments for what it so often is — a tinkering with symptoms.

The drastic incursions of IMF programmes into the economic, financial and budgetary policies of debtor countries mean that the Fund is appropriating central functions of the state; its policies constitute an attack on one of the cornerstones of national sovereignty. These interventions are all the more serious because the IMF is not attempting to bring a rational approach to development policies. Its first priority, as defender of the industrial countries' interests, is to ensure that debtor countries are capable of repaying their debts. The beneficiaries of IMF programmes have always been the foreign creditors who, even if forced to agree to a rescheduling of the debt, could from then on reckon with a steady flow-back of their capital. But because IMF austerity packages do not tackle the causes of indebtedness in developing countries, creditors' hopes that the debtor countries will be put in a position to pay their debts in the long run are disappointed. Sooner

Figure 3. The Vicious Circle of Indebtedness and IMF Intervention.

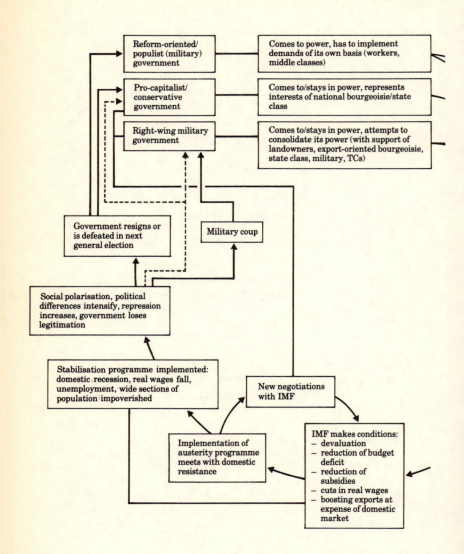

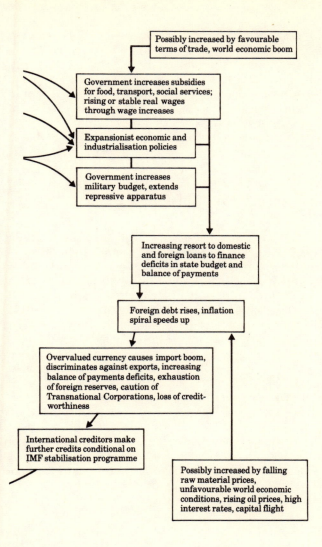

Possibly increased by favourable terms of trade, world economic boom

Government increases subsidies for food, transport, social services; rising or stable real wages through wage increases

Expansionist economic and industrialisation policies

Government increases military budget, extends repressive apparatus

Increasing resort to domestic and foreign loans to finance deficits in state budget and balance of payments

Foreign debt rises, inflation spiral speeds up

Overvalued currency causes import boom, discriminates against exports, increasing balance of payments deficits, exhaustion of foreign reserves, caution of Transnational Corporations, loss of credit-worthiness

International creditors make further credits conditional on IMF stabilisation programme

Possibly increased by falling raw material prices, unfavourable world economic conditions, rising oil prices, high interest rates, capital flight or later the crises erupt again, aggravated by the social and political consequences of IMF interventions, which make crisis management considerably more difficult at every new attempt to rehabilitate the economy.

Thus the IMF fails not only in the field of development policy but also in its task of guaranteeing debtors' long-term ability to repay their debts and thus of ensuring the continued viability of the world monetary and financial system. A reform of IMF terms and conditions policies is urgently needed: in the interests of the developing countries, who have a right to expect that IMF stabilisation policies do not destroy their chances of development, and in the interests of creditors who must be anxious to prevent short-term 'stabilisation' permanently affecting debtors' ability to repay.

The World Bank's Structural Adjustment Loans

In March 1980, the World Bank launched a new kind of loan: the 'structural adjustment loan'. Like IMF loans, they would be tied to conditions, and their purpose would be to finance 'structural adjustment programmes' in developing countries. Such programmes would provide a basis for steady, crisis-free growth — an indirect admission by the Bretton Woods twins that the IMF's traditional stabilisation programmes were not doing their job. Although the granting of structural adjustment loans is not formally dependent on a previous agreement with the IMF (Wright, 1980, p. 22), there is a *de facto* connection. Up to July 1984, 29 structural adjustment loans had been granted, and in each case an IMF loan had been granted previously. As Tanzania in 1981/2, Mauritius in 1982 and Peru in 1984 failed to reach agreement with the IMF, the World Bank also refused to grant them loans (Hofmeier, 1983, pp. 216ff.; *Africa Now*, October 1982, pp. 129f.; LAWR, 20 January 1984).

By introducing these structural adjustment loans, the World Bank, sister organisation of the IMF, entered the territory of balance-of-payments rehabilitation previously reserved to the IMF alone. This marks the final stage in a process in which the IMF has made repeated attempts to live up to its task as manager of balance-of-payments crises in developing countries — attempts which have not had notable success. In 1963 it introduced the Compensatory Financing Facility, thereby acknowledging that developing countries, through no fault of their own, can suddenly be affected by a fall in export income which has to be offset by loans whose terms are not too harsh. Access to compensatory financing was made easier in the course of time and the upper drawing limit was raised; but its financial volume was inadequate in view of the balance-of-payments difficulties faced by many developing countries. The same criticism can be applied to the Oil Facility introduced from 1974 to 1976 to help Third World countries plug — at least partially — the gaps torn in their balance of payments by the oil-price shock. Even the Trust Fund which, from 1976 to 1981, provided loans for the poorest developing countries, was no more than the proverbial drop in the ocean. Despite several increases in quotas, the sums made available for loans by the IMF fell behind the amount by which world trade had expanded and thus did not meet the financing requirements of deficit countries.

The 1970s brought an expansion of facilities tied to lenient terms, but only gradual changes in terms. Then as now, the philosophy of 'tightening one's belt' ruled. Nonetheless, the introduction of stabilisation programmes running for up to three years (the so-called Extended Fund Facility), did indicate that the IMF had realised that short-term packages, which inevitably have a shock effect, are no solution to the structural problems of developing countries.

The IMF's change of heart went beyond the extension of the length of its stabilisation programmes. In view of its chastening experiences with shock therapies, the Fund was increasingly willing to allow the measures it recommended to be translated gradually into action, though without ever questioning the fundamental rightness of the measures themselves. More and more often it agreed to gradual devaluations, to make it easier for governments alarmed by the disastrous effects of devaluation to agree to stabilisation packages.

The IMF has also shown itself to be more flexible in fixing performance criteria — the core of every stabilisation programme, in which targets for domestic credit are set. Instead of rigidly insisting, as before, on predetermined levels being reached, it has increasingly tended to include so-called control clauses in agreements. These clauses enable performance criteria to be adjusted to changing domestic economic conditions during the period of the programme.[32] Criticisms of its deflationary policies may perhaps explain why ever since 1980 the Fund has been at pains to point out that its stabilisation package includes 'supply-oriented' measures which, though primarily designed to stimulate export production, are also aimed at countering domestic economic contraction (Guitián, 1981; Crockett, 1981).

In fact, the Fund nowadays, far more than in the past, insists on the raising of agricultural producer prices, which is in many places undoubtedly a precondition for the expansion of production. On closer inspection, however, these 'supply-oriented' measures (reduction of price controls, tax relief for private companies, reduction of state intervention in the economy) reveal a philosophy based solely on the uncompromising application of free market economy principles. Given the economic and social realities in developing countries (incomplete economic structures, absence of bourgeoisies prepared to invest, inadequate or non-existent social security systems), such measures cannot possibly produce the desired results.

Shifts in emphasis in its loan conditions, the occasional use of more flexible performance criteria, extensions in the length of programmes and the creation of additional facilities with less severe conditions — these changes in the IMF's instruments of credit policy, though long overdue, could not preserve the developing countries from ever-more-frequent debt crises. Since the end of the 1970s, when the more lenient loan facilities were withdrawn, and especially since the Reagan administration took office, the IMF's loan conditions have again become stricter. During the world economic crisis of 1974, the Fund's main concern was to preserve the developing countries as sales markets for the industrial countries by injections of finance. In the world economic crisis of the 1980s, the recipe for the developing countries is 'adjustment', adjustment above all to a drop in demand and in prices for their exports (Larosière, 1982, p. 5). The deficits of debtor countries are too great, the economic problems of the industrial countries too oppressive, and so the latter are not prepared to provide their unreliable trade partners with substantial funds without tying them to severe terms.

In this situation, 'structural change' is the magical formula. By this the Bretton Woods twins mean that deficit economies should be forced to adjust to changed world market conditions — higher energy prices, the inflationary increase in the price of manufactured goods, high interest-rates and reduced demand and reduced prices for raw materials. It also means that social and domestic market-oriented economic policies must be sacrificed for the sake of exports. According to the IMF and the World Bank, this is the only means of achieving a sound balance of payments and eliminating chronic deficits in the Third World.

Since 1980, the World Bank, in close cooperation with the IMF, has been calling for this kind of 'structural change' — towards which the IMF had already been working in its three-year stabilisation programmes. 'Structural change' — on this both organisations agree — requires a longer period of time than traditional IMF programmes. The World Bank's structural adjustment loans last from three to five years. If the process of structural change, in the World Bank's view, promises to be successful, it may, during this period, grant further loans (with new conditions).[33]

Structural adjustment loans are neither 'balance of payments subsidies' nor 'blank cheques' (Steckhan, 1981, p. 912). As in the case of IMF loans, a credit is only granted if the borrower-government signs a letter of intent in which it undertakes to comply with certain conditions. As with IMF loans, structural adjustment loans are paid out in several tranches; and the next tranche is only paid when the agreed measures have been implemented. In the case of the Philippines in 1981, for example, the next tranche was not paid until the government fulfilled its promise to reduce protectionist import controls (Bello et al., 1982, p. 169).[34] Unlike the IMF, the World Bank does not judge compliance with its terms on the basis of exactly quantified macro-economic variables, but on the implementation of specific economic measures such as tax reforms or price increases for certain goods. This practice of formulating and assessing economic goals is undoubtedly an improvement on the IMF method. It means that goals can be formulated which take far fuller account of the specific situation of the developing

Table 4.1 Structural Adjustment Loans (SAL) and IMF Stabilisation Loans (to July 1984)

| Country | Structural Adjustment Loans | | SAL in connection with | IMF Loans |
	Date of Approval	Sum $m	Technical Assistance	Date of Approval
Bolivia	June 1980	50	no	Feb. 1980
Guyana	Feb. 1981	22	yes	July 1981[1]
Ivory Coast	Nov. 1981	150	yes	Feb. 1981[1]
	July 1983	250.7	yes	March 1983
Jamaica	March 1982	76.2	yes	April 1981[1]
	June 1983	60.2	no	
	July 1984	30.1	yes	June 1984
Kenya	March 1980	55	yes	Aug. 1979
				Oct. 1980
	March 1983	60.9	yes	March 1983
Malawi	June 1981	45	yes	May 1980
				Aug. 1982
	Dec. 1983	55	yes	Sept. 1983[1]
Mauritius	May 1981	15	no	Sept. 1980
				Dec. 1981
	Dec. 1983	40	yes	May 1983
Pakistan	June 1982	140	yes	Dec. 1981[1]
Panama	Nov. 1983	60.2	yes	June 1983
Philippines	Sept. 1980	200	no	Feb. 1980
	April 1983	302.5	no	Feb. 1983
Senegal	Dec. 1980	60	yes	Aug. 1980[1]
South Korea	Dec. 1981	250	no	Feb. 1981
	Nov. 1983	300	no	July 1983
Thailand	March 1982	150	no	June 1981
	May 1983	175.5	no	Nov. 1982
Togo	May 1983	40	no	March 1983
Turkey	March 1980	275	no	June 1979
	May 1981	300	no	June 1980
	May 1982	304.5	no	
	June 1983	300.8	no	June 1983
	June 1984	376	no	April 1984
Yugoslavia	June 1983	275	no	Jan. 1981[2]

[1] Extended Fund Facility
[2] Three-year programme, Stand-by Arrangement

Sources: World Bank Annual Reports, IMF Annual Reports, World Bank News and IMF Surveys (various issues)

country than the IMF's performance criteria, which are always identical and vary only in the amounts fixed.

The majority of World Bank terms, however, do not differ greatly from those of the IMF, except perhaps that they go into greater detail (Landell-Mills; 1981, Wohlmuth, 1984). Like the IMF, the World Bank insists on the reduction of trade restrictions, abolition of price controls together with price increases for public goods and services and stimulation of export production by means of tax relief and devaluation. Both organisations regard the reduction of state intervention and the application of the principles of the free market economy as of central importance. Only thus, they argue, can structural change be brought about.

But some World Bank measures go beyond the manipulation of economic incentives and affect specific institutional reforms and state measures to improve certain sectors of the economy. In the case of state enterprises, for example, the World Bank, unlike the IMF, does not confine its conditions to reducing subsidies but insists on training programmes for managers or measures to protect the enterprises from state intervention and increase their managerial independence. In the agricultural sector the World Bank not only demands increases in producer prices but also the reform of the marketing system or expansion of the network of agricultural development banks. Whereas the IMF tries to stimulate export production primarily by devaluation of the national currency, the World Bank applies supporting measures such as export subsidies or specific tax reforms. And whereas the IMF is generally satisfied with alterations to current rates of taxation, the World Bank frequently insists on a wholesale reform of the taxation system and works out detailed plans to this end. Where IMF measures are confined to reducing demand for foreign-exchange consuming oil products by means of price rises, the World Bank tries to encourage debtor countries to invest in finding home energy sources and thus reduce energy requirements in the long run.

Although these conditions may be sensible and necessary in specific cases, they generally overlook the causes of debt crises. The effect of training courses to improve management in state enterprises is bound to be limited when society and the economy are riddled with corruption and nepotism. The profitability of an enterprise may improve if it can make more independent decisions on appointments, dismissals and the determining of sales prices. But the cost of this increase in profitability and the relief for the state budget is the same as with IMF measures: unemployment rises, public goods become too expensive for the poor and private companies are driven to the verge of ruin because they can hardly afford to pay for the intermediate goods produced by state enterprises. The reform of the agricultural marketing system and the expansion of agricultural credit systems are in many places merely cosmetic because the structure of land ownership remains the same. Tax reforms can help to plug gaps in the state budget if previously privileged high-earners are taxed more heavily; but the positive effects of such measures are cancelled out if — as in Turkey in 1982 (cf. Werle, 1983, pp. 145ff.) — companies, land-owners and traders are allowed to offset higher tax payments by raising their prices.

The prospects of success for the production-stimulating measures and institutional reforms ordered by the World Bank are limited not only because they fail to tackle the core of the problem. They are above all restricted by the IMF's deflationary packages, to which World Bank measures are expressly subordinated.[35] World Bank measures aimed at growth have only the scope which the IMF's recession policies, aimed at a short-term balance-of-payments improvement, allows them. Given these priorities, the World Bank's claim that in designing structural adjustment programmes it tries to ensure that the 'impact on the poorest members of society [is] minimized, sounds hollow (World Bank, *Annual Report*, 1982, p. 40). Governments are forced to accept two sets of conditions if they want a structural adjustment credit — the IMF's austerity package which affects the entire economy and the World Bank's detailed conditions for key sectors of the economy. These conditions affect 'the heart of the political management of an economy' (Husain, 1980) and they explain why, from the introduction of structural adjustment loans in March 1980 until July 1984, only 16 countries availed themselves of these loans[36] (Pirzio-Biroli, 1983, p. 127; *UN Chronicle*, 6/1983, p. 49). Governments of developing countries are extremely reluctant to be sandwiched between the IMF and the World Bank, to renounce part of their sovereignty and to commit their economies to a consistent, free-market, export-oriented course. Indeed they are only likely to do so when they have no alternative.

Like IMF loans, the World Bank's structural adjustment loans are not intended to completely erase the deficit in a country's balance of payments, although in some cases the loans are so substantial that they come close to doing so. World Bank loans are primarily intended to act as a 'catalyst for the inflow of other external capital' (World Bank, *Annual Report 1982*, p. 39). The IMF's seal of approval serves primarily to notify international creditors that the debtor-country has regained its solvency. World Bank involvement, on the other hand, indicates to foreign investors that the developing country in question would be a profitable place to invest.

Measures to create an attractive climate for foreign investors and particularly transnational corporations are therefore a central component in structural adjustment programmes. In Mauritius and the Philippines, for instance, the World Bank successfully insisted on the expansion of free production zones — high tax relief, customs exemptions and low wages in these zones were designed to encourage foreign corporations to invest (*World Bank News*, 19 May 1983; *Multinational Monitor*, 2/1981, p. 6).

Increased production for the world market — this is the common denominator in the stabilisation and structural adjustment programmes of the IMF and the World Bank. The object of these programmes is to achieve a satisfactory balance of payments by means of export-oriented economic policies working preferably in close cooperation with transnational corporations (Balassa, 1982; Krueger, 1981). World Bank conditions which stimulate import substitution are confined to the energy sector and — to a lesser extent — domestic food production.

It is unlikely that an expansion of world market production is the key to growth and affluence in all developing countries (Streeten 1982; Frank, 1983). Increased export orientation forces developing countries into ever-greater competition for industrial countries' markets, which are protected by trade barriers. Even the IMF sees the export prospects of the Third World diminishing as protectionism in the industrial countries increases (F&D, 1/1983, p. 5) but it continues to cling to the hope of a new export boom (F&D, 2/1983, p. 12). The struggle for a share of the world market forces developing countries to keep wage-costs — their only international competitive advantage — as low as possible. In many cases this can only be achieved by banning trade unions and by other repressive measures, with the result that the people have few or no political and social rights. It is not only wage-earners, however, who have to pay for this one-sided export orientation. Companies producing for the domestic market are also hit when this contracts as a result of a shift of resources. In the Philippines, the World Bank programme forced through by the Marcos clan was rejected by large sections of the national bourgeoisie (FEER, 9 August 1983, pp. 54ff.).[37]

The World Bank's involvement is greatest in Turkey, which it had granted five structural adjustment loans by the end of 1984. Yet even here, under the joint aegis of the IMF and the World Bank, the number of bankruptcies of companies producing for the domestic market rose sharply. In 1983 the World Bank congratulated Turkey on its 'notable progress' (World Bank, *Annual Report*, 1983, p. 92), but this was because the country doubled its exports in three years. Yet this success was achieved at the cost of a deterioration of living standards, a collapse of the domestic market, massive export subsidies, tax relief and drastic devaluation. The boom is unlikely to last, nor will it, as the IMF claims, restore 'the basis for sustainable growth' (*IMF Survey*, 22 August 1983, p. 245). The war between Iran and Iraq was a major contributory factor in Turkey's export boom; but both countries had to reduce their demand in 1983 because of lack of foreign exchange. The European Community also indicated that it was no longer prepared to accept the artificial improvement in the competitiveness of Turkish products (OECD, 1982a, p. 37).[38] Given these developments, there are good grounds for fearing that the IMF and World Bank policy of short-term balance of payments improvements would jeopardise long-term consolidation 'not only of Turkey's balance of payments but of its economic production basis as a whole' (Kampffmeyer, 1983, p. 49).

Thus the policy of 'structural adjustment' with which the World Bank, too, has been trying to improve developing countries' balance of payments is ineffective as a means of establishing a basis for healthy economic and social development in debtor countries. Frequently it does not even accomplish its self-imposed task of leading the country along the path of crisis-free economic growth. This negative balance was inevitable: to date every structural adjustment programme of the World Bank has been subordinate to the IMF's deflation therapy, and IMF policy, fixated on a short-term balance-of-payments improvement, prevailed over the production-stimulating elements also included in the World Bank packages.

The two sets of conditions imposed by the IMF and the World Bank set clear-cut priorities for domestic economic and financial policy: the first priority is the short-term stabilisation of the balance of payments, the second is 'structural change', entailing above all a shift in emphasis towards export production, and, thirdly, social progress. The IMF and the World Bank appear to believe that social progress appears as a kind of side-effect when a country's foreign trade problems are solved.

To summarise: the structural adjustment policy of the World Bank in cooperation with the IMF is nothing but old wine in new skins. Nonetheless, structural adjustment programmes do contain elements – such as political-institutional reforms and the application of new performance criteria — which could form part of an appropriate development therapy — one in which stabilisation means more than a short-term improvement in the balance of payments and 'structural change' means more than export orientation.

More Loans and Better Terms — a Way out of the Crisis?

From Argentina to Zimbabwe the governments of the deficit countries are all agreed that the IMF's conditions represent a new variant of neo-colonialism, that the Fund does not make enough money available and loads all the burdens of adjustment onto the developing countries — indeed that the world monetary and finance system created in Bretton Woods has outlived its usefulness. Like their criticisms of the world monetary system, the developing countries' demands for a reform of the present order can be followed back to the 1960s. At the first United Nations Conference on Trade and Development (UNCTAD) in 1964, a recommendation was passed calling on the industrial countries to take more account of the developing countries in international monetary policies. Again and again the developing countries have spoken out at IMF and World Bank annual conferences to criticise the present monetary and finance system in general and the policies of the Fund in particular.[39] In 1972 a 'Committee on the Reform of the International Monetary System and Related Issues' — known as the Committee of Twenty — was formed but was unable to agree on any comprehensive proposals for reform. But it was at this committee's recommendation that the Oil Facility, the Extended Fund Facility and the Trust Fund were established and the sums available in the Compensatory Financing Facility were increased (Bird, 1978, pp. 17ff.).

All important decisions in the field of monetary policy — for example the creation of the Special Drawing Rights in 1969 and the dollar's coming off the gold standard in 1971 — were taken outside the IMF, without any participation whatever by the developing countries. These decisions were taken either by the industrial nations in the Group of Ten or by nations acting independently. As a counter-balance to the Group of Ten, the developing countries in the 'Group of 77' set up the 'Group of 24', whose task was to speak on behalf of the Third World countries and to work out recommendations for a reform of monetary policies. But this group's influence was modest compared with that of the Group of Ten, because the countries involved had nothing like the economic stature of their competitors.

Since the conference in Santiago de Chile in 1972, UNCTAD has increasingly become the forum for discussion between the industrial and developing countries on a reform of the world's economy. In 1974, the 'Charter of Economic Rights and Duties of States' was published, focusing world attention for the first time on the Third World and its demands. The increasing indebtedness of the Third World and the increasingly important role played by the IMF brought monetary and finance policies — alongside trade and raw material policies — to the centre of attention at UNCTAD V (1979) and UNCTAD VI (1983) (Bremer Gesellschaft, 1981; DÜ 3/1983, pp.37ff.). The problem of indebtedness was also given prominence at the General Conference of the Non-Aligned Countries in March 1983 and in the second report of the North–South Commission (NZZ, 5 March 1983; Brandt, 1983).

For the developing countries, a new monetary and financial system is an integral part of their demands for a new international economic order (Rweyemamu, 1980).[40] According to the ideas of the Third World countries, the purpose of a new monetary system would be to institute a democratic system of decision-making and control and thus to ensure that the economically powerful industrial countries would no longer be able to impose their wills over the heads of the majority of countries. It was hoped that this new international monetary system would include not only the capitalist countries but also the socialist countries. A new international currency unit would be established as a means of exchange and reserves, taking over the role now played by the few hard currencies — above all the dollar — and gold. The developing countries would receive preferential allocations of the new currency unit and thus boost their reserves, and the dominant role of the US dollar in the international monetary system would be ended. Finally, an automatic system of financial transfers would be instituted between industrial and developing countries to ensure that Third World countries were supplied with adequate funds on reasonable conditions. The Third World also called for the establishment of a new international institution to supervise and control this monetary system — an organisation which would replace the IMF and the World Bank. Universal and democratically organised, this new institution would be responsible for balance-of-payments financing and development financing; it would control the international liquidity supply and adjust it to the development of world trade. This new institution would ensure that not only deficit countries but also countries with positive balance of payments would be required to contribute — in the form of a redistribution of their surpluses.

The meagre results of international conferences in recent years prove that such radical changes of the world monetary and financial system are unlikely to be achieved in the near future, because the industrial countries are more inflexible than ever before. The Bonn government, for example, (Bundesregierung, 1983, p. 24) insists in its fifth overseas development report on the 'protection of the integrity of the IMF, the World Bank and GATT' as the organisational pillars of the present international economic order. With the above-mentioned goals in mind, the developing countries in their preparations for UNCTAD VI again formulated a series of steps towards reform; but not a single one was accepted. The resolutions for UNCTAD VI clearly underline the weakening of the developing countries' negotiating position in the present economic and debt crisis. The resolutions on international monetary issues, for example, stress the IMF's key role in helping to resolve the debt crisis; but they contain no commitment to reform of the IMF. Note was merely taken of the developing countries' 'interest' in preferential treatment in the allocation of Special Drawing Rights (SDRs), the revival of the Trust Fund or the creation of a medium-term financing facility with reasonable conditions (UNCTAD, 1983).

One of the Third World's major demands since the end of the sixties has been for the creation of SDRs to be used for the development of the Third World (Bird, 1982, pp. 201ff.). The SDR, an artificial currency established in 1969, would then be stocked up and used to a far greater extent, and would benefit the developing countries in particular — unlike the current practice whereby SDR allocations are made according to IMF quotas. Industrial countries would then provide loans for the developing countries from their own SDR allocations. The developing countries' interest in the link is so strong because it would enable them to exchange SDR for any hard currency, giving them access to foreign exchange with no strings attached.

The industrial countries are blocking the creation of new SDRs, on the grounds that the link would have an inflationary effect. They argue that the creation of new SDRs or its preferential allocation to Third World countries would increase international liquidity without any corresponding increase in the supply of goods; inevitably this would increase inflation (Bremer Gesellschaft, 1981, pp. 542ff.). The counter-argument here is that a cautiously managed link would only increase inflation if the resultant increase in developing countries' demand occurred when production capacity was being fully used throughout the world. But in fact the danger of inflation is probably slight in view of the deflationary world economy and the considerable fall in international liquidity in relation to world trade. A cautious SDR allocation could lead to a global expansion of import capacity and of trade and thus revive the world economy (Brandt, 1983, p. 63f.).[41]

The developing countries' other demands are similar. The Third World wants more loans on more favourable conditions. It wants the industrial countries to provide the multilateral development and financial institutions with more money, to top up their own bilateral development aid and to adopt a new International Export Credit Insurance.[42] The developing countries wish to see the creation of at least 15 thousand million SDRs per annum, to be allocated according to the IMF quota system. They would also like to see the quotas, especially for the Third World, considerably increased. In addition, they want the Compensatory Financing Facility to be so funded that it can completely compensate for export-related loss of earnings; a credit facility to be established on reasonable conditions to finance medium-term balance-of-payments deficits; a second Trust Fund to be set up, to be financed by further sales of gold. The developing countries also want changes in the conditions of IMF loans. They would like the Fund 'to respect the economic and social goals and priorities' of the developing countries, to extend the period for which programmes run and to move away from its rigid performance criteria (Group of 77, 1983, p. 29). Finally, since the UNCTAD debt conference of 1978, the developing countries have been calling for the reform of the present debt-rescheduling procedures (epd-Entwicklungspolitik, 6/1978, pp. 10ff.; Büttner, 1982, pp. 191ff.). They also propose the replacement of the Club of Paris by a Debt Commission on which industrial and developing countries would be equally represented. The task of this Commission would be to work out recommendations for debt-rescheduling arrangements. The Third World countries hope that such an arrangement would bring more favourable interest-rates, loans with longer repayment periods and a partial remission of their debts.

It would be an illusion, however, to expect an increased, automatic (non-conditional) flow of finance to the developing countries to bring a solution to the problem of debt. More money on more favourable terms — given the polarised, undemocratic social structures in Third World countries — means in the majority of cases more money for prestige projects, the import of luxury consumer goods and more military expenditures — not development policies aimed at meeting the basic requirements of the mass of the population. At the IMF annual conference of 1982, Ghulam Ishaq Khan, the Pakistani Minister of Finance, called for a 'fundamental reform of the world monetary order' (IMF Summary Proceedings, 1982, p. 189).[43] This demand reflects above all the interest of state classes and bourgeoisies in developing countries in consolidating their power, which, in the present system, is endangered by cyclical, debt-related state bankruptcies and the resultant loss of legitimacy. A greater inflow of foreign aid and loans would enable these classes to obtain more foreign exchange with which they would then imitate Western industrialisation models and consumption habits. Further debt crises would be the inevitable result.

What Gunnar Myrdal has criticised about development policy in general also applies to the developing countries' demands for more loans on more favourable terms:

> The truth is that in order to get the sort of development we wish for, the
> thing needed is not distributional reforms by transfer of money via taxes

and subsidies of the kind that might be effective in developed countries; what we need is thorough institutional reform. Land reform is only one part of the necessary reforms. Above all, I should like to say, an effective fight against corruption is needed. (Myrdal, 1981, p. 88.)

The policies of the industrial countries impose all the burdens on the developing countries and insist on them overcoming the crisis by 'tightening their belts'. This merely leads into a cul-de-sac in development terms. Yet the automatic transfer of finance which the Third World is calling for does not solve the debt problem either. It would only benefit the privileged classes in these countries. What is required is a reform which not only, by providing more loans, improves the world market-related prospects for development but also, by specifically designed conditions, restricts the debt-inducing policies of certain social groups by linking financial aid to the implementation of political and economic structural reforms promoting development.

Notes

1. See, for example Felix (1964, p. 371): 'It is by now evident that the stabilisation programs have been largely unsuccessful, particularly in the larger Latin-American countries.' And (ibid., p. 396): 'the IMF-type programs were based on a misappraisal of where some of the leading difficulties lay, as well as on an erroneous normative perspective.' Powelson (1964, p. 189): 'Stabilization is politically unacceptable to much of the nation.' See also: König, 1969, pp. 38ff.; Sunkel, 1964; Hayter, 1971. At a very early stage, Latin American representatives at IMF conferences insisted that the Fund should take more account of the economic and social development priorities of their countries (*IMF Summary Proceedings*, 1964, p. 51; 1965, p. 150).
2. The more recent discussion of the IMF's role was opened in 1974 by Cheryl Payer, who accused the IMF of forcing the developing countries into 'debt slavery'. Criticisms of the IMF continued to be based largely on Latin-American experience. See: Thorp/Whitehead 1979; Foxley/Whitehead, 1980; Diaz-Alejandro, 1981; Griffith-Jones/Seers 1981; Lichtensztejn, 1982. For criticism of fundamental principles see: Knieper, 1979; Gerster, 1982; Sid-Ahmed, 1982; L'Hériteau, 1982. See also: Eckaus, 1977; Dell/Lawrence, 1980; Killick, 1982 and 1984; Dell, 1982; Williamson, 1982; Brandt, 1983.
3. The Terra Nova Statement and the Arusha Initiative are printed in *Development Dialogue*, 1/1980, pp. 29–34 and 2/1980, pp. 10–23. Even conservative governments such as those of Sri Lanka, Bangladesh, Pakistan and Egypt joined in the chorus of criticism. Ronnie de Mel, Sri Lankan Minister of Finance, told the IMF annual conference in 1981: 'conditionality that fails to understand and accommodate the political and social conditions of individual countries can only lead to disaster. The remedy may well prove worse than the disease, if it leads to political and social upheaval.' (*IMF Summary Proceedings 1981*, p. 189.)

4. Wanda Tseng (1984, p. 5) wrote, 'The costs of adjustment . . . must be seen in perspective. In the short run, the costs are the unavoidable sacrifices that accompany the correction of an unsustainable situation . . . Over the medium term, with the attainment of balance of payments viability, adjustment contributes to the full realization of a country's growth potential, permitting higher levels of savings and consumption.'

5. Authors' calculations based on IMF, *International Financial Statistics*, Washington, 1982.

6. Authors' calculations based on IMF, *International Financial Statistics*, Washington, 1982. Another example: the stabilisation programme for Jamaica in force since 1981 has led to a substantial increase in manufactured exports but has still failed to get the country out of its economic crisis.

7. A similarly disastrous development occurred in Argentina since 1976 (see: Beccaria/Carciofi, 1981). According to Werle, (1983, p. 160), there has also been a dramatic rise in the number of company bankruptcies in Turkey.

8. Jamaica, for example, increased its exports of manufactured products as part of various IMF stabilisation programmes, but these sales were confined largely to the restricted market of CARICOM, the Caribbean economic community.

9. If the inflow of foreign exchange remains constant, then devaluation will increase income from exports – expressed in the national currency. State marketing authorities for agricultural products are thus in a position to pay farmers higher prices to encourage them to increase production. State-owned enterprises in the mining industry can also increase their profitability and production thanks to devaluation.

10. The reasons for inadequate supplies from the developing countries are often to be found not in price- or currency-related competitive weakness of their products but in their monocultural orientation, inadequate infrastructure and a land ownership and income-distribution pattern which inhibits production.

11. Guyana, which depends largely on sugar and bauxite for its exports, has been plunged into even greater dependence on these two products in the course of an almost uninterrupted series of IMF programmes since 1967. Liberia, whose economy depends heavily on the export of its iron ore and rubber, has managed only slightly to reduce this dependence after an almost-uninterrupted 20-year period of following IMF guidance.

12. Strictly speaking, the rate of exchange had three levels — apart from those mentioned above, a free currency market for tourists was introduced and a third rate of exchange found its level here.

13. This was the case in Ghana, for example, for almost 10 years (till the *de facto* devaluation of the *cedi* in 1983). The grossly over-valued *cedi* led to a powerful import boom; economic activity shifted increasingly from production to trade, where black market dealings often led to enormous profit margins. Because of the distorted rate of exchange the country's industry was forced to import expensive primary products, even though such products could have been bought locally easily — and if the rate of exchange had been more realistic — more cheaply.

14. Two examples from many: in Argentina the budget deficit was reduced from 10.2% in 1975 to 2.8% in 1977; in Zambia, from 12.7% in 1977 to 5.4% in 1978. Authors' calculations based on IMF, *International Financial Statistics*, Washington, 1982. IMF publications (Beveridge/Kelly, 1980; Kelly, 1983) also prove that

IMF stabilisation programmes reduce both balance-of-payments deficits and budget deficits.

15. In Chile, the rate of inflation dropped from 343.3% in 1975 to 9.5% in 1981. This was only possible because the inflation-reducing austerity measures were backed by the brutal potential for violence of the Pinochet dictatorship.

16. Diaz-Alejandro (1981, p. 128) argues that this has happened in Latin American countries. In Jamaica, too, the forced reduction of state influence in the economy did not provide an incentive for greater private initiative, except in the export industry, where a slight economic recovery began to make itself felt in 1979.

17. In Ghana, for example, the originally wide-ranging plans to privatise 46 state industrial and commercial enterprises in the stabilisation period 1966-9 had to be considerably modified. Finally, 7 such enterprises were put up for sale; only 3 were bought by Ghanaian industrialists. A further 11 companies were partially privatised (Krassowski, 1974, p. 118).

18. The Mobutu regime in Zaire has, in the official rhetoric, given 'top priority' to agriculture since 1967/8. And in the stabilisation programmes of the 70s the *relance de l'agriculture*, the revival of agriculture, was the linchpin of the programme. The share of agriculture in the GDP was still as high as 30.5% in 1980; but here the level of the subsistence economy, 19.4%, was almost twice as high as that of commercial agriculture, 11.1% (Rép. du Zaire, *Note d'information*, Kinshasa, 1981). In Zaire, market production is further hampered by wandering groups of soldiers who set up internal customs posts and impose unofficial 'tithes' on agricultural products.

19. In Chile, unemployment figures were rigged because they took no account of compulsory unpaid holidays which many employees were obliged to take (Rivera, 1981, p. 77); in Turkey the unofficial rate of unemployment was 30% —increasing all the time (Werle, 1983, p. 144).

20. In strong contrast to the positive reports in numerous economic journals, which claimed that in autumn 1983 Mexico was on the way to economic recovery (e.g. *The Economist*, 20 August 1983).

21. African small farmers, still the vast majority of the population, ought to benefit from IMF programmes, because in these countries there are often wide gaps between official and real market prices.

22. The 'state-class' is the social elite which has control over large amounts of state surplus value in the form of national revenue. Unlike the bourgeoisie, however, it does not own the means of production.

23. Transnational corporations which produce for the domestic market also suffer as a result of the contraction of the domestic economy.

24. The pharmaceutical, car, electrical and machine construction industries were soon largely in foreign hands (Sandaglia/Rescher, 1976, p. 446).

25. In the Dominican Republic the 'IMF riots' of April 1984 and February 1985 left more than 55 protesting people dead as the army intervened (NZZ, 15 February 1985).

26. Richard Eckaus (1977, p. 15), Professor of Economics, Massachusetts Institute of Technology, said: 'Where political stability itself is important for development, the prescriptions of austerity and restraint are not helpful when their consequences might well be to cause riots in the streets and bring down the government.'

27. The IMF felt obliged to make a statement that there was no connection between the granting of a Compensatory Financing Facility loan and the

military coup that took place two days previously (*NYT*, 27 March 1976). Only five months later, in August 1976, the standby arrangement was signed.

28. For Brazil, see p. 74; for Chile, see Whitehead, 1979; for Uruguay, see Finch, 1979; for Turkey, see Werle, 1983.

29. Chile was given a standby arrangement in January 1974, four months after the Pinochet coup; in South Korea the IMF loan of March 1980 helped to consolidate the Chun dictatorship which had gained power three months previously.

30. In Peru, the IMF brought about the dismissal of three finance ministers and one central bank governor in 1977 and 1978 (McCauley, 1979, pp. 163, 165). In Jamaica, Finance Minister Coore was dismissed by Premier Manley in March 1978 and in March 1980 his successor, Bell, became a political victim of the dispute with the IMF. In Brazil, Central Bank Governor Langoni resigned in 1983 because, although himself a supporter of austerity measures, he thought the IMF programme went too far.

31. There are even reports of governments absolving themselves by insisting that the IMF, in its letter of intent, should include detailed measures which the government knows to be unacceptable to opposition groups, even within the government (Pirzio-Biroli, 1983, p. 125).

32. The case of Jamaica shows how much the IMF's flexibility depends on the basic political direction of the government concerned: the IMF's 1981 agreement with Seaga contained the flexible performance criteria which the Fund was not prepared to grant the social democratic Manley government two years earlier.

33. By mid-1984 this had happened in Turkey, the Ivory Coast, Jamaica, South Korea, the Philippines, Thailand, Kenya, Mauritius and Malawi (see Table 4.1).

34. In Senegal, the World Bank refused to pay a structural adjustment loan granted in 1980 because the government did not carry out its promise to re-organise the agricultural marketing system (*New African*, August 1983, p. 39).

35. The World Bank justifies this subordination by arguing that 'effective long-term development programs [i.e. World Bank structural adjustment programmes, ed.] cannot be undertaken by a country facing an immediate financial crisis; in these circumstances, priority must be given to stabilization measures' (Landell-Mills, 1981, p. 20).

36. By July 1984, 29 structural adjustment loans worth a total of $4.5 thousand million had been granted. The share of structural adjustment credits in overall credit volume was well below the 10% mark which the World Bank originally set. In February 1983, the World Bank abandoned this target, stating that in future structural adjustment credits would play an even more important part in overall credit policy (World Bank, *Annual Report, 1983*, p. 42) but this statement of intent had not by the end of 1984 led to any notable increase in loans granted.

Contrary to World Bank announcements that the poorest countries would above all be the main beneficiaries of this new credit (*World Development Report, 1981*, p. 82), the beneficiaries to date have been newly industrialising countries and raw-materials exporting countries with medium income (see Table 4.1). At the top of this list we find countries which are pro-Western, geo-strategically exposed or important trade partners for the industrial countries: i.e. Turkey, the Philippines, Thailand, the Ivory Coast, Pakistan and South Korea. Military and repressive police-governments seem to find it easy to qualify for structural adjustment credits.

37. Even a study commissioned by the World Bank concluded that in unilaterally reducing protection for Philippine industry and improving the conditions for foreign investment, the World Bank ran the risk of being criticised as a 'henchman of multinational corporations and in particular of US economic imperialism' (so-called Asher Memorandum, quoted in epd-Entwicklungspolitik, Materialien 2/1981, p. 14).

38. As early as April 1982 the European Community imposed a 12% duty on cotton-wool yarn imports from Turkey (Werle, 1983, p. 129).

39. See 'Summary Proceedings' published by the Fund, containing statements by the Finance Ministers of member countries at IMF annual conferences.

40. 'Reform of the international monetary and finance system has been a major concern in the efforts to evolve a new international economic order. Decisions on the mobilization and allocation of financial resources have wide distributive effects nationally and internationally. Availability of finances of magnitude, form and character necessary to support a process of rapid change in the structure of production in developing countries is essential for rapid progress towards the new order.' (UN, 1982, p. 18.)

41. The USA is scarcely in a position to advance the argument that the link would inflate the world economy. In the 70s in particular, the US Federal Reserve Bank simply printed dollars to finance its budget and trade deficits – and this pushed up inflation throughout the world. The USA's monetary policy has always been based on its domestic economic and financial priorities; and US governments only began to concern themselves with the negative effects of their policies on the world economy and that of developing countries when the international glut of dollars posed dangers to the US economy.

42. This institution's task would be to promote the manufactured products of developing countries (incl. exports to other Third World countries) by granting credit lines to purchaser countries and taking on guarantees for their repayment.

43. 'We must calmly review the premises of the present international monetary system and find some fundamental solution to the creation and distribution of international liquidity, rather than keep refining and sharpening the conditionality for poor countries who have no other alternative but to keep protesting that such conditionality is inherently unfair since developing countries are being made to adjust to a grossly distorted international monetary system, without any attempt to correct the distortions themselves.' (Ghulam Ishaq Khan, the Pakistani Minister of Finance, in *IMF Summary Proceedings*, 1982, pp. 187f.).

5 Ways Out of the Debt Crisis: The Need for a Development-Oriented Policy

No Lasting Solution to Crisis without 'Duty to Adjust' for Surplus Countries

Given the industrial countries' negative attitude to the demands of the developing countries, is it possible and conceivable that the highly indebted countries of Latin America could join forces and simply inform their creditors that repayment of their debts was beyond their economic means and that these debts were therefore – partially or entirely – null and void? Can we expect the formation of a debtors' cartel which will dictate terms to the creditors? Has indebtedness in some countries reached a level which means that the creditors are now dependent on the debtors, enabling the latter as it were to turn the tables and make the creditors liable for the debt debacle? Speculation on these questions has been rife in recent years, particularly at the height of the Mexican and then Brazilian crises in 1982/3. It is now a known fact that at the beginning of September 1982 there were at least two secret meetings betwen the then Mexican president Lopez Portillo and Brazilian and Argentinian government representatives to sound out the possibilities of a debtors' cartel. It is said that Brazil and Argentina finally got cold feet (SZ, 22 June 1983).

Although there may have been thoughts of a debt repudiation and a debtors' cartel at the highest government level, it is highly unlikely that such schemes will ever be implemented. What at first sight may appear to be the untying of the Gordian knot for debtor countries turns out on closer inspection to be a sure way of strangling the country economically. Not only would creditors boycott the country for the foreseeable future — overnight the offending country would have to conduct its foreign trade on a barter basis: the state export credit insurances of the industrial countries would withdraw their guarantees and few foreign exporters would then be prepared to supply on credit, fearing that in their case too the debtor country would break its contract. Creditors would try to cover their losses by confiscating the debtor country's money abroad. Ships and aeroplanes would be confiscated as soon as they landed on foreign territory. Even if countries such as Mexico, Brazil and Argentina might possibly be able to cope in the long term with the foreign trade effects of debt repudiation, the short-term effects of foreign trade isolation, especially in countries which —

like most of the major debtors — are strongly integrated into the world economy, would be catastrophic; so catastrophic that a government would scarcely be able to survive them politically. A deep economic crisis, explosive price rises and serious supply shortages for the lower classes of the population would be the immediate effects of such a spectacular move. This would lead almost inevitably to social unrest and subject the political system to a test it would be unlikely to survive.[1]

Debt repudiation is therefore only an option for countries which are relatively unintegrated into the world market and can have little hope of more finance flowing into the country in the foreseeable future than is flowing out in the form of interest and principal repayments. But even in such a relatively rare case debt repudiation would have drastic and lasting consequences. In 1972 Ghana repudiated most of its medium-term debts and although it reached agreement on more favourable repayment conditions with its creditors two years later, it suffered from its lack of creditworthiness among international financiers for a further ten years (see Chapter 3).

Given these perspectives, the Mexican initiative of the summer of 1982 and the reports of imminent debt repudiations must be interpreted as an attempt to strengthen the debtors' position in rescheduling negotiations. Unilateral moratoriums (temporary non-payment of principal) until agreement on rescheduling could, as already seen, serve this purpose just as well as a joint strategy of debtors in rescheduling negotiations[2] which would overcome their isolation in the face of their creditors. Concerted debt repudiations, however, because of the incalculable risks they bring for the governments of debtor countries, are hardly likely, as creditors are well aware.[3]

The crisis of major debtors, which for the first time jeopardised creditors and above all the banks, has at least led to reflections on how to cope with the Third World's debt catastrophe. The proposals reflect the interest in keeping damage for the banks but above all for the world monetary and financial system as low as possible. The restoration of the health of developing countries' economies is a secondary consideration.

One proposal with innumerable variations is that banks should be given the possibility of transferring their problem loans at discount to a new international fund, to the IMF or to the World Bank. The new holder of these claims — who would also receive a guarantee from creditor states or banks to be liable for losses — would then reschedule the debts in the long term.[4] Former New Zealand Prime Minister Muldoon proposed that the debts of the debtor countries should be transformed into long-term loans at fixed rates of interest which could be bought and sold as bonds (NZZ, 29 January 1983). Others argue for the issue of long-term rescheduling bonds or wish to solve the crisis by restricting the debt-service of the developing country to a certain percentage of export earnings which would be expressed in bonds to be bought and sold.

Others — US economist Karl Brunner, for example (NZZ, 27 May 1983)

— object to any form of regulatory intervention. In cases of insolvency, creditors and debtors should share the costs. In practice this means a 'market economy solution' in which the debtor country pays the (undoubtedly huge) economic, social and political costs of lasting insolvency, whereas the banks are liable for losses and, in the worst case, go bankrupt Other economists and bankers (for example Krahnen, FAZ, BdW, 13 December 1983) believe that the partial transformation of debts into shareholdings — which would make creditor banks co-owners of state enterprises and industrial plants — would solve the crisis.

Hankel (1984, pp. 76ff.) has made an original proposal which would free the developing countries of the necessity to earn foreign exchange to pay off debts. He proposes that debtor countries should pay their unredeemable debts in their national currencies (which would be far easier to earn). They would be booked to counterpart accounts of creditors in debtor countries and the sums would be available for development financing. The creditor banks would cede these irretrievable debts to the governments of creditor countries and would receive appropriate compensation from its development aid budgets.[5]

The implementation of this plan would not, however, as Hankel hopes, be a 'Marshall Plan for the Third World' — the uncoupling of debt servicing from the necessity to earn foreign exchange would certainly not in itself provide a basis for development. The biggest imponderable in his plan is the question of whether the transfer of debt to development aid budgets of creditor countries — despite the substantial increase in these budgets which Hankel calls for — would not be to the detriment of new development projects. Furthermore, there would be the risk of development aid being shifted to newly industrialising countries at the cost of the Fourth World countries that are less indebted to private banks. Like most other proposals, Hankel's plan would amount primarily to a nationalisation of banks' credit risks or even of their losses.

Apart from the Hankel plan and the so-called Lever plan (*The Economist*, 9 July 1983, pp. 19f.) which proposed the creation of a global credit insurance which would in future also cover bank loans and would cancel guarantees if a country risked becoming too heavily indebted, few proposals go beyond the regulation of old debts or have ideas about how debt crises could be avoided in future. There is general agreement that not all claims can be enforced on time if the risk of a collapse of the debtor countries, and their complete insolvency, is to be avoided. All banks which do business with developing countries therefore make large-scale 'value adjustments', the first step towards write-offs, increase their risk reserves and take other precautionary measures. In 1982/3, when Latin America was in the grip of a serious debt crisis, the international banks involved with the region made unprecedented profits — not least through refinancing and rescheduling operations for Latin American countries.[6] The greater the risk, the higher the interest and the greater the profit — this is the law of the market.

There is also general agreement in the North that the debt-service burdens of the developing countries must be adjusted to their real capacity to repay. Some years ago, debt-service ratios of between 20 and 30% were considered high; but today some Latin American countries (theoretically) would have to spend 100% and more of their export earnings on debt-service, new loans would have to be taken up merely to avoid getting into arrears on interest and principal repayments. It is obvious even to creditors that in these circumstances an extension of repayment deadlines and/or a reduction of interest is inevitable.

Finally there is also general agreement that world economic conditions must change if the debtor countries are to overcome the debt crisis. High interest rates — caused above all by the US budget deficit and thus indirectly by the Reagan administration's arms policies — must be reduced; prices for raw materials — the main exports of many developing countries — must rise and remain at certain minimum levels. The Third World must be given the opportunity to restore and to increase its volume of exports, which means that the increasing protectionism of the industrial countries must be opposed. All these are important preconditions for solving the acute crisis of some debtor countries, but the recovery of the world economy and a number of rescheduling operations are not in themselves a long-term solution to the Third World's debt problem.

There is no chance of a more stable development in debtor countries and indeed in the world economy as a whole until qualitative changes in the structure of the world monetary and financial system are made and as long as the adjustment burdens of balance-of-payments deficits are placed on the shoulders of the debtor — the deficit — countries alone. The world economic crisis of the 1930s surely brought home the lesson that the necessary 'adjustments' cannot be made by the indebted countries alone. At that time the debt crisis of Latin America — as well as Germany — was an important factor in the international banking collapse (see Chapter 1).

A lasting solution to the debt crisis can only be found if balance-of-payments surpluses in the industrial countries and in some OPEC countries — which are after all the other side of Third World deficits — are no longer regarded as holy cows and a mechanism is established which forces both surplus and deficit countries to long-term 'adjustment' (Dell/Lawrence, 1980, pp. 96ff.)[7] If a successful strategy for the solution of the international debt crisis is to be worked out, then surpluses as well as deficits must also be regarded as contributing to the crisis.[8] The tendency to regard surpluses as a sacred cow is one of the most fundamental errors of the present world monetary and financial system.

Ideas about ways of making surplus countries contribute to solving balance-of-payments crises were discussed during the talks which led to the foundation of the IMF and the World Bank. J.M. Keynes, the chief British negotiator, presented a plan to skim off balance-of-payments surpluses via an 'International Clearing Union' and to make the money available to deficit countries to help them improve their balance of payments

(Horsefield *et al.*, 1969, III, pp. 19ff.; Knieper, 1976, pp. 108ff.; Andersen, 1977, pp. 27ff.). This plan also reflected the interests of Great Britain, weakened by the Second World War and itself a deficit country. However, the plan was rejected by the United States, which was in a far stronger negotiating position and used the position it had acquired in two world wars as leading Western power for the benefit of US capital.

Keynes' plan proposed that the central banks should establish accounts with the Clearing Union and the money deposited would be used to improve balance of payments. The unit of account — similar to today's Special Drawing Rights — was to be known as Bancor, and it would fix the rates of national currencies in relation to one another. The task of the Clearing Union would have been to grant deficit countries Bancor loans according to their quota (see Chapter 2, note 1); these would be covered by the accounts of the surplus countries. Both debtors and creditors would be required to adjust in the long term. Debtor countries would have to undertake to pay interest on Bancor, devalue their currencies to stimulate exports, supervise capital export and transfer part of their foreign exchange reserves to the Clearing Union to pay off their foreign debts. The surplus countries would also have been required to pay in duties to establish Bancor, to boost their domestic economies by expanding domestic credit and increasing domestic demand, to revalue their currencies and to liberalise imports — all measures designed to reduce their balance-of-payments surpluses in the long term and to lead world trade and production onto an expansionist path, in stark contrast to the IMF's therapy of restoring economic health by shrinking the economy.

The weakness of the Keynes plan lies in its implicit appeal to the enlightened self-interest of creditors to renounce short-term competitive advantages for the sake of a stable long-term world economic development.

> Both the hope for harmonious domestic economic development and for international discipline rely on the perception of an overall world interest and disregard powerful development factors — such as individual and national-capitalistic competition — from which economic crises form, crises which might produce tendencies towards a favouring of export trade and unbridled capital export. (Knieper, 1976, p. 112)

It seems unlikely today that concepts based on the Keynes plan could successfully be put into practice. Nonetheless, the real danger that the Third World debt crisis poses to the world's monetary and financial system could lead the industrial countries to agree to a mechanism for mutual balance-of-payments adjustment which is based partly on the Keynes plan.[9] It would be conceivable, for instance, that IMF member states with surpluses would have to pay a substantial part of their surpluses to fund the Compensatory Financing Facility.

This facility, introduced in 1963 to finance temporary reductions in export earnings for which the economic and financial policies of developing countries' governments were not responsible, has not yet fulfilled its function satisfactorily. True, access to the facility has been liberalised over the years; its funds have risen as a result of quota increases and the upper drawing limit has been raised. In 1981 it was extended to include cereal imports — a response to the spectacular cereal price rises. Yet despite all this the funds mobilised through this facility came nowhere near filling the gaps in the foreign exchange budgets of developing countries.[10] There is no doubt that Third World countries must sooner or later adjust their foreign exchange budgets to a lasting price slump or reduction of sales of their exports and must also adjust to a drastic increase in the price of major imports. To finance balance-of-payments deficits through the IMF in the foreseeable future would amount to making the developing countries chronically dependent on 'social welfare payments' from the international community.

In this process of inevitable 'adjustment' to unfavourable foreign trade conditions, the Compensatory Financing Facility should play a significantly greater role than hitherto. The funds available from the facility would have to be substantially increased and the financing of balance-of-payments deficits would have to take place over a much longer period, enabling the country concerned to adjust to the changes in foreign trade without intolerable social hardships. Regardless of the country's quota, the sum by which the balance of payments was additionally burdened could be financed at first completely, and later, in declining percentages by the Compensatory Financing Facility — depending on what 'adjustment burdens' could be imposed on the debtor country without limiting its development options or endangering the satisfaction of the basic needs of the poor.[11] Here price slumps of export products and drops in export sales, drastic increases in import prices (Dell, 1982, p. 604; Brandt, 1983, pp. 66f.) and in particular the excessive rise in interest costs which has threatened to strangle the economies of Latin America in recent years would also have to be taken into account.

The task of the facility would not simply be to provide — as it has done up to now — partial compensation for export earning reductions diagnosed as temporary; it would also involve financing medium- to long-term adjustment to deteriorating world market conditions and thus help to overcome structural development problems. The conditions for these loans would not in principle differ from those granted to cure deficits caused by internal financial and economic policies. They would as far as possible respect the path to development chosen by the government concerned and be so designed as to enable a medium-term restructuring of production and consumption patterns without endangering the satisfaction of the basic needs of the population.

As balance-of-payments deficits are rarely attributable solely to external factors but are also caused by the economic and financial policies of governments, the granting of a Compensatory Financing Facility loan would normally be tied to the conclusion of an IMF stabilisation programme designed to remove the internal causes of the crisis and containing appropriate conditions — which would be development-oriented, in contrast to current IMF practice. Whether and to what extent the deficit should be financed from the Compensatory Financing Facility or from a standby arrangement would depend on the comparative importance of external and internal factors in causing the crisis — admittedly not always an easy matter to judge. This assessment would have no influence on the conditions of the loan but only — if at all — on the period within which the stabilisation measures would have to be implemented. If the balance-of-payments deficit were largely world-market related, a longer period to adjust to changed world market conditions could be allowed and the country would receive a loan from the Compensatory Financing Facility — but the (now development oriented) stabilisation programme would be necessary nonetheless.

The Compensatory Financing Facility would have to be substantially increased and would be financed by skimming off part of the surplus of countries with positive balances of payments. As their market power in the raw-materials and industrial-goods sectors as well as the finance sector contributes significantly to the deficits of developing countries, the surplus countries ought to make the major contribution to the financing of this facility at least. A mechanism — along the lines of the European Community's STABEX — could be established at global level by means of which the IMF as the control point could operate a non-conditioned transfer of finance from surplus to deficit countries if the latter were manoeuvred into debt crises through no fault of their own (Bremer Gesellschaft, 1981, pp. 295ff.).[12]

Funds to increase the facility's financial volume could also be mobilised by a general increase in quotas; an increase in funds is also urgently required for standby arrangements. The Brandt Commission (1983, p. 59) has argued for an increase in quotas to at least 120 thousand million SDRs in response to the present crisis. This would re-establish the ratio of quotas to world imports for 1975. Pirzio-Biroli (1983, p. 147) argues that quotas should be raised to 300 thousand million SDRs — equivalent to the ratio for the first postwar years.

Additional funds could also be raised by IMF borrowing from governments and — in contrast to its practice to date — borrowing on international capital markets. This procedure would be perfectly compatible with the IMF Fund's statutes (the World Bank has raised money in this way since its foundation).[13] Finally, the finances of the IMF could be improved by moderate creation of Special Drawing Rights, without inflating the world economy. The objective should not be an unconditional allocation of Special Drawing Rights along the lines of the developing countries' 'link' demands, but an increase in the amount of finance available for development-oriented stabilisation programmes.

A significant increase in IMF funds, a reduction of IMF loan interest and an extension of repayment deadlines to prevent debt-service requirements triggering a new crisis after 'stabilisation' — all these are necessary conditions for the solution of the Third World's debt crisis; but such reforms would be inadequate unless accompanied by policies in the debtor countries which reconcile stabilisation with development.

Elements of a Reformed Stabilisation Policy: Development-related Conditionality and Co-liability of Creditors

Whether proposals to make the surplus countries pay an 'adjustment' contribution are realised or not, the IMF will continue to play a key role in the management of debt crises in the Third World. There is no sign that any other institution is likely to take on the task of the international financial policeman or to make such a role unnecessary. There is no indication that the world development fund proposed by the Third World as an agency for supplying the developing countries with more funds at more favourable conditions is likely to materialise.[14] The Bank for International Settlements (BIS) in Basle, which at the height of the debt crisis in 1982/3 provided interim aid several times to heavily-indebted Third World countries such as Brazil, Mexico and Argentina as well as to Hungary and Yugoslavia, never at any time looked like establishing itself as an alternative to the IMF. As the central banks' bank, the BIS intervened because the negotiations between the IMF and the debtor countries were dragging on and the threat of the debtor countries becoming insolvent conjured up fears of the breakdown of the international banking system. The BIS will only provide similar aid again if the international financial system is in acute danger (NZZ, 3 December 1983).

Nor is the Institute for International Finance (IIF), founded by major banks at the beginning of 1983, likely to take on the mantle of the IMF, despite being hailed by the *Financial Times* (28 October 1982) as a 'commercial IMF'. With its small staff of 35 and its budget of US$4 million in 1984, it will at best be able to fulfil its statutory function of gathering and analysing data so as to provide a kind of early warning system for debt crises in debtor countries.[15]

The IMF will continue to play a central part in the solution of debt crises in the 1980s, if only because creditor countries and banks are not prepared to dispense with its disciplinary function.[16] It absolves them of the need to intervene themselves to defend their own interests. At the same time, its comparatively small loans pose no real threat to the banks' business. Up to now, however, the financial policeman, with its rigid austerity programmes, has proved incapable of carrying out its essential task — of stabilising the economies of Third World debtor countries and thereby enabling them to repay their debts in the long term. Short-term economic stabilisation is achieved at the cost of social and political destabilisation. After a brief period of apparent recovery the economic crisis sets in again — often more drastically than before.

The industrial nations are gradually beginning to realise that these destabilising stabilisation policies not only harm the debtor countries but also run counter to the long-term interests of the creditors. Henry Kissinger has complained that IMF conditions often led to 'a cure that is worse than the disease', because they can 'create instability' and 'lead to revolutionary conditions' (*Executive Intelligence Review*, 5 October 1982, p. 51).

The failure of the terms traditionally imposed by the IMF is not, however, an argument in favour of granting loans with no strings attached. It is highly doubtful that loans 'without strings' would be used to solve the structural problems behind debt crises. Furthermore, a 'self-service' fund — a danger against which bankers sometimes feel impelled to warn — would no longer give debtors the seal of creditworthiness which they require. The comparatively small IMF loans would no longer give them access to further sources of credit.

In order to be rational and effective — taking into account the interests both of debtors and creditors — terms would have to aim not only at the manipulation of macro-economic data but the reduction of structural defects in the developing countries. Terms for a stabilisation policy truly worthy of the name would have to contain economic, social and political reforms geared to the situation of the debtor country. Such reforms would break through the crisis-ridden dynamism of the economy and society and guarantee the satisfaction of the basic needs of all sections of the population. Only policies which achieve an (undoubtedly necessary) stabilisation of the balance of payments as well as development can claim to have attacked the root causes of permanent indebtedness and to have restored these countries' long-term ability to repay their debts. We therefore argue in favour of *development-related conditionality* for IMF loans. This is realistic because it takes into account the creditors' interest in the long-term stabilisation of the debtors' economies. And it is reasonable because it recognises that in view of their deformed socio-economic structures these countries also need help from outside if they are to overcome their debt crises.[17]

There is no doubt that development-related conditionality would work out as more interventionist in nature for the governments of developing countries than traditional IMF terms which have been related primarily to monetary goals. It would not only contain more detailed terms than in the past, it would also restrict the mechanisms of self-privilege by the ruling classes if such a restriction appeared necessary for development. The obvious objection is that this conditionality is paternalistic, infringes the sovereign rights of debtor countries and is therefore not compatible with the Fund's statutes, which commit it to strict political neutrality. But experience shows that IMF loan policies often infringe on debtor countries' sovereignty — one need only cite spectacular examples such as Zaire in 1978/9, when an international finance expert was made *de facto* head of the Central Bank at the IMF's behest or Haiti in 1982, where the Fund appointed a member of the World Bank staff as Minister of Finance. The IMF's range of stabilisation measures — even though the terms are strictly monetary — always have profound economic, social and political effects on the situation in debtor countries. The concept of development-related conditionality would merely require the IMF to acknowledge the political impact of its terms, to admit that its practice is already interventionist and to reform its catalogue of conditions in such a way as to combine adjustment with development.

Making loans conditional on the implementation of economic, social and political reforms would not be a fundamental innovation in international financial relations: already in 1961, the USA, alarmed by the Cuban revolution, decided to tie its economic and capital aid within the framework of the 'Alliance for Progress' with Latin American countries to a number of political reforms. The aid-receiving countries were urged to democratise their institutions, private enterprise was to be encouraged and the health, education and above all the agricultural systems were to be reformed.[18] In addition to this the World Bank has been running a loans programme since the mid-1970s designed to help small farmers and to encourage governments to introduce agricultural reforms and reduce discrimination against agriculture.

But a new, development-related conditionality would scarcely rescue the Fund from the cross-fire of Third World criticism, especially if these new policies conflicted with the interests of the ruling classes. Only a comprehensive democratisation of the IMF would invalidate this criticism and increase the legitimacy of its interventions. Two possible solutions present themselves here. One would be to give the developing countries more votes and so to involve them more than hitherto in decision-making processes, thus ensuring more commitment to the Fund's policies. The other would be to include all relevant social groups in the debtor country in the negotiations on a stabilisation programme and then to publish the results with analyses of their possible effects. This would protect the country against excessive demands by the IMF and guarantee that governments did not unload the burdens of the programme onto the poorest sections of the population.

The egalitarian aspect of vote calculation in the IMF — every country has 250 basic votes regardless of its quota[19] — has been eroded by successive quota-increases. When the IMF was founded, basic votes made up 11.5% of overall votes. After the eighth revision of quotas, this has dropped to 4%. Because of their comparatively low quotas, the voting power of individual developing countries, and thus their influence on decisions, has declined steadily. It would therefore appear reasonable to increase the basic votes at least sufficiently to restore them to their original level. Jeker (1978, p. 223) proposes that basic votes should be increased to 15% of the total and not allowed to fall below this level. This ought to be acceptable to the industrial countries as it would not affect their blocking minority. A more radical move would be to revise the formula on which the quotas are established. This formula takes into account variables such as national income, foreign-exchange reserves, fluctuations in external trade and export dependency, giving each of these factors different weightings. As national income scarcely seems a relevant criterion for establishing the amount of a loan when a country has payments problems this factor ought to be replaced by export income fluctuation. This change would give the Third World — which is especially hard hit by fluctuations in export earnings because of the instability of world raw-materials markets — higher quotas and therefore more votes.[20]

The involvement of all relevant social groups in the debtor country in negotiations on a stabilisation programme is at least as important as a means of ensuring greater influence for developing countries in IMF decisions. A political consensus on the programme is only likely to be achieved if the recommended measures are publicly debated and the various social groups have an opportunity to ensure that their interests are taken into account in the stabilisation programme.[21] This practice would also help to ensure that interests of the lower classes were not sacrificed to those of the state classes and the bourgeoisie. The latter goal would not necessarily be guaranteed by the involvement of political parties, churches, trade unions and farmers' organisations because in most developing countries the lower classes are virtually completely unorganised and scarcely have an opportunity to articulate their interests. The marginalised urban and rural classes on whom the burdens of stabilisation policies have to date mostly been unloaded will scarcely be able to speak out even if the structure of the IMF is reformed. The only conceivable corrective here would be world public opinion, which could name the victims and the beneficiaries of the measures, denounce the self-privileging tendencies of the politically dominant classes and discuss the effects which the IMF's conditions would have on development. If negotiations with the IMF were held in public the debtor country would also be protected against excessive terms — those not compatible with development-related conditionality.

Conditionality would be called development-related if it not only corrected specific IMF conditions but also led to an abandonment of the idea implicit in the Fund's stabilisation programme: the idea that the 'streamlining' of the economy, export orientation and redistribution of income in favour of the privileged provide the basis for lasting economic growth, from which sooner or later benefits will trickle through to the poor in the form of welfare. The new conditionality would have to follow developmental guidelines which recognise that the debt crisis in the Third World will only be finally solved when the development crisis which has caused it has been overcome. The historical experience of today's industrialised countries proves that development can only be achieved by the opening up of domestic economic structures, close connections between agricultural and industrial production and domestic mass production based on a widely distributed variety of domestic demand. Minimum levels of self-reliance in the fields of technology, education and research are just as essential as a democratisation of society enabling the underprivileged to articulate their interests and for example an agricultural reform to guarantee self-sufficiency in food supply. Conditionality would strive for the diversification of export trade to prevent sudden world market developments causing financial ruin overnight. Another aim would be to rescue the export sector from its enclave existence and integrate it into the workings of the domestic economy (see Chapter 1).

To establish the foundations of such self-sustaining economies, IMF stabilisation policies ought to aim to gear the production apparatus of debtor countries to production for mass domestic demand. Orientation towards basic needs[22] — laid down in the United Nations Charter of Human Rights and accepted, however half-heartedly, as a basic principle by the World Bank (Tetzlaff, 1980, pp. 1ff.) — should be made a principle of reformed conditionality.

The state will have to play a leading role in planning and directing the economy if stabilisation policies oriented towards basic needs are to be successful.[23] As the majority of people in the Third World live on the land, agriculture should be given priority in development policy. Labour-intensive, technologically uncomplicated small-holder modes of production and the setting up of appropriate marketing structures would be essential components of any conditionality oriented towards basic needs. The main goal of agricultural policy would be self-sufficiency, and the process of industrialisation would have to be subordinated to this objective. Domestic economic cycles would thus be created not by the production of luxury goods and of arms but by the processing of agricultural products and the creation of the necessary production inputs. This would also reduce dependence on imports (food, consumer goods, investment goods) and with it the pressure to export or to raise foreign loans.[24]

Policies aimed at the satisfaction of basic needs are incompatible with the sudden cutback in production and restriction of demand which deflationist IMF therapies usually bring in their train. Expansionist stabilisation policies would take the place of these disastrous recession policies. Such policies would widen the range of goods and services, increase exports or replace imports and thus improve the balance of payments on a higher level. Only a growth strategy would shift the productive apparatus towards the production for mass demand — the only measure by which the satisfaction of basic needs can be achieved.[25]

Development-oriented conditionality — in contrast to the IMF's traditional therapy, which is uniform, with elements differing only in degree — would take account of specific conditions in debtor countries. It would have to consider the composition of imports and exports, the size of the domestic market and the degree of economic concentration, as well as the economy's capacity to react to economic measures. It would also have to look at such factors as per capita income, the development of real wages, the administrative and planning capacities of the state and the political support the government could expect in the implementation of certain measures (Helleiner, 1983, pp. 351f.).

It is obvious that an expansionist stabilisation strategy involving the restructuring of the production apparatus could not bear fruit in the time span normally allowed. In the short and medium term, an increased inflow of foreign capital would be necessary to prevent the strategy failing before sufficient domestic capital could be mobilised.[26] In many cases the level of foreign debt would rise at first, until the establishment of domestic cycles led to a self-sustaining development with low levels of debt.[27] During this phase the IMF — alongside private capital (from banks) and public capital (in the form of development aid) — would have to make a substantial contribution from its own funds to the stabilisation and development financing of the debtor country. This would only be possible if quotas were substantially increased. Finally, interest-rates and repayment deadlines for IMF loans would have to be managed more flexibly to ensure that the burden of debt-servicing did not ruin positive developments at their inception.

Satisfaction of basic needs is the central aspect of a reformed adjustment policy in which stabilisation would have to be coupled with development. In 1980 the US Congress instructed the US Executive Director of the IMF to pursue such a policy. But so far this has not led to any change in IMF conditionality.[28] The performance criteria of a development-oriented conditionality would have to be related to the satisfaction of basic needs. They would no longer be restricted to a few macro-economic variables (such as domestic credit, money supply and foreign indebtedness).

In defence of traditional performance criteria, the IMF argues that the data required are relatively easy to measure and readily available and provide objective information on the state of the economy and thus of the success of stabilisation. It adds that control of these variables is easily possible and their manipulation is an effective method of stabilisation. Furthermore, the Fund takes the view that the performance criteria are as it were a guarantee of the sovereign economic decisions by governments, who can and must decide themselves on where, for example, cuts must be made.[29]

The macro-economic data used as performance criteria do not, however, in developing countries, have the degree of precision and objectivity which the Fund attributes to them. They cannot be measured with the necessary speed. Wishful thinking, speculation and chance are important ingredients in data which the IMF claims to be scientifically substantiated and objective (Jeker, 1980, p. 47; Daniel, 1981, pp. 31ff.; Dell, 1982, p. 610).

Not even a reformed conditionality would be able to dispense with the formulation of goals which the debtor countries would be expected to reach within a certain period. But in establishing performance criteria for a development-oriented conditionality, the fixation on data which claim precision and objectivity that they do not really possess would have to be abandoned. This does not mean that traditional criteria would be irrelevant. They would still have a role to play but they would indicate general directions in which the economy ought to be moving rather than economic targets that had to be met down to the last decimal point. Performance criteria would continue to be fixed, but would be subject to continual revision within the programme, depending also on the development of other variables.

These other variables would be performance criteria designed to measure improvements in the satisfaction of basic needs. One of the merits of the World Bank Structural Adjustment Programme is that it includes targets such as an increase in food production, improvement of administrative capacity and diversification of export production among its performance criteria (see Chapter 4). A reformed IMF conditionality would take up and extend the range of these targets but would not subordinate them to rigid deflation therapies as is the practice with the granting of Structural Adjustment Loans. These targets would instead be guidelines from which micro-economic as well as macro-economic variables could be derived. They would make possible not only overall economic control but also regional and sectoral control of an expansive stabilisation and development strategy.[30]

With the aid of these instruments the IMF's deflationary policies could be abandoned and production- and demand-stimulating policies could be introduced.[31] This does not mean that a bundle of a priori variables should be put together and applied indiscriminately to every country. The main objective would be to break with the uniform stabilisation programmes to date and to formulate performance criteria which take into account the specific causes of development deficits.

Although the performance criteria of developmental conditionality would be far more concrete about specific measures than previous criteria, they would have to respect the political goals of the debtor country and accept its chosen development model as a framework for the working-out of IMF terms — assuming of course that the goals of the government did not conflict with the general consensus on development. To include basic needs-related performance criteria in stabilisation policy, no fundamental changes would have to be made in the laws governing IMF conditionality. In Article 4 of the New Guidelines for the Use of Fund Resources in the Credit Tranches the IMF is required to 'pay due regard to the domestic social and political objectives, the economic priorities and the circumstances of members, including the causes of their balance of payments problems.' Admittedly Article 9 of the Guidelines does state that performance criteria should 'normally' be macro-economic variables, but it adds that — in exceptional cases — additional criteria necessary to achieve the goals formulated in the IMF agreement can be introduced.[32] These goals include 'the promotion and maintenance of a high level of employment and real income' and the 'development of the production potential of all members' (Art.I, 2).

Performance criteria related to basic needs ought, if precise targets could not be defined, to specify development objectives. These could then be correlated with other performance criteria and precisely defined in the course of the stabilisation programme. Performance criteria would be laid down which committed governments to take — or to refrain from taking — certain measures. The imperatives of development related to basic needs and designed to establish internal coherent economic structures, encourage diversification of exports, independent development of technology and democratisation of society, would therefore suggest the following performance criteria (the list does not claim to be exhaustive):

● *Self-sufficiency in food*: in order to increase the self-supplying capacity of the debtor countries and thus to save foreign exchange on food imports, targets could be fixed for food production (or if necessary for certain products). Increases in government-fixed producer prices, the development of marketing structures, easier access to seed and fertilisers, more favourable loans and better expert advice for farmers would be among the variables which would stimulate agricultural production.

● *Mass demand*: mass demand by consumers with a high level of purchasing power is the basis of a stabilisation strategy oriented towards basic needs. Such demand can be stimulated only by agricultural and industrial production geared towards self-sufficiency. Performance criteria would have to be so designed as to create work and income for an increasing proportion of those capable of gainful employment. This would as a rule tend to favour a labour-intensive production technology, with ploughs being preferred to tractors in agriculture, for example. As mass demand depends on a broad distribution of income, this too should be made a performance criterion. More effective methods of tax-gathering and/or the reform of taxation systems which hitherto favoured the wealthy would be steps in this direction and could be made into performance criteria.

● *Basic needs-oriented investment*: productive investment leading to qualitative growth is required if the production apparatus is to be restructured towards the creation of mass demand. Performance criteria could be established for investment on the basis of whether it boosts employment, develops agricultural production and brings about industrialisation. This should be aimed at the processing of agricultural production and the production of pre-products and simple means of production for agriculture.[33] All investments financed from foreign loans would be expected, in the medium term, to bring in or to save at least the amount of foreign exchange by which they increased the burden of debt servicing.[34]

● *Selective world market integration*: it will as a rule only be possible to establish internal coherent economic structures if the nature and the degree of the debtor country's world market integration is changed. Given the present international division of labour and level of world market integration, uncoupling from the world market is not realistic. It would therefore be necessary to examine the areas in which export production is developmentally worthwhile and to work out which imports could be cut back without endangering the development of internal economic structures. Variables here could be the relation of imports and exports to GDP, which would gradually have to be reduced to a developmentally acceptable level. Other performance criteria would be: diversification of export production, as an insurance against abrupt drops in income, and the reduction of import dependence in the food, energy, consumption and/or investment-goods sectors. The primary aims would be a medium-term elimination of the balance-of-payments deficit and the limitation of the burden of debt-servicing to an acceptable level.

● *Socio-political and institutional reforms*: the key element in this strategy – the re-structuring of the production apparatus towards stabilisation and development policies geared to basic needs – can generally be achieved only if it is accompanied by socio-political and institutional reforms. In many cases the economic targets selected as performance criteria will only be reached if production-inhibiting landowning structures are reformed; if the tax system is radically re-structured and a more just distribution of income is achieved; if reforms are introduced to stop mismanagement, corruption and personal privilege and to make state enterprises and public administration more efficient. The World Bank's Structural Adjustment Programmes have shown that it is possible to include such reforms in conditions packages. The task is therefore to develop these first positive steps and to embed them into the basic needs-oriented development concept.

When performance criteria are being formulated, the specific political balance of power in the debtor countries will also have to be considered – in contrast with IMF practice to date. A state-class cannot be expected to introduce reforms which would deprive them of their power-base overnight. A government whose socio-political base is the agricultural bourgeoisie cannot be expected to introduce radical agrarian reforms from one day to the next. Only a conditionality which takes into account the economic, social and political obstacles to the implementation of measures oriented to basic needs, a conditionality which attempts to overcome the self-blocking structures in the developing countries *gradually*, can claim to be combining stabilisation with development. It is quite clear that such a concept cannot contain measures which — even temporarily — reduce the satisfaction of basic needs and load the burdens onto those social groups least responsible for the debt crisis. Development-oriented conditionality means aiming for changes which are realistic in the given political and social constellation in the debtor country; changes which at the same time open up long-term development options. This postulate also means using conditionality to strengthen the social and political forces which could become the driving forces behind development.

A development-oriented conditionality could not dispense with policies designed to achieve a healthy balance of payments and to limit budgetary deficits — goals which the IMF has up to now given precedence over all others, arguing that continuing budgetary deficits aggravate inflation, revalue national currencies, put the balance of payments into the red and thus provoke debt crises.[35] The traditional instruments of IMF policy (as well as the new performance criteria) would therefore have to fulfil the postulates of a development strategy oriented towards basic needs; but at the same time the strategy would seek to achieve a sound balance of payments and a limitation of budget deficits.

A healthy balance of payments cannot be achieved in the medium term if a currency is grossly over-valued. Devaluation would therefore be an element even in a reformed conditionality;[36] but shock therapies which put the satisfaction of basic needs at risk would have to be avoided. The introduction of multiple rates of exchange — a measure which the IMF has accepted in a number of exceptional cases — can be an appropriate response. It allows for the fact that devaluations have a different effect on the competitiveness of raw materials and manufactured goods. It also acknowledges that price rises for indispensable products not replaceable by domestic production (such as medicines) can damage the economy.[37]

Import duties and export subsidies could also be introduced as alternatives or complementary measures alongside multiple exchange rates, provided that such measures were not abused by corrupt state-classes. Import duties and licences, which the IMF has up to now rejected as legitimate instruments of foreign trade policy, can be an appropriate means of protecting domestic sectors from over-powerful world market competition. Exchange controls could also be introduced and applied pragmatically according to administrative capacities and economic requirements in order to prevent an undesirable capital outflow through the transfer of profits and capital flight. These measures ought not to be condemned as sins against the market economy, though traditional IMF ideology has always regarded them as such. Quantitative targets could also be set for the level of foreign-exchange reserves and the increase in foreign indebtedness (as in the traditional IMF package of terms); but they would be points of reference as opposed to mandatory goals.

Limitation of budgetary deficits may make an expansionist stabilisation strategy difficult; but it does not make it impossible. In most state budgets in the Third World there are ways of increasing income by means of tax reforms and better methods of tax collection. Expenditure can also be re-structured in such a way as to finance development oriented towards basic needs. Savings could be made, for example, in often excessive military budgets, in the case of large-scale projects which do not contribute enough to development and in state enterprises which in the long run are not profitable in development terms.[38] Even subsidies — the favourite target for IMF cuts to date — would not be sacrosanct, yet the reduction of subsidies for basic goods ought not to exceed the level by which real incomes rise or the level at which locally produced basic goods (especially foods) are available at reasonable prices and in sufficient quantities.

Despite all budgetary imperatives, it may even be necessary to introduce new subsidies in the stabilisation programme, to soften the impact on the lower classes of price rises caused by devaluation or price liberalisation. The decontrolling of frozen prices — a policy relentlessly pursued by the IMF to date — ought not to be taboo even in a concept of developmental conditionality, but price liberalisations must always be judged in terms of whether or not they provide stimuli to increase production. The IMF regards cuts in real wages achieved by means of decontrolling and sometimes of additional wage guidelines as an essential precondition of successful stabilisation. By contrast, in an expansionist stabilisation strategy, real wages would have to be index-linked to price rises (at least) because only consumers with money to spend can produce the levels of demand necessary for a lasting increase in production.

In the sphere of wages, state control is generally only to be recommended in the fixing of minimum wages. State price and import controls are desirable if they reach the development and stabilisation goal faster than the market does (provided no excessive friction loss is caused, for example by corruption and the creation of a black market). In principle, the aim should be to find the mix of market economy and state intervention which seems appropriate in each specific case, without fixation on one or the other philosophy; at the same time the mode of development the debtor state itself has chosen must be respected as far as possible.

Deficit financing of the state budget will as a rule be indispensable, particularly in the transitional phase in which the transformation of the production apparatus has to be financed; expenditure at this stage will still exceed income. State money-supply, loan and interest-rate policies — for which quantitative guidelines would be fixed — would thus have to be carefully balanced. On the one hand, they would have to ensure that basic-needs-oriented investments could be adequately financed. On the other, they would have to prevent a wave of inflation which would make medium-term restoration of a sound balance of payments unattainable.

There is no doubt that a development-oriented stabilisation policy would need more room for financial manoeuvre than most debtor countries today possess. High debt-service repayments force them to neglect development-oriented measures because the need to earn foreign exchange takes precedence. Only when a debtor country falls into arrears on payments do the creditor countries allow reschedulings. After a short breather, which is virtually useless for development purposes, the debtor country is then confronted with even higher debt-service commitments for the future. Creditors (banks, export insurers, national and international development agencies), whose loan allocation policies are in many cases partly responsible for crises, ought therefore to be made co-liable for the costs of solving the crisis. In fact, this would be an essential complement to a reformed stabilisation policy.[39] Whatever the institutional and technical precautions to be taken, even if the traditional rescheduling procedure remained in force, the crucial change in such a reformed IMF policy would be that the interests of the creditors would no longer be played off against those of the debtor country, and in particular of its most impoverished classes.

This would mean that in rescheduling negotiations the IMF would have to oppose the creditors' principle that rescheduling should be strictly distinguished from development aid and therefore offered at commercial terms. IMF mediation in the past has again and again demonstrated how dependent the creditor countries are on its expertise and on its judgment of the economic capacity of the debtor country. This shows that the IMF is most definitely in a position to make creditors co-liable and to give debtor countries room for manoeuvre and for development. The Fund should insist on more favourable rescheduling conditions being granted by public and private creditors — especially lower moratorium rates of interest but also later repayment deadlines, more years without repayment on the principal and if necessary partial remission of debts.[40] The IMF would at last justify its claim to be an 'honest broker' between debtors and creditors. And the interests of the creditors would not be ignored: the Fund would help them to overcome their short-sighted individual interest in rapid repayment and thus educate them to realise that their common interest is in the long-term stabilisation and thus capacity to repay of developing countries' economies. For only with stably developing economies can economic relations be maintained and sound monetary and financial relations be guaranteed in the long term.

The above reflections on development-oriented stabilisation policies can be summarised as follows:

● *Duty to Adjust for Surplus Countries*: The current practice whereby the deficit countries alone, the weakest members of the international community, are forced to adjust would be replaced by a mechanism whereby surplus countries would also be forced to adjust. What applies to countries with structural deficits should also apply to countries with structural surpluses: a healthy balance of payments cannot be achieved abruptly. Reasonable periods of time are required to carry out structural changes in the economy.

● *Extension of the Compensatory Financing Facility*: The balance-of-payments surpluses of one group of countries would be used to finance the deficits of the other group whenever deficits are (partly) attributable to causes which are beyond the control of the deficit country concerned: deterioration of the terms of trade, reductions in exports because of natural disasters, a fall in demand for imports in industrial countries, protectionist policies, high interest-rate policies by the United States. One possibility would be to pay part of the surpluses into the IMF's Compensatory Financing Facility to compensate for the loss of exports, at first completely, then in gradually reduced amounts. It is essential that deficit countries should in the long term adjust to changes in world market conditions.

● *Increase of the IMF's funds*: If the IMF is to fulfil its function of stabilising debtor countries' economies effectively in the long term, its funds must be substantially increased. It would be advisable not only to increase quotas substantially but to take up loans on private money markets and to allocate additional Special Drawing Rights.

● *Extending stabilisation programmes and repayment deadlines*: By creating the Extended Fund Facility, which is combined with a stabilisation programme lasting up to three years, the Fund recognised in principle that the structural causes of deficits in many countries cannot be remedied in the short term. In a reformed IMF, the length of stabilisation would be further extended, to five to ten years. To avoid the repayment of stabilisation loans bringing on the next crisis, repayment deadlines for IMF loans would be extended and the interest on these loans kept low.

● *Reform of IMF stabilisation programmes/development-oriented conditionality*: Conditions would continue to be attached to the granting of IMF loans. But they would be conditions which no longer sacrificed debtor countries' long-term development options to short-term manipulations of certain variables in the balance of payments. A reformed, development-oriented conditionality would contain terms designed to eliminate structural defects in deficit countries. Reformed stabilisation programmes, unlike traditional IMF stabilisation programmes, would be expansionist. Their central elements would be measures to gear the production apparatus to the satisfaction of mass demand, to establish domestic economic cycles and to improve the satisfaction of basic needs.

● *Democratisation of the IMF and of negotiations on stabilisation agreements*: To increase the acceptability of a reformed IMF stabilisation policy, the developing countries would be given more say in decision-making processes by increasing their voting rights. All social groups involved would participate in the negotiations, which would be held in public.

● *Reform of performance criteria*: Targets which the debtor country would be required to reach within a certain period would also be part of a development-oriented conditionality. The traditional macro-economic performance criteria would be retained, but would be used for orientation purposes rather than being mandatory. They would be complemented by variables relating to increases in food production, export diversification, investment oriented to basic needs and institutional reforms. Reformed performance criteria would respect the development path chosen by the country and translate the requirements for development-oriented stabilisation policies into concrete political targets. In determining performance criteria, the different situations in the debtor countries (including the political balance of power) would have to be taken into account. These measures would have to ensure that the costs of stabilisation programmes were not – as hitherto – unloaded onto social groups who are not responsible for the crisis.

● *Co-liability of creditors*: Financial room for manoeuvre to make the necessary structural changes is an indispensable precondition for development-oriented stabilisation policy. Creditors — who are often co-responsible for crises — would also be required to make their contribution.

As mediator in rescheduling negotiations the IMF would ensure that the agreements which the debtor countries reached with public and private creditors did not force them to earn foreign exchange for debt-servicing to an extent which was incompatible with long-term, basic needs-oriented development policy.

Notes

1. Brazilian economist Celso Furtado concluded that Brazil would definitely not benefit from a debt repudiation (*South*, December 1982, p. 65).

2. In 1984, representatives of the Latin American debtor countries met at a number of conferences to discuss such a strategy but the result was meagre (Quito, February 1984; Cartagena, June 1984; Mar del Plata, September 1984). In February 1985, they gathered in Santo Domingo to coordinate their position on holding a summit with the industrial countries to consider the rescheduling of their debts. Further debtor conferences were held in summer 1985 in Lima and Havana.

3. European banking chief Yassukuvich said in an interview: 'I regard a debt repudiation as highly unlikely. It would completely cut off the country concerned from the rest of the world . . . it would be a siege economy. It would be virtual suicide for the country concerned.' (Ww, 15 July 1983, p. 56.) Meier-Preschany, former Chairman of the Dresdner Bank, replied in similar terms to questions about the 'danger of a debtor cartel': 'I don't think it's likely. There has been pressure to make such a move but as a rule the people there are not so different from us in their philosophy.' (Ww, 15 July 1983, p. 61.)

4. Many of the proposals to relieve the banks of their problem loans must be seen against the background of US legislation which prescribes that loans on which no interest has been paid 60 or 90 days after it is due must be classified as 'dishonoured' and therefore written off.

5. To prevent the irresponsible granting of credits in future, Hankel suggests that the European market should be brought under state control.

6. The profits of the West German Deutsche Bank, Dresdner Bank and Commerzbank rose by 35.4%, 104% and 228.6% respectively from October 1981 to October 1983 (Zeitschrift für das gesamte Kreditwesen, 1/1984, p. 5).

7. A long-term strategy would be unpromising if it ignored the huge budget and current account deficits of the USA. Not only do high interest rates and the overvaluation of the dollar (both of which are consequences of these deficits) intolerably increase the debt-service burden of the Third World but they also suck in capital from all over the world, thus depriving debtor countries of scarce foreign exchange. The impending bankruptcy of major debtors can lead to heavy disturbances of the international monetary and finance system. This can only be prevented if the USA adjusts to its deficits (e.g. by curbing military expenditure).

8. It can be argued that surpluses always occur whenever economies have a limited import capacity compared to their capacity to conquer export markets. The deficits in the balance of payments of debtor countries therefore reflect the structures of surplus economies. Even though this explanation does not apply in all cases, it does at least underline how one-sided the IMF perspective is – a

perspective which always attributes deficits to excessive demand in the debtor countries – except for the case of drops in raw materials prices, which entitle a country to apply for Compensatory Financing Facility loans.

9. On behalf of the developing countries, the Pakistani Minister of Finance, Ghulam Ishaq Khan complained at the 1982 annual meeting of the IMF that creditor countries are not forced to reduce their balance-of-payments surpluses: 'The fatal flaw in the IMF operations at the moment is that despite its formal mandate for surveillance it is in no position to place any conditionality on the surplus countries and as such is obliged to place the entire burden of adjustment on the borrowing developing countries.' (IMF, *Summary Proceedings 1982*, p. 187.)

10. Herrmann (1983) worked out that payments from this facility generally did not take place until four months after the end of the year in which the drop in exports occurred.

11. Williamson (1982, p. 16) proposes three graduated drawing facilities over three years – 100% of the externally caused deficit in the first, 75% in the second and 50% in the third. If no adjustment has occurred by the fourth year, the country should be forced to conclude an IMF stabilisation programme.

12. STABEX is a system for stabilising export earnings. It grants automatic compensatory payments to 57 African, Caribbean and Pacific countries associated with the EEC through the Lomé Agreement when the sales of certain products which earn a high proportion of foreign exchange drop below a certain level. STABEX funds do not have to be repaid by the 35 poorest developing countries; for the other countries STABEX loans are interest-free.

13. It is argued that the IMF should not take up loans on the capital markets because the banks would withdraw from their high-risk transactions with the Third World and would only lend to the IMF as a 'safe' customer. Critics also point out that by taking up loans on the capital markets the IMF could become dependent on the banks and would therefore run the risk of losing its reputation as a crisis manager independent of private interests. (For a discussion of whether the IMF should use private capital markets for re-financing purposes see Gold, 1980, pp. 41ff.; Reich, 1977, pp. 40ff.; Konrad, 1982; Killick 1984, p. 29).

14. It is highly doubtful whether such a fund could solve the fundamental structural problems behind debt crises or even bring the debt problem under control, unless the granting of funds were tied to conditions.

15. Not even this can be guaranteed. The inclination of the 180 member banks to provide all relevant and available data is – for obvious reasons of competition – unlikely to be very great.

The idea of establishing the institute was first mooted in 1982 when, faced with the impending crisis among major debtor countries, the banks were alarmed to discover that no reliable data were available (especially for short-term debts) which would provide a solid basis for decisions on future business transactions. The founding of the IIF was intended to remedy this deficiency. In October 1983, a Japanese counterpart, the 'Japan Centre for International Finance' was founded by Japanese banks (Wels, 1983).

16. Asked which international institution played a key role in solving the debt crisis, Meyer-Preschany, former director of the Dresdner Bank replied: 'The IMF, for the simple reason that it alone can impose discipline.' (Ww, 15 July 1983, p. 61.) Guth, spokesman of the Deutsche Bank board, concedes that the financial system must do more justice to the problems of developing

countries. 'The central role of the IMF' says Guth 'must be brought to bear more powerfully than in the seventies' (FAZ, 27 September 1983).

17. Our proposals therefore differ from those of Sánchez Arnau, for example, which essentially support Third World demands for more loans on more favourable terms.

18. Measures designed to prevent the 'Cubanisation' of Latin America in fact paved the way for the expansion of US capital and turned out to be economic aid to military dictatorships.

19. This is calculated on the basis of 100,000 SDR = 1 vote.

20. It should be noted that a change in the calculation formula could involve a reduction in the Fund's finances unless – as we suggest – it went hand in hand with a general increase in quotas. As a change in the quota automatically involves a change in the sum each country pays to the IMF, a reform would leave the IMF with less 'hard' currency (from the industrial countries) and more 'soft' currency (from the developing countries) than before. This mechanism could be avoided if the calculation of voting rights were uncoupled from the size of quotas.

21. In Argentina, the trade unions lamented in mid-1985 that they had not been consulted in working out the IMF programme (NZZ, 5 July 1985). In Ghana, the TUC went further, in February 1985, by demanding to be involved in negotiating agreements with the IMF and the World Bank alongside government negotiators (WA, 1 April 1985, p. 620).

22. The aims of the basic needs strategy are to eliminate absolute poverty in the world and to enable the poor in the Third World to live in conditions fit for human beings. The question of how precisely basic needs can be defined remains controversial (and this is reflected in the literature). It is generally agreed, however, that food, clothing, accommodation and medical care are absolutely essential needs (Nuscheler, 1982).

23. It must be acknowledged that state intervention in developing countries is often dysfunctional. Bureaucracy, mismanagement, corruption and self-privileging by state-classes frequently hinder development policy geared towards basic needs. But given the absence or the weakness of the national bourgeoisies who own the means of production or invest productively in Africa, Asia and Latin America, and in view of the development-impeding effects of a pure market economy, the state appears to be the only institution in the Third World economies capable of initiating the development and restructuring of the production apparatus towards production for mass demand (Hanisch/Tetzlaff, 1981, p. 16; Elsenhans, 1982, pp. 169ff.).

24. The question of how to re-structure the production apparatus and what concrete form agricultural and industrial policy should take can only be decided in each specific case and will depend on the level of development in the debtor country. Different criteria would apply to newly industrialising countries with well-developed consumer- and investment-goods industries and to countries with less developed or undeveloped industries. But in principle the development of agriculture is as important for Brazil as it is for Bolivia or Bangladesh.

25. Killick (1984) argues the need for a strategy of 'adjustment with growth' which aims to re-orient the production apparatus by means of supply-oriented measures and to achieve a balance in foreign trade on a higher level of economic activity. Satisfaction of basic needs is not the major objective of these authors. In fact they regard it more as a by-product of export-led economic

recovery which would minimise the social costs of 'adjustment' and allow the poor to benefit from improved welfare.

26. Killick et al. (1984, p. 274) and Killick/Sutton (1982, pp. 69f.) also argue, in view of experience with traditional IMF stabilisation programmes, for longer adjustment periods and an increased inflow of foreign capital.

27. Development with low debt levels does not necessarily mean that foreign indebtedness is reduced in absolute terms. For indebtedness to be considered 'low', it must drop compared to GDP; the debt-service ratio, which reflects the pressure to earn foreign exchange, must also be reduced. In absolute terms, the level of debt may in fact rise.

28. As long ago as 1978, in the era of President Carter's human rights policies, Congress tied the granting of US funds for the Supplementary Financing Facility to a US amendment calling on the US Executive Director to ensure that IMF terms encouraged investment and job-creation in areas which satisfied basic demands. The US Congress also called on the American IMF governor to produce an annual report on the impact of IMF programmes on the satisfaction of basic needs. The 1978 rider referred only to IMF programmes financed from the funds of Supplementary Financing Facility. In 1980, when passing the seventh quota increase, Congress extended this stipulation to cover all facilities. US representatives in the IMF are there called upon to ensure that IMF credit agreements are extended beyond the three-year period and that stabilisation programmes take into account their impact on jobs, investment, real per capita income, the distribution of income and social programmes in order to minimise the negative effects on the satisfaction of basic needs. These riders have had next to no impact on political practice. Since President Reagan took up office in 1981 the IMF has taken less notice than ever of the postulate of the satisfaction of basic needs. The reports of the US IMF Governor have not been at all detailed or enlightening in this respect. During Congressional discussions on the eighth quota increase in 1983, the question of the satisfaction of basic needs played only a marginal part (Gerster, 1982, pp. 205ff., and 1982a, pp. 503ff.; Congressional Record, 4 August 1983,H. pp. 6590ff.; ICR 3/1983, pp. 25–7).

29. 'Decisions on the exact implementation of the measures are of course the sole responsibility of the government' (IMF, 1981, p. 2).

30. Killick et al. (1984, p. 272) stress the need for specific micro-economic measures designed to tackle bottlenecks in overall economic development. Dell/Lawrence (1980, p. 137), Sánchez-Arnau (1982, pp. 187ff.), and Pirzio-Biroli (1983, p. 148) all argue against micro-economic variables. They argue that the establishment of micro-economic variables conflicts with the IMF's commitment not to interfere with the sovereignty of member countries.

31. IMF representatives claim that measures to increase the range of goods supplied are already part of stabilisation programmes (Guitián, 1981a, p. 15). But in reality production-stimulating elements continue to play only a small part in demand-depressing IMF therapies.

32. Article 9 runs: 'Performance criteria will be limited to those that are necessary to evaluate implementation of the program with a view to ensuring the achievement of its objectives. Performance criteria will normally be confined to (i) macroeconomic variables, and (ii) those necessary to implement specific provisions of the Articles or policies adopted under them. Performance criteria may relate to other variables only in exceptional cases when they are essential for the effectiveness of the member's program because of their

macroeconomic impact.' (IMF Survey, 19 March 1979, 83)

33. As governments cannot control private investments, it is not possible to set certain goals as performance criteria for private investment. But a reduction of productive investment – apart from seasonal or technical reductions – can be interpreted as a sign that the expansion-oriented stabilisation strategy contains too many depressive elements and is failing to achieve one of its main objectives.

34. There will as a rule be no place in this concept for large-scale projects which do not create jobs, swallow up foreign exchange and have at best prestige value. In fact avoiding such misinvestments could itself constitute a performance criterion!

35. Griffith-Jones (1981), advisor to the Chilean Central Bank during the Allende era, rightly complains of the ignorance of the 'left' on these points and stresses the importance of a sound balance of payments and limitation of budgetary deficits in the economic and financial policies of socialist governments.

36. The degree of overvaluation and thus the amount by which the currency should be devalued is difficult to determine because different rates of exchange apply in the different sectors of the economy of Third World countries. These sectors are only loosely connected with one another. These different rates are reflected only in distorted form in the official rate of exchange. Katseli (1983, pp. 362ff.) recommends a slightly over-valued currency for a transitional period of development in which above-average levels of capital goods imports have to be financed.

37. Kaldor (1983, p. 36) says that 'a general exchange rate adjustment may be called for if, and only if, the labor cost per unit of output . . . of a country's main export product exceeds its world market price at the official rate of exchange.'

38. State enterprises which are in deficit can create an indispensable development push by providing services and pre-products for the reform of the production apparatus, which is why they should not be automatically sacrificed as part of the IMF's uncompromising policy of privatisation. Apart from their social function of providing employment, these enterprises assume an economic function which often is unable to be carried out by a merely 'embryonic entrepreneurial class. In the case of state enterprises which cannot fulfil this function or in the long term cost more than they earn, a decision based on micro- and macro-economic considerations would have to be made to improve efficiency, to privatise or, if necessary, to close the enterprise. The dismissals a closure would entail would have to be compensated for by investments to restructure the production apparatus and to create new jobs.

39. Funds for development finance would have to be increased considerably to prevent the burden of debt-servicing becoming a drag on the debtor country's development. Abbott (1979, pp. 247ff.) proposes that the debt-servicing repayments by developing countries on public loans should be collected in an account at the IMF or the World Bank and that these sums should then flow back to debtor countries in the form of development aid.

40. The rescheduling of government credits for Indonesia in 1970 underlined that rescheduling can create room for developmental manoeuvre (see p. 68).

Appendix 1

Debt Reschedulings of Official and Private Loans 1956–1985 (US$ millions)

	1956	—	1965	1966	1967	1968	1969	1970	1971	1972
Argentina	May 56 422	Jan 61 284	Oct 62 189	Jun 65 90						
Bangladesh										
Bolivia										
Brazil	May 61 407	Jul 64 216								
Cambodia										Jun 2 Oct 2
Central African Republic										
Chile				Feb 65 298						Apr 181
Colombia										
Costa Rica										
Cuba										
Dominican Republic										
Ecuador										
Gabon										
Ghana				Dec 106		Oct 79		Jul 19		
Guyana										
Honduras										
India						Mar 423			Jun 92	Mar 1
Indonesia				Dec 247	Oct 95	Oct 83		Apr 786		
Ivory Coast										
Jamaica										
Liberia										
Madagascar										
Malawi										

73	1974	1975	1976	1977	1978	1979	1980	1981	1982	1983	1984	1985
			970							Jan 6000	Dec 13400*	Jan 2100†
Jun n.a.												
								Apr 444		536		
										Nov 3800	5500	neg*
								Jun 55		Jul 13		
	Mar 509	May 230								Jul 4100		
												neg*
										Jan 107 Sep 1259		
										Dec 430	Jul 254† Dec 103*	
										660		neg†
										Jul 200 Oct 2150	Dec 4300*	neg†
				Jun 105								
Mar 200												
					29				14	24		
										122		
'3	Jun 194	Jun 157	May 169	Jul 110								
											May 275†	
					Jun 126			Mar 103		Jun 166	Jul 172†	
						Dec 30		Dec 25	27	Dec 25		Dec 30-40†
								Apr 142	Jul 103	Sep 195	Mar 160† Oct 180*	
										Sep 24	Oct 36† 57	

	1956	—	1965	1966	1967	1968	1969	1970	1971	1972
Mexico										
Morocco										
Mozambique										
Nicaragua										
Niger										
Nigeria										
Pakistan										May 234
Panama										
Peru							Sep 195 Nov 351			
Philippines										
Poland										
Rumania										
Senegal										
Sierra Leone										
Sudan										
Togo										
Turkey	May 59 442		Mar 65 220							
Uganda										
Uruguay										
Venezuela										
Yugoslavia										
Zaire										
Zambia										

Sources: OECD. 1982. *External Debt of Developing Countries, 1982 Survey*. December. Paris.
Weltbank, *Weltentwicklungsbericht 1983*, Washington D.C., August 1983.
World Bank, *Debt and the Developing World: Current Trends and Prospects*, Washington D.C.,
US General Accounting Office *US Development Efforts and Balance-of-Payments Problems in Develo
Countries*, (GAO/ID-83-13) Washington, February 14 1983.
IMF, *Recent Multilateral Debt Restructuring with Official and Bank Creditors,* (Occasional Paper N
Washington D.C., 1983.

73	1974	1975	1976	1977	1978	1979	1980	1981	1982	1983	1984	1985
											Jun 2000 Aug 22550	Sep 48600*
										Oct 1200		neg*
											Oct 225†	
						582	190	55				
										29	Dec 66†	
										Jul 1830		neg*
07	Jun 650							Jan 263				
												neg*
			Nov 420	821						Jul 450 May 2320	Feb 1500*	neg†
											Oct 1600*	neg†
								4300	4600	Aug 2600	1600*	neg†
									Jul 234 1544	May 195 572		
								Oct 77	Nov 84	Dec 81 92		Jan 100†
		Sep 39				Feb 37						
					Nov 373			Dec 638	Mar 174	Feb 550 Apr. n.v.		
					Jun 170	68			Feb 92	Apr 300 84	Jun n.a.†	
			May 1223		Jul 873	Jul 2640	Jul 3000	3100				
								Nov 27	Dec 10			
										Jul 170		
											Sep 20750*	
										Sep 3800	Mar 800† Nov 1400*	
	Jun 270	Jul 170 Dec 40			Dec 1040	Apr 402		Jul 574		Dec 1280†		
										May 320	Jul 200†	

aris Club (official creditors)
ondon or New York Club (bankers)
not available
negotiations

Appendix 2

Stand-by Arrangements (SBA), Extended Fund Facilities (EFF) and Compensatory Financing Facilities (CFF) 1952 to 1984 and Quotas (after 8th revision, November 1983)

Country	Quota (in m. SDRs)		Date of Approval	Amount (in m. SDRs)
Afghanistan	86.7	SBA	June 1965	6.75
		SBA	August 1966	8.00
		CFF	June 1968	4.80
		SBA	July 1968	7.00
		SBA	October 1969	12.00
		SBA	June 1973	10.00
		SBA	July 1975	8.50
Argentina	1.113.0	SBA	December 1958	75.00
		SBA	December 1959	100.00
		SBA	December 1960	100.00
		SBA	December 1961	100.00
		SBA	June 1962	100.00
		SBA	May 1967	125.00
		SBA	April 1968	125.00
		CFF	March 1972	64.00
		CFF	December 1975	110.00
		CFF	March 1976	110.00
		SBA	August 1976	260.00
		SBA	September 1977	159.50
		SBA	January 1983	1.500.00
		SBA	September 1984	1.419.00
		CFF	December 1984	275.00
Australia	1.619.2	SBA	May 1961	100.00
		CFF	July 1976	332.50
Bangladesh	287.5	CFF	December 1972	62.50
		SBA	June 1974	31.25
		SBA	July 1975	62.50
		CFF	August 1976	39.10
		SBA	July 1979	85.00
		EFF	December 1980	800.00

		CFF	February 1982	60.00
		SBA	March 1983	68.40
Barbados	34.1	CFF	January 1977	3.50
		CFF	October 1977	3.00
		SBA	October 1982	31.88
		CFF	October 1982	12.60
Belgium	2,080.4	SBA	June 1952	50.00
Belize	9.5	CFF	June 1983	3.60
		SBA	December 1984	7.13
Bolivia	90.7	SBA	November 1956	7.50
		SBA	December 1957	3.50
		SBA	May 1959	1.50
		SBA	July 1961	7.50
		SBA	August 1962	10.00
		SBA	September 1963	10.00
		SBA	September 1964	12.00
		SBA	September 1965	14.00
		SBA	December 1966	18.00
		SBA	December 1967	20.00
		SBA	January 1969	20.000
		SBA	January 1973	27.30
		CFF	July 1978	15.00
		SBA	February 1980	66.38
		CFF	January 1983	17.90
Brazil	1,461.3	SBA	June 1958	37.50
		SBA	May 1961	160.00
		CFF	June 1963	60.00
		SBA	January 1965	125.00
		SBA	February 1966	125.00
		SBA	February 1967	30.00
		SBA	April 1968	87.50
		SBA	April 1969	50.00
		SBA	February 1970	50.00
		SBA	February 1971	50.00
		SBA	March 1972	50.00
		CFF	December 1982	498.75
		EFF	March 1983	4,239.38
		CFF	November 1983	64.50
		CFF	May 1984	247.90
Burma	137.0	CFF	November 1967	7.50
		SBA	November 1969	12.00
		CFF	September 1971	6.50
		SBA	February 1973	13.50
		CFF	February 1974	15.00
		SBA	November 1974	31.50
		SBA	May 1977	35.00
		SBA	July 1978	30.00
		SBA	June 1981	27.00

		CFF	December 1982	25.60
		CFF	August 1983	29.15
Burundi	42.7	SBA	January 1965	4.00
		SBA	March 1966	5.00
		SBA	March 1967	6.00
		SBA	March 1968	6.00
		SBA	April 1969	4.00
		SBA	June 1970	1.50
		CFF	June 1970	2.50
		SBA	June 1976	6.50
		CFF	November 1979	9.50
Cameroon	92.7	CFF	July 1976	17.50
Central African	30.4	CFF	February 1976	5.10
Republic		SBA	February 1980	4.00
		CFF	January 1981	9.00
		SBA	April 1981	10.40
		SBA	April 1983	18.00
		SBA	July 1984	15.00
Chad	30.6	CFF	August 1976	6.50
		CFF	January 1981	7.10
Chile	440.5	SBA	April 1956	35.00
		SBA	April 1957	35.00
		SBA	April 1958	10.00
		SBA	April 1959	8.10
		SBA	February 1961	75.00
		SBA	January 1963	40.00
		SBA	February 1964	25.00
		SBA	January 1965	36.00
		SBA	March 1966	40.00
		SBA	March 1968	46.00
		SBA	April 1969	40.00
		CFF	December 1971	39.50
		CFF	December 1972	39.50
		SBA	January 1974	79.00
		SBA	March 1975	79.00
		CFF	August 1976	79.00
		SBA	January 1983	500.00
		CFF	January 1983	295.00
China	2.390.0	SBA	March 1981	450.00
Colombia	394.2	SBA	June 1957	25.00
		SBA	June 1958	15.00
		SBA	October 1959	41.25
		SBA	November 1960	75.00
		SBA	January 1962	10.00
		SBA	January 1963	52.50
		SBA	February 1964	10.00
		SBA	January 1966	36.50
		CFF	March 1967	18.90

		SBA	April 1967	60.00
		SBA	April 1968	33.50
		CFF	September 1968	1.90
		SBA	April 1969	33.25
		SBA	April 1970	38.50
		SBA	April 1971	38.00
		SBA	May 1972	40.00
		SBA	June 1973	20.00
Congo	37.3	SBA	January 1977	4.70
		CFF	February 1977	6.50
		SBA	April 1979	4.00
Costa Rica	84.1	SBA	October 1961	15.00
		SBA	December 1962	22.60
		SBA	February 1965	10.00
		SBA	March 1966	10.00
		SBA	August 1967	15.50
		SBA	July 1976	11.60
		CFF	October 1979	10.00
		SBA	March 1980	60.50
		EFF	June 1981	277.00
		SBA	December 1982	92.25
		CFF	September 1983	18.60
Cuba	—	SBA	December 1956	12.50
Cyprus	69.7	CFF	May 1976	13.00
		CFF	January 1979	9.90
		SBA	July 1980	8.50
Dominica	4.0	CFF	December 1979	0.95
		EFF	February 1981	8.55
		SBA	July 1984	1.40
Dominican Republic	112.1	SBA	December 1959	11.25
		SBA	August 1964	25.00
		CFF	December 1966	6.60
		CFF	September 1976	21.50
		CFF	January 1979	6.00
		CFF	September 1979	27.50
		CFF	May 1982	36.00
		EFF	January 1983	371.25
		CFF	January 1983	42.75
Ecuador	150.7	SBA	June 1961	10.00
		SBA	June 1962	5.00
		SBA	July 1963	6.00
		SBA	July 1964	13.00
		SBA	July 1965	32.00
		SBA	July 1966	13.00
		SBA	April 1969	18.00
		CFF	October 1969	6.25
		SBA	September 1970	22.00

		SBA	July 1972	16.50
		SBA	July 1983	157.50
		CFF	November 1983	85.40
Egypt	463.4	SBA	May 1962	42.40
		CFF	October 1963	16.00
		SBA	May 1964	40.00
		CFF	March 1968	23.00
		CFF	August 1973	47.00
		CFF	June 1976	94.00
		SBA	April 1977	125.00
		EFF	July 1979	600.00
El Salvador	89.0	SBA	October 1958	7.50
		SBA	October 1959	7.50
		SBA	October 1960	11.25
		SBA	July 1961	11.25
		SBA	September 1962	11.25
		SBA	September 1963	5.00
		SBA	October 1965	20.00
		SBA	December 1967	10.00
		SBA	July 1969	17.00
		CFF	December 1969	6.25
		SBA	December 1970	14.00
		SBA	September 1972	8.75
		SBA	June 1980	10.75
		SBA	July 1982	43.00
		CFF	July 1982	32.30
Equatorial Guinea	18.4	CFF	June 1980	6.40
		SBA	July 1980	5.50
		CFF	March 1981	4.70
Ethiopia	70.6	CFF	August 1979	18.00
		CFF	December 1979	18.00
		SBA	May 1981	68.00
Fiji	36.5	SBA	November 1974	3.25
		CFF	July 1977	6.25
		CFF	February 1982	13.25
Finland	574.9	SBA	December 1952	5.00
		SBA	March 1967	93.75
		SBA	June 1975	95.00
France	4,482.8	SBA	October 1956	262.50
		SBA	January 1958	131.25
		SBA	September 1969	985.00
Gabon	73.1	SBA	May 1978	15.00
		EFF	June 1980	34.00
Gambia	17.1	CFF	March 1977	3.50
		SBA	May 1977	2.53
		CFF	November 1978	4.50
		SBA	November 1979	1.60

		SBA	February 1982	16.90
		SBA	April 1984	12.83
Ghana	204.5	SBA	May 1966	36.40
		CFF	November 1966	17.25
		SBA	May 1967	25.00
		SBA	May 1968	12.00
		SBA	May 1969	5.00
		SBA	January 1979	53.00
		SBA	August 1983	238.50
		CFF	August 1983	120.50
		SBA	August 1984	180.00
		CFF	December 1984	58.20
Greece	399.9	CFF	September 1976	58.00
Grenada	6.0	SBA	September 1975	0.50
		SBA	June 1976	0.23
		SBA	November 1979	0.65
		CFF	April 1981	2.10
		SBA	May 1981	3.43
		EFF	August 1983	13.50
Guatemala	108.0	SBA	June 1960	15.00
		SBA	August 1961	15.00
		SBA	January 1966	15.00
		SBA	April 1967	13.40
		CFF	February 1968	6.25
		SBA	April 1968	10.00
		SBA	August 1969	12.00
		SBA	December 1970	14.00
		SBA	March 1972	9.00
		SBA	November 1981	19.10
		SBA	August 1983	114.80
Guinea	57.9	CFF	March 1974	6.00
		SBA	December 1982	25.00
Guinea-Bissau	7.5	CFF	April 1979	1.10
Guyana	49.2	SBA	February 1967	7.50
		SBA	February 1968	4.00
		SBA	March 1969	4.00
		SBA	April 1970	3.00
		SBA	May 1971	4.00
		SBA	May 1972	2.80
		SBA	May 1973	4.00
		CFF	March 1974	5.00
		SBA	May 1974	5.00
		SBA	June 1975	5.00
		SBA	June 1976	7.25
		CFF	December 1976	10.00
		CFF	July 1978	8.75
		SBA	August 1978	6.25
		EFF	June 1979	62.75

		CFF	January 1980	6.25
		EFF	July 1980	100.00
		EFF	July 1981	100.00
		CFF	November 1982	5.93
Haiti	44.1	SBA	July 1958	5.00
		SBA	October 1959	4.00
		SBA	October 1960	6.00
		SBA	October 1961	6.00
		SBA	October 1962	6.00
		SBA	October 1963	4.00
		SBA	October 1964	4.00
		SBA	October 1965	4.00
		SBA	October 1966	4.00
		CFF	August 1967	1.30
		CFF	December 1967	1.00
		SBA	June 1970	2.20
		SBA	June 1971	3.00
		SBA	July 1972	4.00
		SBA	July 1973	4.00
		SBA	August 1974	4.00
		SBA	August 1975	4.75
		SBA	August 1976	6.88
		SBA	August 1977	6.90
		EFF	October 1978	32.20
		CFF	December 1981	17.00
		SBA	August 1982	34.50
		SBA	November 1983	60.00
Honduras	67.8	SBA	November 1957	3.75
		SBA	January 1959	4.50
		SBA	March 1960	7.50
		SBA	May 1961	7.50
		SBA	June 1962	7.50
		SBA	July 1963	7.50
		SBA	August 1964	7.50
		SBA	January 1966	10.00
		SBA	January 1968	11.00
		SBA	February 1969	11.00
		SBA	June 1971	15.00
		SBA	June 1972	15.00
		EFF	June 1979	47.60
		CFF	January 1982	23.30
		SBA	November 1982	76.50
		CFF	November 1982	23.10
Hungary	530.7	SBA	December 1982	475.00
		SBA	January 1984	425.00
Iceland	59.6	SBA	February 1960	5.62
		SBA	February 1961	1.62
		SBA	March 1962	1.62
		CFF	November 1967	3.75

		CFF	November 1968	3.75
		CFF	March 1976	11.50
		CFF	December 1982	21.50
India	2,207.7	SBA	March 1957	72.50
		SBA	July 1962	100.00
		SBA	July 1963	100.00
		SBA	March 1965	200.00
		CFF	December 1967	90.00
		CFF	February 1974	62.00
		CFF	August 1980	266.00
		EFF	November 1981	5,000.00
Indonesia	1,009.7	SBA	August 1961	41.25
		SBA	August 1963	50.00
		SBA	February 1968	51.75
		SBA	April 1969	70.00
		SBA	April 1970	46.30
		SBA	April 1971	50.00
		SBA	April 1972	50.00
		SBA	May 1973	50.00
		CFF	January 1983	65.10
		CFF	July 1983	360.00
Iran	1,117.4	SBA	May 1956	17.50
		SBA	October 1960	35.00
Iraq	504.0	CFF	November 1967	17.50
Israel	446.6	SBA	November 1974	32.50
		SBA	February 1975	32.50
		CFF	August 1976	65.00
		SBA	October 1976	29.25
		CFF	September 1978	72.40
Italy	2,909.1	SBA	April 1974	1,000.00
		SBA	April 1977	450.00
Ivory Coast	165.5	CFF	March 1976	26.00
		EFF	February 1981	484.50
		CFF	September 1981	114.00
		SBA	August 1984	82.75
Jamaica	145.5	SBA	June 1963	10.00
		SBA	June 1973	26.50
		CFF	March 1974	13.25
		CFF	September 1976	13.25
		CFF	November 1976	13.25
		SBA	August 1977	64.00
		EFF	June 1978	200.00
		CFF	June 1978	15.75
		EFF	June 1979	260.00
		CFF	September 1979	31.75
		EFF	April 1981	477.70
		CFF	April 1981	37.00
		CFF	August 1982	19.40

199

		SBA	June 1984	64.00
		CFF	June 1984	72.60
Jordan	73.9	CFF	November 1971	4.50
		CFF	January 1973	2.85
Kampuchea	25.0	CFF	March 1972	6.25
		CFF	April 1973	6.25
Kenya	142.0	EFF	July 1975	67.20
		CFF	September 1976	24.00
		SBA	November 1978	17.25
		SBA	August 1979	122.48
		CFF	October 1979	69.00
		SBA	October 1980	241.50
		SBA	January 1982	151.50
		SBA	March 1983	175.95
Korea	462.8	SBA	March 1965	9.30
		SBA	March 1966	12.00
		SBA	March 1967	18.00
		SBA	April 1968	25.00
		SBA	April 1969	25.00
		SBA	March 1970	25.00
		SBA	January 1971	25.00
		SBA	January 1972	30.00
		SBA	April 1973	20.00
		SBA	May 1974	20.00
		SBA	October 1975	20.00
		CFF	June 1976	40.00
		SBA	May 1977	20.00
		SBA	March 1980	640.000
		CFF	July 1980	160.00
		SBA	February 1981	576.00
		CFF	January 1982	106.20
		SBA	July 1983	575.78
		CFF	June 1984	279.70
Laos	29.3	CFF	December 1975	3.25
		CFF	June 1976	3.25
		SBA	August 1980	14.00
Liberia	71.3	SBA	June 1963	5.70
		SBA	June 1964	4.40
		SBA	June 1965	4.00
		SBA	June 1966	6.00
		SBA	June 1967	4.40
		SBA	June 1968	3.20
		SBA	June 1969	2.00
		SBA	March 1972	4.00
		SBA	May 1973	4.00
		SBA	August 1974	4.00
		SBA	January 1976	5.00
		SBA	March 1979	9.25
		CFF	December 1979	20.50

		SBA	September 1980	65.00
		SBA	August 1981	55.00
		CFF	June 1982	7.00
		SBA	September 1982	55.00
		CFF	September 1982	27.70
		SBA	September 1983	55.00
Madagascar	66.4	SBA	December 1977	9.43
		SBA	June 1980	10.00
		CFF	June 1980	29.20
		SBA	April 1981	76.70
		SBA	July 1982	51.00
		CFF	July 1982	21.80
		SBA	April 1984	33.00
		CFF	June 1984	14.40
Malawi	37.2	CFF	August 1979	9.50
		SBA	October 1979	26.34
		CFF	November 1979	9.50
		SBA	May 1980	49.88
		SBA	August 1982	22.00
		EFF	September 1983	100.00
Malaysia	550.6	CFF	August 1976	93.00
		CFF	September 1981	189.75
		CFF	March 1983	12.20
Mali	50.8	SBA	July 1964	9.90
		SBA	August 1967	6.50
		SBA	August 1968	5.00
		SBA	October 1969	5.00
		SBA	July 1971	4.50
		CFF	March 1980	5.10
		SBA	May 1982	30.38
		SBA	December 1983	40.50
Mauritania	33.9	CFF	August 1976	6.50
		SBA	May 1977	4.71
		CFF	January 1980	10.50
		SBA	July 1980	29.70
		SBA	June 1981	26.00
Mauritius	53.6	CFF	July 1977	11.00
		SBA	February 1978	7.97
		SBA	October 1979	73.03
		SBA	September 1980	35.00
		CFF	April 1981	40.50
		SBA	December 1981	30.00
		SBA	May 1983	49.50
Mexico	1,165.5	SBA	April 1954	50.00
		SBA	March 1959	90.00
		SBA	July 1961	90.00
		CFF	November 1976	185.00

		EFF	January 1977	518.00
		EFF	January 1983	3,410.63
Nepal	37.3	SBA	February 1976	4.50
		CFF	July 1978	9.50
		CFF	September 1980	10.49
Netherlands	2,264.8	SBA	September 1957	68.75
New Zealand	461.6	CFF	May 1967	29.20
		SBA	October 1967	87.00
		CFF	July 1975	50.50
		CFF	April 1976	50.50
		CFF	December 1976	50.50
Nicaragua	68.2	SBA	November 1956	3.75
		SBA	October 1957	7.50
		SBA	September 1958	7.50
		SBA	November 1960	7.50
		SBA	March 1963	11.25
		SBA	April 1964	11.25
		SBA	March 1968	19.00
		SBA	May 1969	15.00
		SBA	August 1970	14.00
		SBA	February 1972	10.75
		SBA	May 1979	34.00
		CFF	May 1979	17.00
		CFF	October 1979	17.00
Niger	33.7	CFF	July 1983	12.00
		SBA	October 1983	18.00
		CFF	October 1983	12.00
		SBA	December 1984	16.00
Pakistan	546.3	SBA	December 1958	25.00
		SBA	March 1965	37.50
		SBA	October 1968	75.00
		SBA	May 1972	100.00
		SBA	August 1973	75.00
		SBA	November 1974	75.00
		CFF	July 1976	90.50
		SBA	March 1977	80.00
		CFF	April 1977	27.00
		EFF	November 1980	1,268.00
		EFF	December 1981	919.00
		CFF	August 1982	180.20
Panama	102.2	SBA	July 1965	7.00
		SBA	May 1968	3.00
		SBA	January 1969	3.20
		SBA	February 1970	10.00
		SBA	March 1971	14.00
		SBA	June 1972	9.00
		SBA	August 1973	9.00
		SBA	October 1974	9.00

		SBA	November 1975	9.00
		CFF	December 1976	18.00
		SBA	April 1977	11.25
		SBA	June 1978	25.00
		SBA	March 1979	30.00
		SBA	April 1980	90.00
		SBA	April 1982	29.70
		SBA	June 1983	150.00
		CFF	June 1983	58.90
Papua-New Guinea	65.9	CFF	June 1976	10.00
Paraguay	48.4	SBA	July 1957	5.50
		SBA	July 1958	1.50
		SBA	August 1959	2.75
		SBA	October 1960	3.50
		SBA	December 1961	5.00
		SBA	November 1964	5.00
		SBA	September 1966	7.50
		SBA	January 1968	8.00
		SBA	January 1969	7.50
Peru	330.9	SBA	February 1954	12.50
		SBA	February 1955	12.50
		SBA	February 1956	12.50
		SBA	February 1957	12.50
		SBA	February 1958	25.00
		SBA	March 1959	13.00
		SBA	March 1960	27.50
		SBA	March 1961	30.00
		SBA	March 1962	30.00
		SBA	March 1963	30.00
		SBA	March 1964	30.00
		SBA	April 1965	30.00
		SBA	March 1966	37.50
		SBA	August 1967	42.50
		SBA	November 1968	75.00
		SBA	April 1970	35.00
		CFF	June 1972	30.75
		CFF	May 1976	61.50
		SBA	November 1977	90.00
		SBA	September 1978	184.00
		CFF	September 1978	61.50
		SBA	August 1979	285.00
		EFF	June 1982	650.00
		SBA	April 1984	250.00
		CFF	April 1984	74.70
Philippines	440.4	SBA	April 1962	40.40
		SBA	April 1963	40.40
		SBA	April 1964	40.40
		SBA	April 1965	40.40
		SBA	April 1966	26.70

		SBA	January 1967	55.00
		SBA	March 1968	27.50
		SBA	February 1970	27.50
		SBA	March 1971	45.00
		SBA	May 1972	45.00
		SBA	May 1973	45.00
		CFF	May 1973	38.75
		SBA	July 1974	38.75
		SBA	May 1975	29.06
		EFF	April 1976	217.00
		CFF	April 1976	77.50
		SBA	June 1979	105.00
		CFF	June 1979	44.20
		SBA	February 1980	410.00
		CFF	March 1980	93.30
		SBA	February 1983	315.00
		CFF	February 1983	188.55
Portugal	376.6	CFF	July 1976	58.50
		SBA	April 1977	42.40
		CFF	July 1977	29.25
		SBA	June 1978	57.35
		SBA	October 1983	445.00
		CFF	October 1983	258.00
		CFF	July 1984	54.60
Rumania	523.4	SBA	October 1975	95.00
		CFF	April 1976	95.00
		SBA	September 1977	64.13
		CFF	September 1977	47.50
		CFF	April 1979	41.25
		CFF	May 1980	121.25
		SBA	June 1981	1,102.50
Rwanda	43.8	SBA	April 1966	5.00
		SBA	April 1967	2.00
		SBA	April 1968	3.00
		SBA	April 1969	2.00
		SBA	October 1979	5.00
Saint Lucia	7.5	CFF	March 1981	2.70
Saint Vincent	4.0	CFF	April 1981	1.30
Senegal	85.1	CFF	November 1978	21.00
		SBA	March 1979	10.50
		EFF	August 1980	184.80
		SBA	September 1981	63.00
		CFF	September 1981	42.00
		SBA	November 1982	47.25
		SBA	September 1983	63.00
Sierra Leone	57.9	SBA	November 1966	7.50
		SBA	January 1968	3.60
		SBA	March 1969	2.50

		CFF	March 1976	7.00
		CFF	September 1976	5.50
		SBA	June 1977	9.02
		SBA	November 1979	17.00
		EFF	March 1981	163.70
		CFF	February 1983	20.70
		SBA	February 1984	50.20
Solomon Islands	5.0	CFF	April 1979	1.05
		SBA	June 1981	2.00
		CFF	October 1982	1.60
		SBA	June 1983	2.40
Somalia	44.2	SBA	May 1964	4.70
		SBA	January 1965	5.60
		SBA	January 1966	2.80
		SBA	January 1967	5.00
		SBA	January 1968	7.00
		SBA	January 1969	6.00
		SBA	January 1970	3.98
		SBA	February 1980	11.50
		SBA	July 1981	43.13
		SBA	July 1982	60.00
South Africa	915.7	SBA	April 1958	25.00
		SBA	July 1961	75.00
		SBA	January 1976	80.00
		SBA	August 1976	152.00
		CFF	November 1976	160.00
		SBA	November 1982	363.00
		CFF	November 1982	636.00
Spain	1,286.0	SBA	August 1959	25.00
		SBA	August 1960	25.00
		SBA	February 1978	143.19
		CFF	February 1978	98.75
Sri Lanka	223.1	SBA	June 1965	30.00
		SBA	June 1966	25.00
		CFF	March 1967	19.50
		CFF	April 1968	19.30
		SBA	May 1968	19.50
		SBA	August 1969	19.50
		SBA	March 1971	24.50
		CFF	January 1972	19.45
		CFF	June 1973	18.60
		CFF	February 1974	5.90
		SBA	April 1974	24.50
		CFF	November 1976	15.80
		SBA	December 1977	93.00
		EFF	January 1978	260.30
		CFF	June 1981	25.30
		SBA	September 1983	100.00

205

Sudan	169.7	CFF	June 1965	11.25
		SBA	September 1966	28.50
		SBA	September 1967	10.00
		SBA	December 1968	12.00
		SBA	March 1972	40.00
		SBA	August 1973	24.00
		SBA	August 1974	24.00
		CFF	March 1975	18.00
		CFF	May 1976	26.70
		CFF	September 1978	21.30
		EFF	May 1979	427.00
		CFF	November 1979	36.00
		CFF	November 1980	21.80
		CFF	April 1981	45.70
		SBA	February 1982	198.00
		SBA	February 1983	170.00
		CFF	March 1983	39.10
		SBA	June 1984	90.00
Swaziland	24.7	CFF	June 1983	9.00
Syria	139.1	SBA	May 1960	7.50
		SBA	March 1962	6.60
		SBA	March 1964	18.50
		CFF	September 1967	9.50
		CFF	January 1972	12.50
Tanzania	107.0	SBA	August 1975	10.50
		CFF	April 1976	21.00
		CFF	May 1979	20.25
		SBA	September 1980	179.60
		CFF	September 1980	15.00
Thailand	386.6	CFF	August 1976	67.00
		SBA	July 1978	45.25
		CFF	July 1978	68.75
		SBA	June 1981	815.00
		CFF	July 1981	186.00
		SBA	November 1982	271.50
Togo	38.4	CFF	August 1976	7.50
		SBA	June 1979	15.00
		SBA	February 1981	47.50
		SBA	March 1983	21.38
		SBA	May 1984	n.a.
Tunisia	138.2	SBA	October 1964	14.25
		SBA	November 1965	5.60
		SBA	December 1966	9.60
		SBA	December 1967	9.61
		SBA	January 1969	6.00
		SBA	January 1970	7.50
		CFF	August 1977	24.00

Turkey	429.1	SBA	January 1961	37.00
		SBA	March 1962	31.00
		SBA	February 1963	21.50
		SBA	February 1964	21.50
		SBA	February 1965	21.50
		SBA	February 1966	21.50
		SBA	February 1967	27.00
		SBA	April 1968	27.00
		SBA	July 1969	27.00
		SBA	August 1970	90.00
		CFF	November 1975	37.75
		CFF	April 1976	37.75
		SBA	April 1978	300.00
		CFF	May 1978	74.50
		SBA	July 1979	250.00
		CFF	February 1980	71.60
		SBA	June 1980	1,250.00
		SBA	June 1983	225.00
		SBA	April 1984	225.00
Uganda	99.6	SBA	July 1971	10.00
		CFF	April 1976	20.00
		CFF	August 1979	5.00
		SBA	January 1980	12.50
		CFF	January 1980	25.00
		SBA	June 1981	112.50
		SBA	August 1982	112.50
		SBA	September 1983	95.00
United Kingdom	6,194.0	SBA	December 1956	738.53
		SBA	December 1957	738.53
		SBA	December 1958	738.53
		SBA	August 1961	500.00
		SBA	August 1962	1,000.00
		SBA	August 1963	1,000.00
		SBA	August 1964	1,000.00
		SBA	November 1967	1,400.00
		SBA	June 1969	1,000.00
		SBA	December 1975	700.00
		SBA	January 1977	3,360.00
Uruguay	163.8	SBA	June 1961	30.00
		SBA	October 1962	30.00
		SBA	June 1966	15.00
		CFF	February 1968	9.50
		SBA	March 1968	25.00
		SBA	May 1970	13.75
		CFF	May 1972	17.25
		SBA	June 1972	20.00
		SBA	May 1975	17.25
		CFF	March 1976	25.90
		SBA	August 1976	25.00
		SBA	September 1977	25.00

		SBA	March 1979	21.00
		SBA	May 1980	21.00
		SBA	July 1981	31.50
		CFF	August 1982	55.30
		SBA	April 1983	378.00
USA	17,918.3	SBA	July 1963	500.00
		SBA	July 1964	500.00
Venezuela	1,371.5	SBA	April 1960	100.00
Vietnam	179.8	CFF	January 1977	31.00
Western Samoa	6.0	SBA	November 1975	0.50
		CFF	November 1975	0.50
		CFF	November 1976	0.50
		SBA	January 1977	0.50
		CFF	February 1977	0.50
		SBA	February 1978	0.73
		CFF	November 1978	1.25
		SBA	August 1979	0.75
		SBA	June 1983	3.38
		CFF	June 1983	1.15
		SBA	July 1984	3.38
Yemen Arab Rep.	43.3	CFF	February 1983	9.75
Yemen, P.R.	77.2	CFF	May 1976	2.50
		CFF	July 1982	15.38
Yugoslavia	613.0	SBA	January 1961	30.00
		SBA	July 1965	80.00
		SBA	January 1967	45.00
		SBA	February 1971	51.75
		SBA	July 1971	83.50
		SBA	May 1979	69.25
		CFF	May 1979	138.50
		CFF	February 1980	138.50
		SBA	June 1980	200.00
		SBA	January 1981	1,662.00
		SBA	April 1984	370.00
Zaire	291.0	SBA	July 1967	27.00
		CFF	July 1972	28.25
		SBA	March 1976	40.96
		CFF	March 1976	56.50
		SBA	April 1977	45.00
		CFF	May 1977	28.25
		SBA	August 1979	118.00
		EFF	June 1981	912.00
		CFF	March 1982	106.90
		SBA	December 1983	228.00
		CFF	December 1983	114.50
Zambia	270.3	CFF	December 1971	19.00
		CFF	August 1972	19.00

		SBA	May 1973	19.00
		CFF	November 1975	19.00
		CFF	June 1976	19.00
		SBA	July 1976	62.00
		CFF	April 1977	19.00
		SBA	April 1978	250.00
		CFF	May 1978	48.75
		EFF	May 1981	800.00
		CFF	October 1981	59.30
		CFF	December 1982	34.00
		SBA	April 1983	211.50
		CFF	May 1983	97.20
		SBA	July 1984	225.00
Zimbabwe	191.0	SBA	April 1981	37.50
		SBA	March 1983	300.00
		CFF	March 1983	56.10

Sources: Joseph Gold, *The Stand-by Arrangements of the International Monetary Fund*, Washington, D.C. 1970; *IMF Report: Compensatory Financing Facility*, (IMF Pamphlet Series No. 38), Washington D.C. 1980.

Bibliography

Abbott, George C. (1979), *International Indebtedness and the Developing Countries*, New York.

Abs, Hermann-Joseph (1981), Länderrisiken im internationalen Kreditgeschäft, in: *Die Bank*, No. 12, 588–94.

Aldcroft, Derek (1978), Die zoer Jahre: Von Versailles zur Wall Street, 1919–1929, DTV-Geschichte zur Weltwirtschaft im 20. *Jahrhundert*, Vol. 3, Munich.

Andersen, Uwe (1977), Das internationale Währungssystem zwischen nationaler Souveränität und supranationaler Integration. Entwicklungstendenzen seit Bretton Woods im *Spannungsfeld der Interessen*, Berlin.

Aschinger, Franz E. (1973), *Das Währungssystem des Westens*, 2nd ed., Frankfurt/Main.

Avramovic, Dragoslav (1983), The Debt Problem of Developing Countries at end 1982, in: *Aussenwirtschaft*, No. 1, 65–86.

Balassa, Bela (1982), Structural Adjustment Policies in Developing Economies, in: *World Development*, Vol. 10, 1, 23–38.

Baran, Paul (1971), *Zur politischen Ökonomie der geplanten Wirtschaft*, Frankfurt/Main.

Barclays Review (1981), *IMF - Do its Functions Conflict?*, Vol. LVI, No. 2.

Beccaria, Luis/Carciofi, Ricardo (1981), Recent Experiences of Stabilisation: Argentina's Economic Policy 1976–81, in: *IDS Bulletin*, Vol. 13, 1, 51–9.

Bekolo-Ebe, Bruno (1979), Les mesures de 'stabilisation' du FMI et le déséquilibre extérieur dans les pays en voie de développement, in: *Présence africaine*, No. 110, 13–28.

Belliveau, Nancy (1976), What the Peru Experiment Means, in: *Institutional Investor*, October, 145–8.

Bello, Walden/Kinley, David/Elinson, Elaine (1982), *Development Debacle: The World Bank in the Philippines*, San Francisco.

Betz, Joachim (1983), Verschuldungskrise der Dritten Welt?, in: *Jahrbuch Dritte Welt*, Vol. 1, Munich, 30–44.

Beveridge, W.A./Kelly, Margaret (1980), Fiscal Content of Financial Programs Supported by Stand-by Arrangements in the Upper Credit Tranches 1969–78, in: *IMF Staff Papers*, Vol. 27, 2, 205–49.

Bird, Graham (1978), *The International Monetary System and the Less Developed Countries*, London/Basingstoke.

_____ (1982), Developing Country Interests in Proposal for International Monetary Reform, in: Tony Killick (ed.), *Adjustment and Financing in the Developing World: The Role of the International Monetary Fund*, Washington, D.C., 198–232.

Bitterman, Henry J. (1973), *The Refunding of International Debt*, Durham/North Carolina.

BIS (Bank for International Settlements) (1983), 53rd Annual Report, Basle.

Blaisdell, Donald (1966), *European Financial Control in the Ottoman Empire*, New York.

Bogdanowicz-Bindert, C. (1983), Debt: Beyond the Quick Fix, in: *Third World Quarterly*, Vol. 5, 6, 827–38.

Brandt, Willy (ed.) (1981), *North-South: a Programme for Survival*, London.

_____ (1983), *Common Crisis: North-South Cooperation for World Recovery*, London.

Brau, Eduard (1981), The Consultation Process of the Fund, in: *Finance and Development*, No. 4, 13–16.

Bremer Gesellschaft für Wirtschaftsforschung e.V. (ed.) (1981), *Auswertung der Dokumentation der fünften Welthandels und Entwicklungskonferenz Manila 1979*, Baden Baden.

Brzoska, Michael (1983), Research Communication: The Military External Debt of Third World Countries, in: *Journal of Peace Research*, No. 3, 271–7.

Büttner, Veronika (1982),. Externe Verschuldung von Entwicklungsländern: Konfliktbereiche und Lösungsmöglichkeiten im *Rahmen einer Nord-Süd-Politik*, Ebenhausen.

Bundesregierung (1983), *Fünfter Bericht zur Entwicklungspolitik der Bundesregierung*, Bonn, March.

Calderón, Hugo (1981), Veränderungen in der Klassenstruktur der chilenischen Bourgeoisie 1970–1980, in: Calderón, Hugo/Jaime Ensignia/Eugenio Rivera, *Chile. Der Monetarismus an der Macht*, Hamburg, 13–58.

Canitrot, Adolfo (1980), Discipline as the Central Objective of Economic Policy: An Essay on the Economic Programme of the Argentine Government since 1970, in: *World Development*, Vol. 8, 11, 913–28.

Cizauskas, Albert C. (1979), International Debt Renegotiation: Lessons from the Past, in: *World Development*, Vol. 7, 2, 199–210.

Corm, Georges (1982), L'endettement des pays en voie de développement: origine at mécanismes, in: J.C. Sánchez Arnau (coordonateur), *Dette et Développement*, Paris, 29–99.

Crockett, Andrew (1981), Stabilization Policies in Developing Countries: Some Policy Considerations, in: *IMF Staff Papers*, Vol. 28, 1, 54–79.

_____ (1982), Issues in the Use of Fund Resources, in: *Finance and Development*, No. 2, 10–15.

Daniel, Philip (1981), The New Recycling: Economic Theory, IMF Conditionality and Balance of Payments Adjustment in 1980s, in: Stephany Griffith-Jones/Dudley Seers (eds.), *'Monetarism'. Its Effects on Developing Countries*, IDS Bulletin, Vol. 13, 1, 27–37.

Dell, Sidney (1980), The International Environment for Adjustment in Developing Countries, in: *World Development*, Vol. 8, 11, 833–42.

_____ (1982), Stabilization: The Political Economy of Overkill, in: *World Development*, Vol. 10, 8, 597–612.

Dell, Sidney/Lawrence, Roger (1980), *The Balance of Payments Adjustment Process in the Developing Countries*, New York.

Deutsche Bundesbank (1981), Internationale Organisationen und Abkommen im Bereich von Währung und Wirtschaft (*Sonderdrucke der Deutschen Bundesbank Nr. 3*), 2nd ed., Frankfurt/Main.

Diaz Alejandro, Carlos (1981), Southern Cone Stabilization Plans, in: William R. Cline/Sidney Weintraub (eds.), *Economic Stabilization in Developing Countries*, Washington, D.C., 119–47.

Dinham, Barbara/Hines, Colin (1983), *Agribusiness in Africa*, London.

Ducruet, J. (1964), *Les capitaux européens au Proche-Orient*, Paris.

Eaton, Jonathon/Gersovitz, Mark (1982), *Country Risk: Economic Aspects,* New Haven (York University, Economic Growth Center, Discussion Paper No. 401).

Eckaus, Richard S. (1977), Is the IMF Guilty of Malpractice?, in: *Institutional Investor* (International edition), September, 13–15.

Elsenhans, Hartmut (1982), Die Überwindung von Unterentwicklung durch Massenproduktion für den Massenbedarf – Weiterentwicklung eines Ansatzes, in: Dieter Nohlen/Franz Nuscheler (eds.), *Handbuch der Dritten Welt*, Vol. 1, Hamburg, 152–182.

_____ (1982a), Ambivalente Rolle des Staates, in: *epd-Entwicklungspolitik*, No. 22, a-c.

Eshag, Eprime/Thorp, Rosemary (1965), Economic and Social Consequences of Orthodox Economic Policies in Argentina in the Post-War Years, in: *Bulletin of the Oxford University Institute of Economics and Statistics*, Vol. 27, 1, 1–44.

FAO (1981), *Trade Yearbook*, Rome.

_____ (1982), *The State of Food and Agriculture, 1981*, Rome.

Feiss, Herbert (1930), *Europe: The World's Banker*, New Haven.

Felix, David (1964), Monetarists, Structuralists, and Import-Substituting Industrialization: A Critical Appraisal, in: Werner Baer/Isaac Kerstenetzky (eds.), *Inflation and Growth in Latin America*, Homewood/Ill. (USA), 370–401.

Fieldhouse, David (1977), Die Kolonialreiche seit dem 18. Jahrhundert, *Fischer Weltgeschichte*, Vol. 29, Frankfurt/Main.

Finch, David (1981), *Review of Upper Credit Tranche Stand-By Arrangements Approved in 1978-79 and Some Issues Related to Conditionality*, Washington, D.C.

Finch, M.H.J. (1979), Stabilisation Policy in Uruguay since the 1950s, in: Rosemary Thorp/Laurence Whitehead (eds.), *Inflation and Stabilisation in Latin America*, London, 144–80.

Foxley, Alejandro/Whitehead, Laurence (eds.) (1980), *Economic Stabilization in Latin America: Political Dimensions*, Oxford.

_____ (1981) Stabilization Policies and Their Effects on Employment and Income Distribution: A Latin American Perspective, in: William R. Cline/Sidney Weintraub (eds.), *Economic Stabilization in Developing Countries*, Washington, D.C., pp. 191–233.

Frank, André-Gunder (1983), Some Limitations of NIC Export Led Growth from a World Perspective, in: *Ifda-Dossier*, No. 33, 82–5.

Frieden, Jeff (1981), Third World Indebted Industrialization, International Finance and State Capitalism in Mexico, Brazil, Algeria and South Korea, in: *International Organization*, Vol. 35, 3, 407–31.

Galeano, Eduardo (1980), *Die offenen Adern Lateinamerikas*. Wuppertal.

Garcia-Thoumi, Ines (1983), ODA from Developed Countries, in: *Finance and Development*, No. 2, 28–30.

Gerster, Richard (1982), *Fallstricke der Verschuldung. Der Internationale Währungsfonds und die Entwicklungsländer*, Basle.

——————— (1982a), The IMF and Basic Needs Conditionality, in: *Journal of World Trade Law*, Vol. 16, 497–517.

Girvan, Norman/Bernal, Richard (1982), The IMF and the Foreclosure of Development Options: The Case of Jamaica, in: *Monthly Review*, Vol. 3, 9, 34–48.

Glaubitt, Klaus/Lütkenhorst, Wilfried (1980), Private Direktinvestitionen und das Verschuldungsproblem der Entwicklungsländer, in: Hans-Bernd Schäfer (ed.), *Gefährdete Weltfinanzen*, Bonn, 199–223.

Gold, Joseph (1970), *The Stand-By Arrangements of the International Monetary Fund*, Washington, D.C.

——————— (1972) *Voting and Decisions in the International Monetary Fund*, Washington, D.C.

——————— (1979), *Conditionality*, Washington, D.C. (Pamphlet Series No. 31).

——————— (1980), *Financial Assistance by the International Monetary Fund: Law and Practice*, Washington, D.C.

——————— (1982), The Relationship between the International Monetary Fund and the World Bank, in: *Creighton Law Review*, Vol. 15, 2, 499–521.

——————— (1983), Nonpolitical Character of Fund: Political Considerations Are Prohibited by Articles of Agreement when the Fund Considers Requests for Use of Resources, in: *IMF Survey*, 23 May, 146–8.

Goreux, Louis H., (1980) *Compensatory Financing Facility*, Washington, D.C. (Pamphlet Series No. 34).

Greayer, Anthony B. (1978), Private Lending to LDCs by Great Britain in the Nineteenth Century: A Guide to the Future?, in: Miguel S. Wionczek (ed.), *LDC External Debt and the World Economy*, Mexico, 295–318.

Griffith-Jones, Stephany (1981), *The Role of Finance in the Transition to Socialism*, London.

Griffith-Jones, Stephany/Seers, Dudley (eds.) (1981), Monetarists and the Third World, *IDS Bulletin,*, Vol. 13, 1.

Group of 77 (1983), *The Buenos Aires Platform: Final Document of the Fifth Ministerial Meeting of the Group of 77*, Buenos Aires 28 March – 9 April 1983.

Group of Thirty (1982), *Risks in International Bank Lending. First Report of the International Banking Study Group of the Group of Thirty*, New York.

Guitián, Manuel (1981), *Fund Conditionality: Evolution of Principles and Practices*, Washington, D.C. (Pamphlet Series No. 38).

——————— (1981a), Fund Conditionality and the International Adjustment Process: A Look into the 1980s, in: *Finance and Development*, No. 2, 14–17.

Guth, Wilfried (1965), Zum Rückzahlungsproblem der Entwicklungsländer. Ansatzpunkte für eine realistische Entwicklungspolitik, in: *Jahrbuch für Nationalökonomie und Statistik*, Vol. 178, 158–68.

——————— (1980), Das internationale Kreditgeschäft der Banken und seine Probleme, in: *Die Bank*, No. 7, 308–16.

Hanisch, Rolf/Tetzlaff, Rainer (1981), Der Staat in Entwicklungsländern als Gegenstand sozialwissenschaftlicher Forschung, in: Hanisch, Rolf/Tetzlaff, Rainer (eds.), *Staat und Entwicklung*, Frankfurt/Main, 13–53.

Hankel, Wilhelm, (1984), Die Schuldenkrise, ein Problem der Dritten oder der Ersten Welt? Umschuldung oder Schuldenerlass?, in: *Blätter für deutsche und internationale Politik*, No. 1, 64–79.

Hardach, Gerd (1973), Der 1. Weltkrieg 1914–1918, *DTV-Geschichte der Weltwirtschaft*, Vol. 2, Munich.

Hardy, Chandra S. (1982), *Rescheduling Developing-Country Debts, 1956–1981: Lessons and Recommendations*, Washington, D.C.

Haumer, Hans (1971), Die Stabilisierungspolitik des IWF unter besonderer Berücksichtigung Lateinamerikas, in: *Aussenwirtschaft*, No. 4, 392–427.

Hayter, Teresa (1971), *Aid as Imperialism*, Harmondsworth.

Helleiner, G.K. (1983), Lender of Early Resort, the IMF and the Poorest, in: *The American Economic Review*, Vol. 73, 349–53.

Herrmann, Roland (1983), *The Compensatory Financing System of the International Monetary Fund: An Analysis of its Effects and Comparisons with Alternative Systems* Kiel.

Hofmeier, Rolf (1983), Tanzania – 'Entwicklungsmodell' oder Entwicklungsbankrott?, in: *Jahrbuch Dritte Welt*, Vol. 1, Munich, 204–20.

Holthus, Manfred (1980), Die Entwicklung der Auslandsverschuldung, in: Hans-Bernd Schäfer (ed.), *Gefährdete Weltfinanzen*, Bonn, 107–30.

_____ (1981), Verschuldung und Verschuldungsfähigkeit von Entwicklungsländern, in: *Hamburger Jahrbuch für Wirtschafts- und Gesellschaftspolitik*, Vol. 26, 239–55.

Hood, Wm C. (1982), Surveillance over Exchange Rates, in: *Finance and Development*, No. 1, 9–12.

Horsefield, J.K. et al. (1969), *The International Monetary Fund, 1945–1965: Twenty Years of International Monetary Co-operation*, Washington, D.C.

Hürni, Bettina (1981), Die Sonderfazilitäten im Internationalen Währungsfonds (IWF): Verwendung und Nutzen, in: *Schweizerische Zeitschrift für Volkswirtschaft und Statistik*, No. 117, 55–74.

Huff, Richard (1982), The Rescheduling of Country Debt: Is a More Formalized Process Necessary?, in: *Group of Thirty* (1982), 49–56.

Husain, S. Sahid (1980), Interview with S. Sahid Husain (Vice-president of the World Bank), in: *New York Times*, 26 May.

IMF (1974), *International Monetary Reform: Documents of the Committee of Twenty*, Washington, D.C.

_____ (1979), *Technical Assistance Services of the International Monetary Fund*, Washington, D.C. (Pamphlet Series No. 30).

_____ (1981), *External Indebtedness of Developing Countries*, Washington, D.C. (Occasional Paper No. 3).

_____ (1982), The Fund's Technical Assistance, in: *Finance and Development*, No. 4, 10–15.

_____ (1983), *Recent Multilateral Debt Restructurings with Official and Bank Creditors*, Washington, D.C. (Occasional Paper No. 25).

_____ (1983), Debt Rescheduling: What Does It Mean?, in: *Finance and Development, No. 3, 26–30*.

_____ (1984), *World Economic Outlook: Revised Projections of the Staff of the International Monetary Fund*, Washington, D.C. (Occasional Paper No. 32).

Jahn, Wolfgang (1980), Die Bewertung von Länderrisiken, in: *Die Bank*, No. 11, 500–2.

Jeker, Rolf (1978), Voting Rights of the Less Developed Countries and the IMF, in: *Journal of the World Trade Law*, Vol. 12, 218–27.

(1980), Conditionality and Stand-by Credits of the International Monetary Fund and the Less Developed Countries, in: *Aussenwirtschaft*, No. 1, 34–52.

Johnson, Omutunde/Salop, Joanne (1980), Distributional Aspects of Stabilization Programs in Developing Countries, in: *IMF Staff Papers*, Vol. 27, I, 1–23.

Jorge, Antonio/Salazar-Carillo, Jorge/Higonnet, René P. (eds.) (1983), *Foreign Debt and Latin American Economic Development*, New York.

Junne, Gerd (1976), *Der Eurogeldmarkt*, Frankfurt/Main.

Kaldor, Nicholas (1983), Devaluation and Adjustment in Developing Countries, in: *Finance and Development*, No. 2, 35–7.

Kampfmeyer, Thomas (1983), Entwicklungsperspektiven der türkischen Aussenwirtschaftsbeziehungen, in: *Aussenwirtschaft*, No. 1, 39–63.

Katseli, Louka T. (1983), Devaluation: A Critical Appraisal on the IMF's Policy Prescriptions, in: *The American Economic Review*, Vol. 73, 359–63.

Kelly, Margaret (1983), Fiscal Deficits and Fund-supported Programs, in: *Finance and Development*, No. 3, 37–9.

Killick, Tony (1982), *Adjustment and Financing in the Developing World: The Role of the International Monetary Fund*, Washington, D.C./London.

——————— (ed.) (1984), *The Quest for Economic Stabilisation. The IMF and the Third World, and The IMF and Stabilisation: Developing Country Experiences*, London.

Killick, Tony/Sutton, Mary (1982), Disequilibria, Financing, and Adjustment in the Developing Countries, in: Tony Killick (ed.), *Adjustment and Financing in the Developing World: The Role of the International Monetary Fund*, Washington, D.C./London, 48–72.

Kincaid, Russell (1983), What are Credit Ceilings?, in: *Finance and Development*, No. 1, 28–9.

Kindleberger, Charles (1981), Debt Situation of the Developing Countries in Historical Perspective (1800–1945), in: *Aussenwirtschaft*, No. 4, 372–80.

Klein, Thomas M. (1973), Economic Aid and Rescheduling, in: *Finance and Development*, No. 3, 17–20 and 34f.

Kneitschel, D./Burdach, Th. (1974), *Auslandsverschuldung in Lateinamerika. Entwicklung und Perspektiven unter besonderer Berücksichtigung der Rückzahlungsfähigkeit*, Hamburg.

Knieper, Rolf (1976), *Weltmarkt, Wirtschaftsrecht und Nationalstaat*, Frankfurt/Main.

——————— (1979), Zurichtung nationaler Politik durch internationales Recht? Die Bereitschaftskreditabkommen des Internationalen Währungsfonds, in: *Kritische Justiz*, No. 3, 270–90.

König, Wolfgang (1969), *Devisenkurspolitik in Lateinamerika*, Hamburg.

Konrad, Anton (1982), Should the IMF Resort to Private Markets for Credit Refinancing?, in: *Intereconomics*, Vol. 17, 2, 71–4.

Krassowski, Andrej (1974), *Development and Debt Trap: Economic Planning and External Borrowing in Ghana*, London.

Krippendorff, Ekkehart (1975), *Internationales System als Geschichte*, Frankfurt/Main.

Krueger, Anne O. (1981), Loans to Assist the Transition to Outward-looking Policies, in: *The World Economy*, Vol. 4, 3, 271–81.

——————— (1983), The Effects of Trade Strategies on growth, in: *Finance and Development*, No. 2, 6–8.

Kulischer, Alfred (1976), *Allgemeine Wirtschaftsgeschichte des Mittelalters und der Neuzeit*, Vol. 2, 5th ed., Munich.

Landell-Mills, Pierre M. (1981), Structural Adjustment Lending: Early Experiences, in: *Finance and Development*, No. 4, 17–21.

Landes, D. (1958), *Bankers and Pashas: International Finance and Economic Imperialism in Egypt*, London.

Larosière (1982), A Conversation with Mr. de Larosière, in: *Finance and Development*, No. 2, 4–7 and 45.

Lateinamerika 6 (1982), *US-Intervention und kapitalistische Gegenrevolution*, Tilman Evers et al. (eds.), Berlin.

Lateinamerika 7 (1983), *Fortschritt der Destruktivkräfte – Ökologische Krise und Gegenwehr*, Michael Ehrke et al. (eds.), Hamburg.

Lelart, Michel (1982), Les mécanismes compensatoires au FMI, in: *Revue Tiers Monde*, Vol. XXIII, 91, 619–28.

Lewis, Vivien (1982), How the Paris Club Deals with Debtors, in: *The Banker*, Vol. 132, 682, 67–9.

L'Hériteau, Marie-France (1982), Endettement et ajustement structurel: la nouvelle cannonière, in: *Revue Tiers Monde*, Vol. XXIII, 91, 517–48.

Libby, Ronald T. (1976), External Co-optation of a Less Developed Country's Policy Making: The Case of Ghana 1969–72, in: *World Politics*, Vol. 21, 1, 67–89.

——————— (1976a), The International Monetary Fund's 'Rehabilitation' of Ghana (1966–69), in: *The African Review* (Dar es Salaam), Vol. 6, 4, 65–76.

Lichtensztejn, Samuel (1982), Zur Stabilisierungspolitik in Lateinamerika, in: Tilman Evers *et al.* (eds.), *Lateinamerika 6*, Berlin, 80–113.

Lipson, Charles (1981), The International Organization of Third World Debt, in: *International Organization*, Vol. 35, 4, 603–31.

Luxemburg, Rosa (1975), Die Akkumulation des Kapitals, in: *Gesammelte Werke*, Vol. 5, Berlin/GDR.

Madeley, John (1982), Third World Debt and Western Society, in: *Contemporary Review*, Vol. 240, 1395.

Manley, Michael (1977), Less Compromise . . . More Purpose, Address to the Royal Commonwealth Society in London, June 9, Agency for Public Information, Kingston/Jamaica.

Martner, Gonzalo D. (1982), Rénégociations de Dettes, in: J.C. Sánchez Arnau (Coordonateur), *Dette et Développement*, Paris, 175–84.

McCauley, Robert (1979), A Compendium of IMF Troubles: Turkey, Portugal, Peru, Egypt, in: Lawrence G. Franko/Marilyn J. Seiber (eds.), *Developing Country Debt*, New York, 143–84.

McMullen, Neril J. (1979), Historical Perspectives in Developing Nations Debt, in: Franko G. Lawrence/Marilyn J. Seiber (eds.), *Developing Country Debt*, New York, 3–16.

Mendelssohn, M.S. (1983), International Debt Crisis: the Practical Lessons of Restructuring, in: *The Banker*, Vol. 133, 689, 33–8.

Morrell, Jim (1983), *A Billion Dollars for South Africa*, Washington, D.C. (Center for International Policy).

Morrell, Jim/Gisselquist, D. (1978), *How the IMF Slipped $464 Millions to South Africa*, Washington, D.C. (Center for International Policy).

Morrell, Jim/William Jesse Biddle (1983), *Central America: The Financial War*, Washington, D.C. (Center for International Policy).

Myrdal, Gunnar (1981), Relief Instead of Development Aid, in: *Intereconomics*,

Vol. 16, 2, 86–9.

Nashashibi, Karim (1983), Devaluation in Developing Countries: the Difficult Choices, in: *Finance and Development*, No. 1, 14–17.

Nohlen, Dieter/Nuscheler, Franz (1982), Was heisst Entwicklung?, in: Nohlen, Dieter/Nuscheler, Franz (eds.), *Handbuch der Dritten Welt*, Vol. 1, Hamburg, 48–72.

Nowzad, Bahram (1981), *The IMF and its Critics*, Princeton, N.J. (Essays in International Finance No. 146).

Nuscheler, Franz (1982), 'Befriedigung der Grundbedürfnisse' als neue entwicklungspolitische Lösungsformel, in: Nohlen, Dieter/Nuscheler, Franz (eds.), *Handbuch der Dritten Welt*, Vol. 1, Hamburg, 332–58.

Nyerere, Julius (1980), No to IMF Meddling: President Nyerere's New Year Message 1980 to the Diplomats Accredited to Tanzania, in: *Development Dialogue*, 1980: 2, 7–9.

OECD (1974), *Debt Problems of Developing Countries*, Paris.

————— (1982), *External Debt of Developing Countries, 1982 Survey,* Paris.

————— (1982a), *Economic Surveys: Turkey 1981*, Paris.

————— (1984), *External Debt of Developing Countries, 1983 Survey*, Paris.

OECD/DAC (1983), *Development Co-operation*, Paris.

Payer, Cheryl (1974), *The Debt Trap*, New York/London.

————— (1982), *The World Bank: A Critical Analysis*, New York.

Pirzio-Biroli, Corrado (1983), Making Sense of the IMF Conditionality Debate, in: *Journal of World Trade Law*, Vol. 17, 2, 115–53.

Please, Stanley (1982), *Adjustment Programs – The World Bank's Role*, Paper prepared for a seminar jointly sponsored by the Central Bank of Kenya and the International Monetary Fund, Nairobi, 3–5 March (unpublished).

Powelson, John (1964), *Latin America: Today's Economic and Social Revolution*, New York.

Reich, Cary (1977), Why the IMF Shuns a 'Super' Role, in: *Institutional Investor* (international edition), September, 35–41 and 200.

Reichmann, Thomas (1978), The Fund's Conditional Assistance and the Problems of Adjustment 1973–75, in: *Finance and Development*, No. 4, 38–41.

Reichmann, Thomas/Stillson, Richard (1977), How Successful are Programs Supported by Stand-by Arrangements?, in: *Finance and Development*, No. 1, 22–5.

Rey, Romeo (1979), Peru und der Internationale Währungsfonds, in: *Lateinamerika-Berichte*, No. 21, 29–38.

Rhein, Wolfram v. (1980), Ausgewählte Probleme bei der Beurteilung von Länderrisiken, in: *Sparkasse*, No. 6, 180–6.

Rippy, J.-Fred (1959), *British Investment in Latin America, 1822–1949*, Minneapolis.

Rivera, Eugenio (1981), Die chilenische Wirtschaftspolitik und die Umwandlung der Ökonomie unter der Militärregierung 1973–1980, in: Hugo Calderón/Jaime Ensignia/Eugenio Rivera (eds.), *Chile. Der Monetarismus an der Macht*, Hamburg, 59–99.

Rossiter, Caleb (1983), *Would an Anti-Apartheid Amendment 'Politicize' the IMF?*, Washington, D.C. (Center for International Policy).

Rweyemamu, Justinian F. (1980), Restructuring the International Monetary System, in: *Development Dialogue*, 1980: 2, 75–91.

Sampson, Anthony (1981), *The Money Lenders: Bankers in a Dangerous World*,

London.

Sánchez Arnau, J.C./Martner, Gonzalo/Sid-Ahmed, Abdelkader (1982), Vers une politique alternative pour faire face aux problèmes de la dette du Tiers Monde, in: Sánchez Arnau, J.C. (coordonateur), *Dette et Développement*, Paris, 185–205.

Sandaglia,Ferdinand/Rescher, Hubertus (1976), Aspekte der brasilianischen Entwicklung seit 1964, in: *Blätter für deutsche und internationale Politik*, No. 4, 438–51.

Schäfer, Hans-Bernd (1979), *Typologie und Bewertung der Wirkungen der deutschen Umschuldungen bei öffentlichen und öffentlich abgesicherten Forderungen an Entwicklungsländer*, Berlin (Forschungsauftrag des BMZ).

––––––––––– (1980), Die Diskussion um die Neuordnung internationaler Umschuldungen, in: Hans-Bernd Schäfer (ed.), *Gefährdete Weltfinanzen*, Bonn, 249–65.

Schubert, Alexander (1982), Von der Verschuldungskrise zum internationalen Finanzchaos?, in: *Weltpolitik*, Vol. 2, 66–88.

––––––––––– (1983), Die Auswirkungen der Ölpreis – und der Aussteigerungeu auf die Entwicklunglander, in: Simonis, Udo Ernst (ed.), *Entwicklungständer in der Finanzkrise. Probleme und Perspektiven*, Berlin, pp. 233–50.

––––––––––– (1983a), Internationale Kreditumschuldungen. Flickschusterei im Weltmassstab, in: *Links*, No. 156.

Senghaas, Dieter (1982), *Von Europa lernen. Entwicklungsgeschichtliche Betrachtungen*, Frankfurt/Main.

Sid-Ahmed, Abdelkader (1982), La conditionalité des tirages sur le Fonds monétaire international, in: Sánchez Arnau, J.C. (coordonateur), *Dette et Développement*, Paris, 101–57.

Sidhom, Michel (1979), Les thérapeutiques de redressement économique du FMI, in: *Problèmes économiques*, 19 Décembre, 3–6.

Steckhan, Rainer B. (1981), Weltbankkredite zur für den Strukturwandel in der Dritten Welt, in: *Zeitschrift für das gesamte Kreditwesen*, No. 20, 908–13.

Streeten, Paul (1982), A Cool Look at 'Outward Looking' Strategies for Development, in: *The World Economy*, Vol. 5, 2, 159–69.

Sunkel, Osvaldo (1964), Comment, in: Werner Baer/Isaac Kerstenetzky (eds.), *Inflation and Growth in Latin America*, Homewood, Ill., 423–7.

Terra Nova Statement (1980), in: *Development Dialogue* 1980: 1, 29–34.

Tetzlaff, Rainer (1980), *Die Weltbank: Machtinstrument der USA oder Hilfe für die Entwicklungsländer? Zur Geschichte der modernen Weltgesellschaft*, Munich/London.

Thorp, Rosemary/Whitehead, Laurence (eds.) (1979), *Inflation and Stabilisation in Latin America*, London

Tseng, Wanda (1984), The Effects of Adjustment, in: *Finance and Development No. 4, pp. 2–5*.

UN (1982), *Towards the New International Economic Order: Analytical Report on Developments in the Field of International Economic Cooperation since the Sixth Special Session of the General Assembly*, New York.

UNCTAD (1979), *The Balance of Payments Adjustment Process in Developing Countries: Report to the Group of Twenty-four*, UNDP/UNCTAD-project INT/75/015, 2 January.

––––––––––– (1983), *Resolutions, recommendations and decisions of the Sixth Session*, Belgrade, 6 June to 2 July.

UNCTC (1983) (United Nations Center on Transnational Corporations), *Transnational Corporations in World Development*, Third Survey, New York.

U.S.ACDA (1983) (U.S. Arms Control and Disarmament Agency), *World Military Expenditure and Arms Transfers*, Washington, D.C.

U.S. General Accounting Office (1983), *U.S. Development Efforts and Balance-of-Payments Problems in Developing Countries*, Washington, D.C. (GAO/ID-83-13).

Villarreal, René (1983), *La contrarrevolución monetarista*, Mexico.

Wagner, Antonin (1980), Euromarktverschuldung der Entwicklungsländer – Chance oder Gefahrenherd?, in: Hans-Bernd Schäfer (ed.), *Gefährdete Weltfinanzen*, Bonn, 143–60.

Wels, Alena (1983), The 'Ditchley Institute' Maps out its Role, in: *The Banker*, Vol. 133, 693, 27–32.

Werle, Rainer (1983), *'Modell' Türkei: Ein Land wird kaputtsaniert*, Hamburg.

Whitehead, Laurence (1979), Inflation and Stabilisation in Chile 1970–7, in: Rosemary Thorp/Laurence Whitehead (eds.), *Inflation and Stabilisation in Latin America*, London, 65–109.

Whitehead, Laurence/Thorp, Rosemary (1979), A Comparative Perspective, in: Laurence Whitehead/Rosemary Thorp (eds.), *Inflation and Stabilisation in Latin America*, London, 264–80.

Wilkens, Herbert (1983), The Debt Burden of Developing Countries, in: *Intereconomics*, Vol. 18, 2, 55–9.

Williamson, John (1982), The Lending Policies of the International Monetary Fund, Washington, D.C. (Institute for International Economics).

Wohlmuth, Karl (1984), IMF and World Bank Structural Adjustment Policies: Cooperation or Conflict? in: *Intereconomics*, Vol. 19, 5, 226–34.

World Bank (1981), *Accelerated Development in Sub-Saharan Africa: An Agenda for Action*, Washington, D.C.

_____ (1981a), *Development in and Prospects for the External Debt of the Developing Countries: 1970–1980 and Beyond*, Washington, D.C.

_____ (1984), *Debt and the Developing World: Current Trends and Prospects* (An Abridged Version of World Debt Tables 1983–84), Washington, D.C.

_____ (1984a), *Toward Sustained Development in Sub-Saharan Africa: A Joint Program of Action*, Washington, D.C.

_____ *Annual Report*, various issues, Washington, D.C.

_____ *World Debt Tables*, various issues, Washington, D.C.

_____ *World Development Report*, various issues, Washington, D.C.

Wright, Peter E. (1980), World Bank Lending for Structural Adjustment, in: *Finance and Development*, No. 3, 20–3.

Wulf, Herbert (1983), *Aufrüstung und Unterentwicklung. Aus den Berichten der Vereinten Nationen*, Reinbek.

Index

Carter 62, 107, 184n26
Central African Republic 36, 39n6
Cereal Import Facility 49, 52
Chad 39, 39n6
Chile 8ff, 10, 23, 34, 35, 53, 61, 72n13,
130ff, 136ff, 140, 158n14, 159n18,
159n27; in history 16
China 19, 23, 45ff, 46
Chun 159n27
CIA 98, 101, 106, 113
Clausen 5
Clearing Union 42, 165ff
cleptocracy 4, 36ff, 97-105
Colombia 8, 17, 23, 35, 72n13
colonialism and debt crisis 3, 26
Committee of Twenty (in IMF) 153
companies, foreign *see* transnational
corporations *and* direct investment
Compensatory Financing Facility (IMF)
4, 49, 52, 61ff, 72n17, 103, 146, 153,
156, 166ff, 180, 182n7
conditionality 47, 52, 54-63, 157n3,
161n41; development-oriented 89,
168, 169-82; *see also* adjustment,
expansionist
Congo 23
Coore 108, 160n28
corruption 29ff, 61, 98-105, 115, 122,
133, 138, 150, 157, 177, 179, 184n21
Costa Rica 23, 140
crawling peg devaluation *see* devaluation
credit, domestic 54, 56ff, 60, 130, 133,
137, 142
creditors co-liability 4, 179ff
Credit Tranche (IMF) 47ff, 52, 60
creditworthiness 10, 21-6, 53, 61, 63, 65,
72n17, 74, 76, 81, 83ff, 97, 101, 112,
115, 128, 139ff, 144ff, 163, 170
Cuba 23, 40n14, 45, 62, 106, 111, 171
Cyprus 23
Czechoslovakia 44

debt: short-term 8, 12, 114; Third World
5-13, 12
debt crisis: causes of 3, 26-39, 54, 150,
168, 170; in history 13-21; proposals to
solution 163-5; Third World 5-13, 95
debtors cartel 162, 182n3
debt repudiation 40n14, 114, 121ff,
162ff, 182n3
debt service 1, 8ff, 12, 22, 26, 55, 66ff,
76, 91, 94, 114, 116ff, 132, 164, 168ff,
174, 176ff, 179ff
debt-service ratio 8ff, 11, 22, 89, 165,
184n25
deflation (therapy) *see* stabilisation

programme
demand, domestic 20, 55ff, 85, 89, 132,
137ff, 150, 172ff, 176, 181, 184n21
destabilisation, political 61, 105-13,
169ff; *see also* social conflict
devaluation 42, 54ff, 58, 77, 83ff, 102ff,
107ff, 121, 126n49, 129ff, 147, 150,
152, 158n8, 158n12, 177, 179
development: aid 6, 67, 118, 164, 174;
definition 143; gigantomania 37ff,
76, 91-7, 101; inhibiting factors 19-21,
31; strategy/model 13, 75, 129, 167,
173, 175, 178, 181
direct investment 6, 28ff, 36, 56ff, 77,
123n3, 131, 160n35; *see also*
transnational corporations
Dominican Republic 23, 35, 139
Duncan, D.K. 111
Duvalier, Jean-Claude 36, 104

Ecuador 23, 133, 139
Egypt 6, 10, 23, 37, 93, 95, 139, 141,
157n3; in history 14ff, 20, 40n12
El Salvador 23, 35, 62, 72n18
England: in history 13ff, 40n12, 100
Erb, Richard 62
Ethiopia 23, 34, 35, 39
Eurodollar market 6, 9, 28
European Community (EC) 85ff, 91, 152,
160n36, 183n11
Evaristo Arns 79
Executive Board (IMF) 46ff, 50, 53, 57,
59ff, 65, 72n20, 77
Executive Directors (IMF) 46ff, 62ff,
72n17; *see also* USA: Executive
Director
export: diversification 34, 59, 131, 173,
175ff, 177, 181; earnings/income 6, 9,
21, 27, 49ff, 58, 135, 146, 172, 180;
industrialisation 33, 91; production
95ff, 130ff, 138, 143, 147, 150ff,
158n7, 158n10, 159n15, 166, 172,
176ff, 184n23; structure 22, 123n4
Extended Fund Facility (IMF) 48, 52, 53,
58ff, 78, 80, 103, 147, 149, 153, 181

Figueres, Pepe 140
Figueiredo 80ff
food: imports 32, 34, 91ff, 101, 132,
176; production 31ff, 34, 135, 152,
176, 181; *see also* agriculture *and*
agricultural reform
France 13ff, 39n1, 40n12, 45ff, 46,
100, 102ff
Frimpong-Ansah, J.H. 122
Furtado, Celso 123n5, 124n12, 182n1